D0205954

C.

1

324.6 L   c.1

Lunardini, Christine A.,
  1941-

From equal suffrage to
  equal rights

8/87

West Hartford Public Library
West Hartford, Conn.

The American Social Experience Series
GENERAL EDITOR: JAMES KIRBY MARTIN
EDITORS: PAULA S. FASS,
STEVEN H. MINTZ, CARL PRINCE,
JAMES W. REED & PETER N. STEARNS

FROM EQUAL SUFFRAGE TO EQUAL RIGHTS

Alice Paul and the
National Woman's Party, 1910–1928

CHRISTINE A. LUNARDINI

NEW YORK UNIVERSITY PRESS
NEW YORK AND LONDON
1986

WEST HARTFORD PUBLIC LIBRARY
DISCARDED

Copyright © 1986 by New York University
All rights reserved
Manufactured in the United States of America

Library of Congress Cataloging-in-Publication Data

Lunardini, Christine A., 1941–
From equal suffrage to equal rights.

(The American social experience series ; 5)
Bibliography: p.
Includes index.
1. Paul, Alice, 1885–   . 2. Suffragettes—United
States—Biography.   3. National Woman's Party—
History.   4. Women's rights—United States—History.
I. Title.   II. Series.
JK1899.P38L86   1986   324.6′23′0924 [B]   86-2499
ISBN 0-8147-5022-2 (alk. paper)

Clothbound editions of New York University Press books are Smyth-
sewn and printed on permanent and durable acid-free paper.

Book design by Ken Venezio

To
Christine Hildegard Cavanaugh Lunardini

Contents

Acknowledgments

This book was begun twelve years ago as a senior thesis project when I was an undergraduate at Mount Holyoke College. To me, Paul's foresight and courage were immediately appealing and it amazed me that no one had yet "discovered" this remarkable woman. After the tumult and social activism of the 1960s, Paul seemed no less a heroine for our time than she had been in her own time. It was truly my good fortune to find such a richly rewarding subject. My baptism as a historian came about with this project, but when I began my graduate studies at Princeton University, I assumed that my relationship with Alice Paul and the National Woman's Party had come to an end. Except for the persistent and persuasive encouragement of friends at Princeton, that might well have been the case. Fortunately, by the time I was ready to make a serious commitment to a dissertation topic, attitudes toward "women's history," even at so traditional an institution as Princeton, had changed. It was no small irony that the process by which change occurred bore certain similarities to the themes with which I was dealing in my research, but suffice it to say that I happily renewed my interest in Paul and the NWP. The result—almost twelve years after my first inquiry—is this book, the publication of which is gratifying for two reasons. First, it is the culmination of truly a labor of love that permits me to tell the story of Alice Paul and the National Woman's Party. And second, it provides me at long last with the opportunity to thank family, friends, colleagues, and mentors who have encouraged and assisted me along the way. While they are in no way responsible or at fault for whatever mistakes I may have made, they deserve the lion's share of credit for what I have done right.

I am, of course, indebted (more literally in some cases than others) to the institutions and foundations that offered financial support, without which I could not have completed this book. In particular, Mount Holyoke College, Princeton University, the American Association of University Women, the Woodrow Wilson Foundation, and the Helena Rubenstein Foundation all have my deep gratitude.

Professors Susanna Barrows (University of California at Berkeley), Phyllis Palmer (George Washington University), Charles Trout (Colgate), and Joe Ellis, all of whom were once members of the History Department at Mount Holyoke College, encouraged me early on to undertake the task of historian and story-teller in a serious way. At Princeton University, my advisor, Chair Professor Arthur S. Link, George Henry Davis '86 Professor of History, with whom I did not always see eye-to-eye, and for whom I have enormous respect, taught me the importance of being a good historian, and allowed me to tell the story my way. Professors Nancy J. Weiss and Lynn Gordon (University of Rochester), provided support and encouragement for which I thank them.

Friends and colleagues read all or part of this manuscript at various stages and offered many good and useful suggestions, many of which I had the good sense to incorporate here in the final manuscript: Professor Lynn Gordon, Professor Nancy J. Weiss, Perry K. Blatz, Professor Thomas J. Knock (Southern Methodist University), Maureen Callahan, Louis Rose, Professor James Amelang (University of Florida at Gainsville), Margaret Douglas Link, Professor Ben Barker-Benfield (SUNY, Albany), Professor Ellen DuBois (SUNY, Buffalo), Professor Nancy Cott (Yale University), Edward Bever, and Elizabeth Craven.

Certain friendships have made all the difference in the world. While I can never adequately thank them for their generous gift of friendship, I take great pleasure in the attempt. Professor Catherine Clinton, (Harvard University), and Maureen Callahan, Senior Vice President (International, of The Refco, Group, Ltd.), my classmates from graduate school days, have long been my most supportive friends. They, more than anyone else, encouraged me to do what I wanted to do. They have both exhibited integrity and courage under fire—qualities they hold in common with the subject of this book—and insisted always that I could do better than I thought I could. They have been— and are still—my best friends and my best critics.

Other good friends to whom I owe much include Tom Knock, Ed Bever, Perry and Katie Blatz, Bill and Jeffrie Husband, Gail Miller and Mario Clement, Lou Rose, Jim Amelang, and Leona Halvorsen. All of them, at various times, have been good listeners, good advice-givers, and good friends.

For those members of my family, who have put up with me the longest and have undoubtedly seen me at my best and worst, "thank you" is an inadequate expression of my gratitude. My mother, Christine Cavanaugh Lunardini, encouraged me at every step; my aunt, Mary Cavanaugh Lunardini, knew, I hope, that I was deeply grateful for her support over the years; my sister, Pat Lunardini, who has had to endure my older-sister sisterly advice and has remained my good friend even so; my brother Larry and sister-in-law, Donna, of Sacramento, California, who have provided me an escape refuge ever since they settled in the Golden West. Thanks also to Bob and Susan Lunardini of Jackson, Mississippi; Virgil and Rosemary Lunardini of Hanover, New Hampshire; Helen Lunardini Close of Auburn, California; Kevin Lunardini, and Joe and Mai Lunardini of Chicopee, Massachusetts, and Patsy Ferriter of Holyoke, Massachusetts.

Not least, my special thanks go to Jonathan Jude Lunardini, Abigail Lunardini, and Noah Callahan Bever, who, over the years, have done exceedingly well what children do best: helped me to maintain a sense of humor and a sense of what is truly important.

Introduction

By 1910, the American woman suffrage movement had lost the urgency and excitement which its two stalwarts, Susan B. Anthony and Elizabeth Cady Stanton, had generated in their heyday. Their successor, Anna Howard Shaw, was a fiery speaker but a lackluster leader. During her presidency of the National American Woman Suffrage Association (NAWSA), the suffrage movement became mired at the state and local level, settling into the low-keyed, plodding pace that characterized it until 1913. Shaw was eventually succeeded by Carrie Chapman Catt, a much more dynamic leader, but one who remained faithful to the old methods when she assumed command of NAWSA. As late as 1913, Catt noted: "I have always felt that I *enlisted for life* when I went into the movement."[1] The already decades-old suffrage struggle, Catt believed, was not likely to be settled in her lifetime.

Events belied such a pessimistic prediction. Between 1913 and 1920, the suffrage movement experienced a revitalization of dramatic proportions. By the end of 1915, the locus of the suffrage struggle shifted from the state to the national level, marking a distinct turning point. A suffrage victory in New York State in 1917 signaled the long sought-after break in the ranks of the previously impenetrable eastern states. And, by the fall of 1918, the issue was so charged that the President of the United States pleaded for its passage as an emergency war measure. Success of the suffrage amendment, declared Woodrow Wilson in an address to the Senate, was "vital to the winning of the war. . . ."

It is vital to the right solutions which we must settle and settle immediately."[2] By the summer of 1919, the federal amendment had passed both houses of Congress and was ratified just one year later by the requisite number of states.

This turn-around in the fortunes of women suffrage was in part a function of the time, occurring as it did in the same decade that witnessed the peaking of progressive reform and a cataclysmic world war. But these events, while an accurate description of conditions prevailing at that time, are not adequate explanations for the success of woman suffrage coming when it did. Progressive reformers had long advocated suffrage through state constitutional amendment. But progressive reform began to wane without ever having embraced a federal suffrage amendment. And as for the war, hostilities had almost ended before suffrage was added to the emergency war measures list. To understand fully the success of woman suffrage it is necessary to look beyond the circumstance of time, to the transformation that occurred within the ranks of the suffrage movement itself. A reexamination of the women responsible for this transformation helps to shed new light on the militant suffrage movement destined to have such a profound effect.

When Alice Paul assumed leadership of NAWSA's Congressional Committee, there was little in her upbringing to predict the effect that she would have, either on the suffrage movement or on the people with whom she worked. Alice Paul possessed many of the same social and educational characteristics of other women suffragists. Her marital and educational status, while unusual, were not extraordinary. She never married, but neither did many of her contemporaries; she collected a string of degrees that eventually included two law degrees and a Ph.D., but there were others as versatile. Yet Paul was an extraordinary personality, perhaps the single truly charismatic figure in the twentieth-century suffrage movement. Certainly she was the engine that powered the militant suffrage movement. She successfully mobilized both impatient younger women and discontented older women. To these women, Paul represented the force that made them willing to take uncommon risks, including imprisonment and possible estrangement from families, friends, and peers.

In *The Sociology of Religion*, written in 1922, Max Weber might have used Alice Paul as his model in developing the concept of the charismatic leader. Such a person, Weber concluded, challenged the established order in ways both constructive and destructive, established boundaries by drawing on legitimacy from sources within her- or himself, and disregarded public opinion.[3] This certainly applied to Paul. When faced with law or custom that, if observed, would surely have nullified a particular plan of action, Paul simply proclaimed the constraint "absurd" and proceeded to do exactly as she pleased.[4] When public opinion turned against her, as it did during the suffrage parade in 1913, and again in 1917 when she picketed the White House while the country was at war, she either ignored the opposition or turned it to her own advantage. When crowds watching the suffrage parade turned riotous, the resultant publicity greatly benefited both her organization and the suffrage movement in general.[5] Similarly, attacks on White House picketers by hostile crowds during World War I generated publicity that sometimes rivaled the war news for front page coverage.[6] Marshall McLuhan's controversial discourse on understanding media may have been decades away, but for Alice Paul in the second decade of the twentieth century, there was no doubt that publicity *was* the event.

In attempting to explain Paul, historians have often dismissed her as either well-meaning but harmless, or as an irritating thorn in the side of the suffrage movement which ultimately proved harmful. At best she is accorded minimal credit for advancing suffrage.[7] Others have gone so far as to label her as pathological—a personality who appealed only to persons on the fringes of the suffrage movement.[8] The tendency to accept this explanation is understandable but unjustified. Those who responded to Paul were sufficiently alienated from society's customs and dictates concerning women that they willingly followed a leader who advocated what were considered extreme tactics. Attempts by women to improve their status in society and to secure their rights have always drawn criticism. Aggressive action is doubly damned because it is a trait that, when attributed to women, is considered negative. But, as S. N. Eisenstadt points out, "The search for meaning, consistency, order is not always something extraordinary, something which exists only . . . among pathological personalities, but also in all stable social situations . . . focused within some specific parts of the social structure and of an individual's life space."[9] American society, in the early twentieth century, was capable of producing disorientation and alienation in women, particularly middle-class women who had the means, the motivation, and the opportunity to take an active public role. Their response to Alice Paul can be understood as a symbol of their search for balance and equality in a world they perceived to be disorderly. Indeed, women sought order in the same way that progressive reform has been characterized as a search for order in a disorderly society.[10] And Paul herself was motivated not by an unrealistic obsession that could justly be called pathological, but by a logically developed expectation of equality for both sexes. Her charismatic appeal clearly made her more effective in pursuing that goal.

Paul, although she professed to be unaware of her power or the source of it, nevertheless used her unfailing ability to motivate people.[11] "I cannot say that I personally like to do the things that Alice Paul set us to do," wrote one bemused worker, "But . . . I helped to picket the White House, to keep the watch fires burning near Suffrage Headquarters and to pester congressmen and senators and did my little best to swell all sorts of parades and demonstrations."[12] More commonly, the women who worked in Paul's organization did so with great enthusiasm and were more than willing to follow Paul's instructions to the letter.

If it is true that Paul did not understand the source of her power, she nevertheless was aware of it. More importantly, she used this power to great effect. One suffrage volunteer vividly recalled how newcomers to the organization met Alice Paul for the first time. They were assigned tasks about the headquarters but not specifically told which job they were being trained for or what precisely was to be expected of them. All the time, Paul received reports from her lieutenants on the volunteer's progress, performance, and potential.

And then Miss Paul sent for you. I will never forget that first interview. Miss Paul sat at a desk in a room seemingly completely dark except for a small desk lamp. . . . I felt she deliberately created the atmosphere of the tough executive. There was no subtlety about her. Direct, blunt, she asked why I wanted to do this, she wanted to probe sufficiently without wasting time, to discover if I had any weaknesses and to what extent she and the movement could depend upon me."[13]

This volunteer left the interview with a sense of deep commitment, not only to the suffrage organization, but to Alice Paul as well.

Paul was more concerned about enthusiasm for the movement than with an individual's specific talents.[14] Ardent feminism was the criteria for acceptance in those to whom she entrusted responsibility. Class, social standing, education, or experience did not particularly concern her. Thus, although her organization, like most suffrage groups, was largely white and middle class, dedication to feminism was the common bond.[15]

Nevertheless, Paul harbored many of the same biases and prejudices associated with her elite, white, upper middle-class milieu. Clearly she was more comfortable with people from her own background with whom she could speak with no self-consciousness of her desire to find a quiet, secluded home where one might still find "some American people left."[16] While she claimed long-standing friendships with both blacks and Jews, at the same time she had a reputation for particularly noticeable prejudices against both groups.[17]

In her personal life, Paul was often as undecipherable as she appeared to be in her public life. In truth, the personal and the public were hard to separate. At a time when most women were "other directed," Paul apparently had made the ego-identify shift to an individualistic ethic necessary for development as a strong member of society capable of functioning in the public sphere.[18] Rarely introspective, Paul applied her abilities to the task at hand in businesslike fashion. Her intellectualism and purposefulness made her appear aloof, coldly efficient, and abrupt to the point of insensitivity and rudeness. Frequently, however, what appeared to be insensitivity was only absent-mindness regarding everyday amenities. When it was pointed out to her that a volunteer worker had left in anger because Paul had presumed too much and acknowledged gratitude too little to suit the disgruntled woman, Paul overcompensated by profusely thanking other workers, and even went so far as to apologize for uncommitted transgressions.[19]

Despite her refusal to dwell on adversity or obstacles, Paul was not immune to attacks leveled against both her and her organization, especially when they came from other women. Paul never forgot an incident in 1914, just after she had embarked on the first anti-Democratic party campaign. She went to Mississippi to participate in a conference with NAWSA and other suffrage groups. Instead, she was treated as a pariah by the other conferees who were convinced that Paul's proposal would cause irreparable damage to the movement. The profound sense of isolation that she experienced was still with her sixty years later. "I remember going down in the morning for breakfast, and here were all these people from all different states in the Union, and I remember that not one human being spoke to me. I just felt *such* an outcast, and for a long time we were regarded in that way."[20]

Although she had many devoted admirers and loyal co-workers and friends, Paul had few intimate, long-term relationships. Most of her close friends were women who worked with her in the American and international women's movements. Although she never married, she certainly had no conflicts with the institution.[21] Her closest friend throughout her long career was Elsie Hill, a Connecticut congressman's daughter who came to work for Paul in 1913. They struck up an immediate friendship and worked together almost constantly from then on. Much later, after the deaths of Elsie's husband and Alice's sister Helen, with whom she had made her home in the 1940s, the two friends shared a home, continuing their work together on behalf of women until Elsie's death in the late 1960s.[22]

Despite recent scholarship which suggests that some relationships between women reformers and activists may have had a sexual component, this was almost certainly not the case with Paul and Hill.[23] Personally, Paul was as conservative as the most circumspect Victorian matron appeared to be. She never hesitated to censor co-workers or to monitor their behavior about even the pettiest matter. She refused, for example, to allow her workers to smoke in the main floor offices of the suffrage headquarters. Although she suffered smoking in the upper, more secluded rooms, even this privilege was revoked when important visitors were scheduled.[24] On more substantive issues, such as birth control, abortion, and divorce, party workers clearly understood that they were not to express their own personal opinions. Paul chastised members for making statements which she had not personally authorized.[25] All other issues took a back seat to suffrage. Paul insisted that the organization stick to its single-issue framework. In many instances, this strategic and tactical stance was reinforced by her personal conservatism and sense of morality which, for example, caused her to view with disdain those persons who advocated the right to sexual preference.[26] Such an attitude most likely precluded similar relationships in her own life.

The contours of Paul's life suggest that she monitored her own actions as relentlessly as she governed her workers—surely a strange practice for an advocate of women's freedom. Her followers, however they may have chafed under her tight rein, did not view her as arrogant, presumptive, or unfaithful to their cause—at least not until after suffrage had been achieved and new political lines were drawn in the women's movement. Regardless of how her public image changed over time, Paul always maintained a larger vision, one that transcended her own conservatism. "I think if we get freedom for women, then they are probably going to do a lot of things that I wish they wouldn't do; but it seems to me that isn't our business to say what they should do with it. It is our business to see that they get it."[27]

Freedom, for Alice Paul, extended beyond suffrage. Ultimately, it meant working to secure an equal rights amendment. Her goal was to remove all legal inequalities from the statute books throughout the country. Such a goal was, and is, profoundly revolutionary in nature. Equal suffrage was the most radical demand of the nineteenth-century women's movement because it propelled women into the public sphere.[28] Just so, the struggle for equal rights in the twentieth century demands a radical redefinition of power relationships, one directed primarily at the public sphere, but which has important and unavoidable consequences for the private sphere.

Following the passage of the suffrage amendment in 1919, and its subsequent ratification in 1920, American women were in the strongest position that they had yet experienced since the inception of the women's movement. It had taken seventy years to achieve that step and in the course of those seventy years, many women had become radicalized. But radicalization came slowly. Years earlier, in 1872, Susan B. Anthony had expressed her desire to see "some terrific shock to startle the women of the nation into a self-respect which will compel them to see the absolute degradation of their . . . position; which will compel them to break the yoke of bondage and give them faith in themselves; which will make them proclaim their allegiance to women first."[29] The cataclysmic shock that Anthony so fervently prayed for never came, but the pervasive inequality that faced women in all aspects of their lives did shake them out of their lethargy. For a brief time, women acted in unison to gain control of their destiny, or an aspect of it. Yet, in the shift from the struggle for equal suffrage to that for equal rights, they could not sustain their unity. The dissolution of the unity they had achieved, after seventy long years of heroic effort, began at the moment of their triumph.

Why this was so has been the focus of some discussion by historians of the women's movement. But the conclusions reached, however tentative, have been largely influenced by the limitations inherent in defining the parameters of their inquiries. A great deal has been written about the contributions made by the National American Woman Suffrage Association under the leadership of the very able Carrie Chapman Catt. In writing the history of the last years of suffrage through the prism of NAWSA activity, the contributions of the National Woman's Party have been either overlooked, dismissed, or misjudged. Yet it is vital to understand fully and to integrate into the history of suffrage, the role played by the NWP in order to understand fully why it was that the women's movement seemed to dissolve rather than strengthen in the 1920s. The ideological conflicts that were a constant undercurrent during the suffrage years erupted full-blown in the 1920s and set the tone that would dominate the women's movement for the next thirty-five years, thereby insuring that the search for equal rights would be as hard fought a cause as suffrage had been. Alice Paul wrote and introduced the Equal Rights Amendment in 1923. By the time of her death in 1977, it seemed finally that the ERA would indeed become a part of the Constitution, but with three states left to ratify the amendment, time ran out. It may be ironic, but hardly coincidental, that some of the underlying causes for the failure of the ERA in the 1970s and 1980s correspond precisely with the underlying causes for dissension in the women's movement of the 1920s.

CHAPTER I

WEST HARTFORD PUBLIC LIBRARY

Breaking with the Past: The New Suffragists

By 1913, a new generation of women—the *New Suffragists*—were ready to take their place in the ranks of the American women's movement.[1] They were among the first and second generations of women to enjoy the opportunities for higher education that had opened up with the initiation of co-education in colleges and universities like Oberlin and Berkeley, and with the founding of the prestigious women's colleges, from Mount Holyoke to Barnard.[2] They were also the beneficiaries of the decades of voluntary, organized club affiliation which had helped to sharpen their political skills and administrative talents. In a broader vein, industrialization, advances in technology, unprecedented immigration, and rapid urbanization combined to alter significantly women's perceptions of society as well as their status in that society.[3] New attitudes and perceptions led women to question old assumptions on issues such as marriage, family, work, and career. The *New Suffragists* were the products of the combined social, political, and economic changes of the preceding half century.

The more involved women became, either in their own careers or jobs, or in the problems they perceived in society, the more apparent became the multiple disadvantages that they faced simply because they were women. For many women, the suffrage movement was the political focus of their new awareness, critical to their aspirations for active participation in the affairs of society. And, perhaps predictably, the changes in society that created a new landscape for women also worked to change the way in which some of them perceived the strategy that the suffrage movement should adopt.

The arguments used by suffragists in their efforts to secure the vote had shifted in the 1890s. When the vote became a goal of the women's movement in the mid-nineteenth century, women had claimed it as a natural right, nothing more and nothing less.[4] In the latter decades of the century, the rationale changed. Women, long the recognized keepers of the flame, would use their votes to help create a better society by acting as a moral balance of power. Temperance, protective legislation for women and children, better city and state government—all of these would be acted upon in a positive fashion by women voters. As an additional incentive, participation in the rights of citizenship would make women better wives and mothers.[5]

Strategically, this shift in the rationale for suffrage proved to be beneficial. On principle, it was ultimately counter-productive to real equality. Once women gave up their claim to suffrage as their natural right as full and equal citizens, it was difficult to maintain that men and women were in fact equal. For most women, however, this was not a problem since it squared with their own beliefs in any case. They forged ahead secure in the belief that they would indeed create a better world.

Just after the turn of the century, new fissures began to appear in the suffrage movement. A growing sense of dissatisfaction developed among some women over the way in which NAWSA conducted its suffrage campaign. NAWSA's strategy of individual state campaigns seemed to grow increasingly more cumbersome and tired, and increasingly less realistic with each defeat. NAWSA conducted well over 400 state campaigns intended to induce state legislators to submit constitutional amendments to their electorates. An additional 300 campaigns were waged to persuade state party leaders to include suffrage planks in their party platforms. The overwhelming majority of these costly and disspiriting campaigns ended in failure.[6] Following Wyoming's entry into the Union as a suffrage state in 1890, three more states enfranchised women during that decade: Colorado in 1893, and

Idaho and Utah in 1896. But between 1896 and 1910, they remained the only four suffrage states—testimony that state-by-state methods were both cumbersome and slow to produce results. In November 1910, Washington state voters extended the franchise to women, and California followed suit in October 1911.[7]

While NAWSA leaders and most of its membership were in a celebratory mood following the California victory, others were far less sanguine. In their view the at best incremental gains achieved by NAWSA provided little cause to pursue the same strategy, and they were wary of remaining enmeshed in state work. In Massachusetts, Maud Wood Park, a NAWSA officer, suggested not only a move toward greater emphasis on federal work, but also toward less tried and tired tactics as well.[8] New York's Harriot Stanton Blatch, the daughter of women's rights pioneer, Elizabeth Cady Stanton, organized the first American suffrage parade as she, too, expressed willingness to adopt less genteel methods and to shift the focus to federal work.[9] Dora Lewis, of main-line Philadelphia society, and Caroline Katzenstein, both members of the Philadelphia Equal Franchise Society, were similarly chafing under NAWSA's tight rein.[10] And in California, Alice Park Lock agreed wholeheartedly with Lydia Kingsmill Commander of New York, that the time was ripe to "appeal to the women voters in the West" to use their political power in helping to secure a federal suffrage amendment.[11] For these and many other women, their impulse to seek new tactics reflected a common disaffection with the moribund NAWSA campaign.

Despite the grass-roots sentiment for federal suffragism exhibited by many of its members, NAWSA was not prepared to undertake a major shift in emphasis away from state work. NAWSA had affiliations in every state, almost all major cities, and many smaller cities and towns. It could boast of a vast machinery to work on behalf of suffrage. The campaign run by each state affiliate was generally aimed at the state's political party machines, or at the state legislature. The campaigns were, as a rule, run independently of any other state campaign, and frequently lacked thorough organization or planning. NAWSA's national office provided some guidelines, but it had no real overall strategy beyond encouraging the continuation of such campaigns, supplying speakers, and raising money. In those instances when a state did en-franchise women, NAWSA and the successful affiliate considered the work finished in that state. It did not occur to NAWSA to reap the benefit of the new political power held by the female voters in the state.[12]

Indicative of their decentralized approach to the suffrage campaign, NAWSA's national headquarters in 1910 was located not in Washington, New York, Chicago, or another equally appropriate location, but on the ground floor of the courthouse in Warren, Ohio. Shortly after Susan B. Anthony retired in 1900, Harriot Taylor Upton, NAWSA's national treasurer, made relocation in Warren—her hometown—the price for her continued service.[13] It was Alva Belmont who finally persuaded the board to move the headquarters to New York, a location better suited to the serious and vibrant nature of the organization's work. Mrs. Belmont, a generous supporter of suffrage, rented the entire twentieth floor of a new office building in Manhattan, part of which was occupied by the New York State Suffrage Association. Belmont's offer to subsidize the rent for NAWSA may have been more significant in the board's decision than either the opportunity to operate from such an important base, or the potential for more effective organization due to the presence of a state affiliate.[14]

Although the choice of the location for headquarters reveals the reluctance of the leaders of NAWSA to depart from old concepts, publicly they avoided negative comments about the merits of a federal amendment. They simply did not see it as a legitimate means to achieve their ends. To be sure, NAWSA paid lip service to the idea of a federal amendment. They even took advantage of opportunities as they arose to make a case for federal action. Catt, for example, testified before the Senate Committee on Woman Suffrage in 1910: "Ordinary fair play should compel every believer, no matter what are his views on woman suffrage, to grant to women the easiest process of enfranchisement and that is the submission of a federal amendment."[15] But this was more in deference to Susan B. Anthony than it was a serious indication of a change of direction. Even the establishment of a congressional liaison committee in 1910, called the Congressional Committee, did not signal change.

Elizabeth Kent, the wife of a California congressman, William Kent, agreed to head the committee. And although Mrs. Kent herself was a strong advocate of a federal amendment, she accepted her new assignment with the understanding that very little would be expected of her. By NAWSA's own admission, "no busier woman could have been selected and beyond making excellent arrangements for the hearings [before Congress], the committee was not active."[16] NAWSA's budget for congressional work was $10.00 per year, and Mrs. Kent reported that she generally had a surplus at year's end.[17]

The concession to federalism made by NAWSA in establishing the Congressional Committee created a misconception that the organization was vigorously pursuing an amendment on all fronts. In truth, its leaders were reluctant—partially out of inertia, partially out of sporadically incremental gains—to reorient the machinery already in place in the states. The winning over of five suffrage states between 1910 and 1912 produced two reactions.[18] On the one hand the victories provided a much-needed boost to NAWSA members whose morale had been badly waning. At the same time, the victories sparked a vigorous interest in a federal amendment, particularly among younger women. Buoyed by the potential that they saw for their own lives and confident that victory could be obtained in the short run, the *New Suffragists*, in concert with some of the older generation of suffragists, became the core of the militant suffrage movement in the United States. Suprisingly, the source of inspiration for the *New Suffragists* came not from the conservative American suffrage tradition, but from the much more aggressive British woman suffrage movement.[19]

The British suffragettes,[20] under the leadership of the Pankhursts—Emmeline, and her two daughters, Christabel and Sylvia—began their militant campaign in 1905. Christabel, a young lawyer, originated the militant strategy. Beginning with the mild action of "questioning" Members of Parliament and the Cabinet when they appeared in public, the suffragettes gradually escalated their activity to the point of minor violence, such as window smashing and rock throwing. The Women's Social and Political Union (WSPU) and the Pankhursts, who founded the organization, soon made suffrage a national issue in England.[21]

Prior to this time, the British suffrage movement had worked for constitutional change along conventional paths in much the same way as NAWSA. The impatience of youth, however, soon triggered the event that acted as the catalyst for the radicalization of many suffragettes. "Christabel Pankhurst and Miss Annie Kenney went to a meeting of one of the great liberal leaders, Sir Edward Grey," recalled Lady Emmeline Pethick-Lawrence some years later. "At the close of Sir Edward's meeting, they rose to put a question. . . . They put it at the proper time . . . and in the proper way. But instead of receiving an answer [they] were flung out of the hall . . . with great violence and held a demonstration in the street, and were arrested and sent to prison. That is how what is called militancy began."[22]

The model for militancy provided by the Pankhursts included all of the elements subsequently adapted to the American situation, as well as some that were not incorporated, notably violence and zealous martyrdom. Even at the height of their militant campaign in 1917, American suffragists never advocated a policy of violent militance, though violence was often directed at them. Nor could the Americans claim a martyr to the cause quite like Britain's Emily Davison, whose fatal act of protest was to throw herself in front of the King's galloping horse at the Derby in 1913, though they could claim an equally effective martyr—Inez Milholland—some three years later.[23] The three main tactics employed by the Americans were drawn directly from the British movement: first, holding the political party in power responsible for failure to enact a suffrage amendment; second, publicity; and third, protest suitable to focus attention on the demand for a federal amendment.[24]

The independence, courage, and audacity of the British women captured the imagination of the *New Suffragists* in America. Inez Haynes Irwin reported her own reaction to the English movement: "When in England, the first militant of Mrs. Pankhurst's forces threw her first stone, my heart went with it. . . . At last the traditions of female patience . . . had gone by the board. Women were using the tactics that, through all the ages men had used; the only tactics that were sure to bring results; rebellion and violence."[25] Mrs. Pankhurst had a similar effect on many who heard her speak. When she first spoke in Hartford, Connecticut, Mrs. Pankhurst galvanized Katharine Houghton Hepburn. Hepburn later recalled the seminal event "as one of the most remarkable speeches I have ever heard." She pointed to it as the catalyst of her involvement in the suffrage movement. "I remember so well [it was] the first time I even thought of [suffrage] as something I must work for myself."[26] With this, Hepburn had started down the road of militant feminism that would lead to her split with NAWSA, her presidency of the Connecticut branch of the National Woman's Party, and finally her tireless spreading of the gospel of Margaret Sanger and the birth control movement.

But even before the word had reached American shores, there were Americans in England and on the Continent who witnessed first-hand the actions of the suffragettes, and in some cases worked with them. Their views, unhampered by the critical filter of the British government and a frequently unsympathetic press, had a profound influence on the *New Suffragists*.

Harriot Stanton Blatch, perhaps the first American to be influenced by the Pankhursts, married English businessman William Henry Blatch, in 1882. For the next twenty years, the Blatch's lived in Basingstoke, England, a small town west of London. Every bit her mother's daughter, Harriot threw herself into a variety of social and political movements, including the Women's Local Government Society and the Fabian Society. She was most impressed, however, with the work of the Women's Franchise League, the suffrage group organized by Emmeline Pankhurst in 1889. During her stay in England, Blatch's home was open to a stream of feminists, socialists, and other assorted radicals. By the time she returned to the United States in 1902, both Blatch and her daughter, Nora, had forged strong international ties with many of England's soon-to-be-militant feminists, including the Pankhursts and the Pethick-Lawrences. Both Blatches were quick to defend militant feminism at home and were instrumental in bringing Emmeline Pankhurst to the United States some years later for her first speaking tour.[27]

The historian, Mary Ritter Beard, accompanied her husband, Charles Austin Beard, to England in 1900. While Charles attended Oxford and helped to found Ruskin Hall, Mary Beard went to work with the Pankhursts. From them, she gained a respect for both the English brand of suffragism and the concerns of working-class women. Her interest in both issues remained very much alive when she returned to the United States in 1902.[28]

Alva Belmont, embittered by the public reaction to her divorce from

William Kissam Vanderbilt (grandson of Cornelius Vanderbilt), and her remarriage a year later to Oliver Hazard Perry Belmont (the son of the wealthy utilities and street-railway magnate, August Belmont), readily embraced militant suffragism. Visits to her daughter Consuelo, the Duchess of Marlborough, brought her into contact with Mrs. Pankhurst and "her great army." Belmont's admiration for the Pankhursts and her anger and outrage at the hypocritical public reaction to her personal life, became the catalysts that transformed her from an insulated society hostess into an ardent feminist. "Yes, I am a militant and I glory in it," she revealed to a friend, adding that she felt only pity for those who wanted "the old-fashioned woman you have cowed into a submissive nonentity."[29]

Elizabeth Robins, the American actress and writer, was a convert first to suffragism and then to militant suffragism, following her settlement in England. She served on the Board of the WSPU and directed much of her creativity toward publicizing the movement. The popularity of her play, *Votes For Women*, and a successful novel, *The Convert*, both of which appeared in 1907, helped to persuade many others of the justness of her cause. Robins, like Mary Beard, saw the needs of working-class women as an integral concern of the suffrage movement, a belief that her sister-in-law, Margaret Dreier Robins, the head of the Women's Trade Union League in America, may have helped to shape. Elizabeth Robins played a significant role in propagandizing American women with her many essays and articles which both explained and justified militant suffragism.[30]

Sara Bard Field's introduction to militancy came through her friendship with Emma Wold, one of the organizer's of the Oregon College Equal Suffrage League. Wold, a Norwegian immigrant and cousin of Henrick Ibsen, impressed Field immediately with her feminist background. Wold spent several years in the WSPU and had endured arrests, imprisonment, and forced feedings. The poet and romanticist in Field responded to Wold's courage, and Sara soon agreed to take on the task of organizing Oregon for suffrage.[31]

Lucy Burns, who worked closest with Alice Paul during the final years of the American suffrage campaign, gave up a promising academic career in favor of political activism after working with the Pankhursts in 1909. Burns was in Germany to attend graduate school.

mother's situation, however, and it undoubtedly influenced Alice's determination to be independent and self-sufficient.[46]

In any event, Donald Paul did not approve of Alice's suffrage activity. Tacie Paul may have withheld public approval of Alice in order to maintain harmony within the family.[47] Despite her reluctance in proffering public support for Alice—and her desire not to offend her brother-in-law—Tacie Paul did support Alice financially, which allowed her to devote herself full-time to the suffrage cause.[48]

The elder Pauls raised their children in an atmosphere of discipline, achievement, and service. In keeping with Quaker teaching, neither music nor dancing were a part of the children's childhood experience.[49] They knew that their Irish maids went off to dances, but assumed that only "a sort of common people" engaged in such activity.[50] After her arrival at Swarthmore, however, Alice did take dance classes and attended the dances sponsored by the college for the women students, as was the custom of the times. But Paul's recreation centered on sports, especially tennis. Suffrage co-worker Mabel Vernon, a year ahead of Paul at Swarthmore, remembered Alice as a rather shy, sports-oriented young woman. In contrast to the sickly pallor that later caused much concern and comment, Vernon described Alice as healthy and vigorous in appearance as a college student.[51]

Paul read voraciously, especially in the classics. She haunted the local Friends Library, consuming literature with a passion. As a young girl, she read every line written by Charles Dickens "over and over and over again."[52] Dickens' social commentary undoubtedly helped to shape her own sense of justice. Her love of literature stayed with her throughout her life, though in the hectic days of the suffrage campaign she found little time to read extensively. Her well-known reading habits gave rise to a story, attributed to co-worker Anne Martin, which circulated around suffrage circles. According to Martin, one of Paul's sacrifices during the campaign was to stay away from Washington bookstores, to keep no books in her room, and to refrain from reading *anything* not specifically related to suffrage. Miss Paul, it was said, did not want to be tempted by anything that might cause her to give less than 100 percent to the suffrage cause.[53]

At Swarthmore, Paul chose biology as her major because, as she later explained, it was something about which she knew nothing.[54] From

Traveling to England for a brief holiday, she met Emmeline, Christabel, and Sylvia, and was so inspired by both their cause and their charismatic appeal that she gradually abandoned her graduate work entirely in order to organize for the WSPU. The chief organizer for the Congressional Union and later the National Woman's Party, Burns spent more time in prison—both in America and in England—than any other American suffragist.[32]

The woman most directly responsible for transferring militant tactics to the American campaign was, of course, Alice Paul. The founder of the National Woman's Party, Paul became the dynamic that propelled American suffragism to its successful end. A remarkably private person for so visible a public figure, an air of mystery seemed always to surround her. An article in *Everybody's* magazine, at the height of the American campaign, attempted to uncover the "real" Alice Paul amidst the myriad contradictory descriptions of her that made the rounds of both suffrage and political circles. The author concluded with obvious frustration and exasperation, "There is no Alice Paul. There is suffrage. She leads by being . . . her cause."[33] Most contemporary journalists assigned to cover Paul were baffled by her and often attempted to make her more—or less—than human. "I tried to imagine Alice Paul married," one such writer confided to her readers, "and I almost succeeded when I heard she was taking dancing lessons last Spring."[34] To associate Paul with the ordinary events of middle-class life, however, was beyond the writer's ability. She went on to predict that Paul would follow the fiery road to revolution. To this journalist and many of her contemporaries, Paul's political activities and the events of everyday life were clearly contradictory, if not mutually exclusive.

Paul, idolized and idealized by her suffrage followers, often appeared paradoxical. Alternately described as "exceedingly charitable . . . and patient," and "cold, austere, and a little remote," she elicited profound and unquestioning loyalty from her friends and co-workers and intense distrust and skepticism from her enemies.[35] More than one unsympathetic observer described her singlemindedness as "fanaticism." Exasperated by Paul's campaign against the Democrats in the summer of 1914, and its attendant publicity, Mrs. Medill McCormick, a NAWSA officer, described Paul as an "aneamic fanatic, well-intentioned and conscientious . . . but almost unbalanced because of her physical condition." McCormick attributed the younger woman's frail appearance to Paul's refusal to spend more than thirty cents a day on food. This, McCormick claimed, was Paul's attitude toward suffrage *par excellence*. "She will be a *martyr* whether there is the slightest excuse for it in this country or not, and I am really convinced that she will die for the cause, but it will be because of her 30 [cent] meals."[36]

Paul's followers were as lavish in their praise of her as her detractors were in their criticism. "I know of no other modern leader with whom to compare her," activist Doris Stevens once observed. "I think she must possess many of the same qualities that Lenin does. . . . Cool, practical, rational. . . . And if she has demanded the ultimate of her followers, she has given it herself."[37] Maud Younger, the "millionaire waitress" from California who was founder and president of the waitress' union in San Francisco, and a tireless and skilled suffrage organizer, could not say enough about Paul's executive abilities. "She has in the first place, a devotion to the cause which is absolutely self-sacrificing. She has an indomitable will. . . . She has a clear, penetrating, analytic mind which cleaves straight to the heart of things. . . . She is a genius for organization, both in the mass and in detail."[38] In a similar vein, Lucy Burns, Paul's second in command, noted: "Her great assets, I should say, are her power to make plans on a national scale; and a supplementary power to see that it is done down to the last postage stamp."[39]

In substance, both views of Paul were accurate, although not necessarily in their particulars. The complexities of her personality revealed in such opposite opinions can better be understood in the context of her background and upbringing. Born on 11 January 1885, in the small Quaker community of Moorestown, New Jersey, nine miles east of Philadelphia, Alice was the oldest child of William M. and Tacie (Parry) Paul. Opposition to authority was nothing new to the family, even before Alice came along. The family tree included, on her mother's side, William Penn, and, on her father's side, the Winthrops of Massachusetts.[40] The first Paul to settle in New Jersey had left England precipitately, after prolonged religious and political conflict with the Crown.[41]

Alice's father was a successful businessman who served as president

of the bank that he helped to found, the Burlington County Trust Company. He also held directorships on the boards of several local companies, invested in several profitable real estate ventures, and owned a working farm. Alice's mother was the daughter of one of the founders of Swarthmore College. Indeed, Tacie Parry would have been among the first women to graduate from Swarthmore, but she left college in her senior year to marry William Paul. Alice followed in her mother's footsteps, first attending a Quaker school in Moorestown, and then enrolling at Swarthmore. Both Pauls were active and devout Quakers and adhered to traditional Quaker beliefs, including that of equality between the sexes.[42] One of Alice's earliest memories involved accompanying her mother to suffrage meetings at a neighbor's home in Moorestown.[43] In addition to Alice, the Pauls had three other children: William, Jr., Helen, and Parry Haines Paul.

Not a great deal is known about Paul's relationship with her parents. Although she was sixteen years old when her father died suddenly of pneumonia, her recollections of his death were vague, and she would say only: "I just remember that life went on."[44] William Paul's opinion of his oldest daughter was revealed in a magazine article in 1916. An interviewer, seeking hometown opinion regarding Paul's suffrage activity, asked Mrs. Paul how she viewed her daughter. "Well," she replied, "I remember that Mr. Paul used to say that whenever there was anything hard and disagreeable to do, 'I bank on Alice.' "[45] The article left the impression that Mrs. Paul had somewhat ambivalent views of her daughter's militance.

Mrs. Paul's ambivalence may have stemmed less from any real questions she had regarding Alice's suffrage work than they did from her desire to keep peace in her family. Following her husband's death, her brother-in-law, Donald Paul, took over many of the family's financial affairs. The family was well-off, to be sure, but in keeping with the custom of the times, Donald Paul took upon himself his late brother's obligations to his family. Like many middle-class women, Tacie Paul had limited knowledge of the family's finances, and neither the experience nor the confidence necessary to take over when faced with the crisis of her husband's sudden death. The circumstances probably did not affect Alice in an immediately direct way since she had already left home for college. She was nevertheless aware of

an early age, then, she incorporated into her life an axiom that remained with her: There was, she believed, little to be gained from redoing something already done. Biology represented new ground to cover, and thus suited her sense of progression. Still, her commitment to biology was superficial, at best, for she never really considered a career in science. Her introduction to politics and economics came only in her senior year, when the college hired Professor Robert Brooks. Alice was immediately attracted to both disciplines and she did so well in his classes that Brooks recommended her for a College Settlement Association fellowship at the New York School of Philanthropy (later the Columbia University School of Social Work).[55]

After graduating from Swarthmore in 1905, Paul spent several years pursuing her studies, and in social work. She fulfilled her year at the New York School of Philanthropy, then enrolled at the University of Pennsylvania where in 1907 she earned a master's degree in sociology with minor fields in economics and political science. Her academic interest in the problems faced by women because of their legal status began to take shape while she was at the University of Pennsylvania. Research that ultimately became her doctoral dissertation entitled "Towards Equality," begun at this time, was an examination of the legal status of women in Pennsylvania.

Paul interrupted work on her doctorate in order to accept a second fellowship to study social work, this time at Woodbridge, England, the central training school for Quakers. As with biology, her commitment to social work was not very deep. She arrived in England in the fall of 1907 with the belief that she was only marking time. "I knew in a very short time that I was never going to be a social worker, because I could see that social workers were not doing much good in the world. . . . You knew you couldn't *change* the situation by social work."[56]

While she was in England, however, Paul found the cause that integrated and brought into focus her family heritage, service-oriented Quaker education, and interests in economics, political science, and the status of women. Christabel Pankhurst spoke at the University of Birmingham where Paul was fulfilling the academic requirements of her fellowship. Suffrage, then even less popular than it was respectable, incited the mostly male student audience to rowdy behavior.

Christabel was shouted down, and embarrassed Birmingham officials were forced to cancel her speech. The reaction to Christabel's attempt to speak both angered and surprised Paul. There was, of course, no opposition to the suffrage meetings she had attended as a child with her mother. And although her research on the status of women ought to have prepared her for such resistance to the idea, it shocked her nevertheless to witness the opposition first-hand. For Paul, such resistance was foolish and ill-informed. If her fellow students were so intolerant, the suffragettes "had anyway one heart and soul convert . . . that was myself."[57]

When Paul finished her work at Woodbridge, a representative of the Charity Organization Society of London invited her to become a case worker in the working-class district of Dalston. There, in the fall of 1908, Paul took part in her first suffrage parade and began an association with the WSPU which lasted for two years. During that time she became thoroughly versed in the strategy and tactics of militant suffragism. She participated in demonstrations which led to her arrest and imprisonment. Along with her English comrades, she took part in hunger strikes to protest the British government's treatment of suffrage prisoners.[58] It was a profoundly formative period in her political education. Prior to this, Paul exhibited little interest in political activism and belonged to no American suffrage organization.

It was in Europe that Paul first met Lucy Burns, the redheaded Irish American from Brooklyn who was to become her alter ego in the American suffrage campaign. Burns had graduated from Vassar, attended Yale's graduate school briefly, then returned to Brooklyn to teach English at Erasmus High School. Lucy resigned her teaching position in 1906 in order to study languages in Europe. She went first to the University of Berlin for two years, then on to the University of Bonn in 1908, for one year. But, much like Alice Paul, Lucy Burns seemed to be drifting along without a real focus. During a vacation break from her studies, Lucy traveled to England where she met the Pankhursts, developed an intense interest in their suffrage activities, and decided to continue her studies at Oxford. In 1909, she enrolled at Oxford, ostensibly to begin work on her doctorate. In fact, she spent little time in study, preferring instead to throw herself into the thick of the suffrage campaign. For the next three years, until her return to

the United States in 1912, Lucy worked with the WSPU as an organizer, primarily in Edinburgh. There, she gained invaluable experience that served the American cause well in later years.

Alice Paul first met Lucy Burns in a London police station. Both
had been arrested for demonstrating. As they stood about the station,
waiting for the police to process their cases, Alice noticed the tiny
American flag pinned to Lucy's lapel. She introduced herself and the
two young women, seating themselves on a tabletop, quietly compared suffrage experiences, ignoring the stationhouse bedlam around
them as though the entire situation was perfectly ordinary. As they
discussed the American movement, it became clear to both that they
shared many of the same hopes for the situation at home. It was a
propitious meeting and the beginning of a mutually rewarding alliance.[59]

In both style and appearance, they provided a striking contrast.
Burns, much the better diplomat of the two, possessed a quick wit
and a ready sense of humor. Paul came across as much more businesslike, perhaps due to her irrepressible shyness. Lucy Burns, with
her red hair, sturdy build, and Irish features, appeared equal to any
task. Alice Paul was slight and almost timid-looking. She suffered periodic bouts of ill-health which, on several occasions, required hospi-
talization. Many of her health problems stemmed from hunger strikes
in which she participated as a suffrage prisoner.[60] Mabel Vernon recalled her shock at seeing Paul on the latter's return from Europe. In
contrast to the Swarthmore days, Paul was wraithlike and seemed on
the verge of collapse. The painful and dangerous forced feedings, in
addition to the hunger strikes and her general disregard for developing
good nutritional habits, had taken a fearsome toll.[61] It was Paul's
physical appearance that prompted Ruth Hanna McCormick's unin-
formed observations about Paul's alleged propensity for martyrdom.
Under the proper set of circumstances, perhaps McCormick's view
might have pervailed. Certainly, Paul was intensely single-minded and
determined to see the cause succeed at almost any cost. But she was
also pragmatic and carefully assessed the pros and cons of risky situations with great trepidation. When Emmeline Pankhurst asked her in
the spring of 1909 to take part in a demonstration that would almost
certainly lead to arrest and imprisonment, Paul recalled: "I remember

hesitating the longest time and writing the letter [accepting the invitation] and not being able to get enough courage to post it, and going up and walking around the post office, wondering whether I dare put it in."[62] Of course, she did.

Burns was impressed with Paul's "extraordinary mind, extraordinary courage, and remarkable executive ability," but she believed nevertheless that the shy Quaker had two serious disabilities that would hamper her effectiveness in a grueling political campaign. The first was her apparent ill-health, and the second was a "lack of knowledge about human nature. . . . I was wrong in both," Burns later acknowledged.[63] For her part, Alice Paul always insisted that Lucy was far more courageous than she. Paul pointed out on several occasions that Lucy never hesitated to run the risk of possible arrest and incarceration as a result of picketing activity, despite her intense fear of the rats and other creatures that invariably found their way inside the prisons.[64]

Paul and Burns worked so well together that observers often attributed to them one mind and spirit. One suffragist, when asked to describe the differences between the two, found more similarity than disparity in their beliefs. She had no problem in defining the difference in their temperaments, however—differences that perhaps help to shed light on their particular world views. "Both saw the situation exactly as it was, but they went at the problems with different methods. Alice Paul had a more acute sense of justice, Lucy Burns a more bitter sense of injustice. Lucy Burns would become angry because the President or the people did not do this or that. Alice Paul never expected anything of them."[65]

After her imprisonment in Halloway Prison in England, in 1910, Paul returned to the United States and resumed graduate study at the University of Pennsylvania. She left England with a prison record and ill-health.[66] Lucy, on the other hand, remained in Europe to continue organizing for the WSPU. The two were not re-united until 1912, when they joined forces to work on the American scene.

Other American women associated with the Pankhursts included nursing pioneer, Lavinia Dock; labor organizer, Josephine Casey; historian and United States Senate candidate, Anne Martin; socialite Eleanor Doddridge Brannon and her mother, Elizabeth Brannon; and patron of the arts and heiress, Louisine Havemeyer. All were active in the militant suffrage movement.[67] Collectively, they conformed in background to the description of the modern American woman—the New Woman—then emerging. Twelve of the fifteen either attended or were graduated from college, and seven went on for graduate or professional training. Ten were married at least once, five were divorced, and four remarried. Nine of the ten married women had children, all but one had more than one child. All worked at paid jobs at one time or another; four listed their occupation as writer, although nearly all of them wrote for publication at some point in their lives. In addition, there were one lawyer, two historians, an actress, a nurse, a labor organizer, an architect, and two teachers. All belonged to suffrage organizations. Several were also involved in volunteer club work, club membership, professional organizations, and alumni associations.[68]

As a group, these women were singularly independent and aggressive. They confronted society on its own terms, found those terms unacceptable, and determined to follow the path that they perceived led most directly to their emancipation, regardless of the barriers encountered. It is hardly surprising that, given the opportunity to work with or observe the English suffragettes, the Americans would applaud and imitate the directness and aggressiveness of their English sisters.

These were the *New Suffragists:* women who were better educated, more career-oriented, younger, less apt to be married, and more cosmopolitan than their counterparts of the previous generation. Still, these differences between the the Old Suffragists and the *New Suffragists* should not be overdrawn. The critical factor that distinguished Old from New was their brand of feminism. For both groups, suffrage was the issue around which they rallied. However, for the younger generation the fight for suffrage was one means to challenge a social system that attempted to refute their feminist ideology and deny them their identities. Among the *New Suffragists,* militancy was the chief weapon. In this respect, they were united with Alice Paul. No longer would they beg for their rights. They would, henceforth, demand them. No longer could these *New Suffragists* look to an Anna Howard Shaw or a Carrie Chapman Catt for inspiration and leadership. Their new role model was Alice Paul, and they rallied under her banner.

CHAPTER 2

Pageants and Politics

The extent to which the idea of militancy had become an understandable, if not acceptable, method of pursuing equal suffrage, was very much in evidence at the NAWSA convention of 1910. Alice Paul had only recently returned from England and a stint in Halloway Prison. The former prisoner spoke to the delegates' meeting at the Arlington Hotel in Washington, on "The English Situation." The English suffragettes, proclaimed Paul, were at the "storm center of our movement." They were, said Paul, fighting the battle for women the world over, and they were doing so by using new and innovative tactics. "The essence of the campaign of the suffragettes," Paul noted, "is opposition to the government. . . . It is not a war of women against men, for the men are helping loyally, but a war of women and men together against the politicians."[1]

In identifying politicians as the enemy, and by endorsing the militant tactics of the suffragettes, Paul provided an alternative to the tone set by the NAWSA hierarchy. Earlier in the convention, President William Howard Taft delivered an address of welcome to the delegates. No supporter of woman suffrage, Taft considered his appearance at the convention merely a part of his ceremonial duties as President of the United States. In the course of his speech, Taft referred to suffragists as "hottentots," which elicited numerous hisses from the audience.[2] Shocked at what she considered appalling behavior from the delegates, Anna Howard Shaw, then the president of NAWSA, scolded the audience in no uncertain terms and directed the corresponding secretary immediately to dispatch a letter of apology to Taft. She made no reference to the witless remark that had sparked the outburst. The letter of apology expressed NAWSA's "great sorrow that anyone present, either a member or an outsider, should have interrupted [Taft's] address by an expression of personal feeling."[3]

Paul's address, following the Taft incident, received high marks from the delegates. Perhaps the members were in a mood to let the NAWSA leadership know where they stood, after being rebuked by Shaw. On the other hand, there was genuine support for more aggressive action. Not all who heard and applauded her speech were willing to embark immediately on a militant course of action, but many of them were completely sympathetic to the Pankhursts' response to governmental intransigence. Within a short time, receptiveness to the Pankhurst message of militancy increased dramatically. "I went to [a suffrage] meeting," recalled Katharine Houghton Hepburn, "in [a] Theatre which seated 1620 people. There were only about 200 people in the audience. . . . Later on after they had begun their militant tactics we had meetings for Mrs. Pankhurst at [the same] Theatre—filled the theatre and turned away hundreds of people."[4]

To be sure, most American suffragists believed that the American condition was so different from the English that militancy would not be necessary. Part of their resistance to more aggressive tactics stemmed from the affirmation of a conservative approach that accompanied each of the state victories, as infrequent as they were. More importantly, most suffragists were convinced that Americans were much more reasonable and were willing to enter into good-faith discussions of the merits of the issue. This belief was reinforced by prosuffrage males who warned suffragists against resorting to militant tactics, or run the risk of jeopardizing their cause. "The sex," intoned Frederick Sullens, the editor of the *Jackson* (Mississippi) *Daily News*, "must show a capacity for self-government, and in this respect the policy of the suffrage association in the United States offers a pleasing contrast to that of Great Britain. The cause is a great one but it does not require martyrs to immolate themselves upon the altar of law. While we may cherish a secret admiration for the dauntlessness and the mettle of the woman who declares that she will starve in prison, at the same time clear reason leads us to doubt the logic and effectiveness of such tactics."[5] Paul's Washington audience clearly subscribed to the philosophy of the Frederick Sullenses. While they were openly sympathetic to the idea of militancy, most women in the hall were decidedly uninterested in becoming actively involved in such a course.

In any event, Paul herself was not yet ready to launch a campaign. In the two years that elapsed between the NAWSA convention of 1910 and Lucy Burns' return from England in 1912, Paul threw herself into the work of completing her doctoral dissertation begun several years earlier at the University of Pennsylvania. The completion of that task and Lucy's arrival in the United States were fortuitously timed, and Paul lost little time in traveling to the Long Island home where Lucy was settling in. Their mutual impatience was evident as they discussed how they might successfully apply English tactics to the American movement. The time had come, they agreed, to implement such a plan.

Both Paul and Burns firmly believed that holding the political party in power responsible for the fate of a federal suffrage amendment made even more sense in the United States than it did in England. Surveying the situation in 1912, they could see that with six full-suffrage states and two million women voters, there already existed a ready-made voting bloc, potentially powerful, that could be mobilized. The obvious objection to such a plan was that by holding the entire Democratic or Republican party responsible for their amendment, women might end up voting against prosuffrage congressmen and senators because they belonged to the offending party. Paul never considered that a serious objection, however, since—as she reasoned—any congressman or senator elected to office from a suffrage state would be, by definition, prosuffrage. Whatever their privately held views on the issue, their public stance *had* to be prosuffrage. Moreover, it was clear to Paul and Burns that under the existing suffrage strategy, there was absolutely no incentive which compelled suffrage state congressmen to use their influence to help persuade their neutral, apathetic, or antisuffrage fellow party members to change their views and their votes. By making the whole party accountable for failure to pass an amendment, and by mobilizing women voters to vote accordingly, suffrage state congressmen would have ample reason to exert their influence on recalcitrant party members—if not for the sake of the party, then certainly for the sake of retaining their own seats.[6]

Over the course of the next few weeks, several more meetings took place between Alice Paul and Lucy Burns, both on Long Island and in Moorestown. After prolonged discussion, they agreed that the next step would be to present a proposal to NAWSA at its annual convention, to be held, appropriately enough, in Philadelphia. The exact nature of the original proposal, which was submitted to Anna Howard Shaw and other NAWSA leaders, is not entirely clear. What is clear is that the Paul/Burns proposal encountered a great deal of resistance. The extent to which the proposal outlined in precise terms an anti-Democratic party campaign and/or other forms of militancy did not sit well with NAWSA. The committee turned down the proposal out-of-hand. NAWSA leaders were not about to embark on a blatantly militant course of action, and certainly viewed as premature any suggestion of an anti-Democratic party campaign, since Woodrow Wilson had only just been elected President and would not take office for several months.

NAWSA leaders learned quickly—as indeed, the entire country would soon discover—that neither Paul nor Burns could be easily dissuaded. They sought out the one person at the convention whose reputation and integrity were universally respected: the even-then legendary Jane Addams. Addams listened as the younger women pleaded their case. Perhaps because her own career was such a monument to the unorthodox, Jane Addams agreed to champion their cause before the NAWSA committee, *if* Paul and Burns would tone down their proposal at least enough to placate the faint of heart among the committeewomen. True to her word, Addams' interceded on their behalf. Alice Paul was appointed the new chairman of the Congressional Committee, replacing Mrs. Kent, who had let it be known that she wished to step down. Lucy Burns was named vice-chairman of the Committee.[7]

The plan that NAWSA leaders finally found acceptable authorized Paul to organize a massive suffrage parade in Washington, D.C., for the following March. It was to coincide with Woodrow Wilson's inauguration. Paul was given a free hand in choosing the members of her committee and in implementing all preparations for the parade. NAWSA also granted her Committee permission to use NAWSA resources in the work of the Committee. NAWSA laid down only one major stipulation: Paul was to understand that her Committee could expect no funding whatsoever from the NAWSA treasury. The Congressional Committee would have to raise all its own operating expenses through its own efforts.[8] Paul not only readily agreed to this condition, but she made it clear that she was willing to work for nothing, and would ask nothing of the national treasury, if NAWSA agreed to accept the more moderate proposal.[9]

Even so, these negotiations hardly boded well for a good relationship between NAWSA and the new chairman of the Congressional Committee. NAWSA made it clear to Paul and her associates that the parent organization would not give up its current strategy, and more to the point, that it had little real interest in trying to secure a federal amendment at the present time. While NAWSA may have felt compelled to accede to Jane Addam's efforts, its refusal to fund any Congressional Committee activity signaled its disinterest in a federal focus. And, by insisting on a severely modified proposal from Paul, NAWSA made it equally clear that it rejected militancy as strongly as it embraced the more cautious state-by-state constitutional approach.

Despite the constraints imposed upon them, Paul and Burns lost little time in putting together their Committee. Burns first sought out one of her Vassar classmates, the dynamic Crystal Eastman. Eastman, a complete feminist and pacifist, as well as a proclaimed socialist, had gone to Columbia for a master's degree in sociology after graduating from Vassar in 1903. She soon realized her preference for law over sociology, however, and quickly enrolled at New York University Law School. After earning her law degree, Eastman went to work for Paul Kellogg, on the famous "Pittsburgh Survey," the first in-depth study of the effects of industrialization on the lives of blue-collar workers. As a consequence of her work with Kellogg, Governor Charles Evans Hughes appointed Crystal to the New York State Employers Liability Commission. From this post, she launched a successful drive to persuade the state legislature to adopt a workman's compensation law in New York.

Among her friends, Eastman's most notable characteristic was her unyielding commitment to feminism and equality between the sexes. Her life was a constant effort to confront mores and conventions which she found personally repugnant and socially backward. That she was able to do so with grace, style, and intelligence was a measure of her stature as a woman.[10] It was also a tribute to the philosophy of her parents, who encouraged both Crystal and her brother, Max Eastman (the editor of *The New Masses*, and prominent in radical political and literary circles), to strive always to overcome socially imposed inequality.[11] But hers was not a battle easily waged, for she recognized the dilemma posed by society for the modern woman, who, noted Eastman, could no longer find satisfaction in traditional domesticity. "She wants money of her own. She wants work of her own. She wants some means of self-expression, perhaps, some way of satisfying her personal ambitions. But she wants a husband, home, and children, too. How to reconcile these two desires in real life, that is the question."[12] Eastman could view the dilemma with particular clarity because her own marriage was foundering at the time. In 1911, Eastman had moved to Wisconsin with her insurance-agent husband, Wallace Benedict, mostly in an effort to strengthen their relationship and hold the marriage together. Never one to stand on the sidelines, she worked in local Wisconsin suffrage organizations for a year. But, by 1912, Crystal knew that life in Wisconsin was not for her, and she longed to return to the mainstream of social activism. When her friend and classmate contacted her, Eastman was more than ready to move back to the East Coast.[13]

Mary Ritter Beard also responded to the call. After she and Charles returned from England, both enrolled in the graduate school of Columbia University. Mary Beard's career as a graduate student in sociology was short-lived, however, both because she objected to what she considered the narrowness of academic life, and because of the pressures of parenting. After the birth of her second child, no longer encumbered by academic demands, Beard rekindled her interest in the condition of working-class women, which had been ignited when she was in England. She joined the Women's Trade Union League (WTUL), and was one of the organizers of the shirtwaistmakers' strike in 1909. Beard also belonged to the Woman Suffrage party of New

York, and edited its publication, *Votes For Women*. Like Crystal Eastman, Mary Beard needed little persuasion to join forces with Paul and
Burns in the Congressional Committee.[14]

The fifth person to serve on the Congressional Committee, at Alice
Paul's request, was Dora Kelley Lewis of Philadelphia. Born in Philadelphia during the Civil War, Dora Kelley's first memory was of her
father, Captain Henry Kelley, the day he returned from the war. Unfortunately, that is also one of the only things known about Dora Kelley's early life. She lived in Philadelphia most of her life, and married
Lawrence Lewis, Jr., in 1883. Both the Kelley and the Lewis families
were prominent in Philadelphia society. Lawrence Lewis, a young and
promising attorney, died at the age of thirty-two, when he fell under
the wheels of a train. Thus, in 1890, at the age of twenty-seven, Dora
Kelley Lewis was a widow with three young children to raise, Louise,
4, Robert, 3, and Shippen, 2.[15] Paul met Lewis when both were
members of the Philadelphia Equal Franchise Society. By that time,
Lewis had already navigated successfully the shoals of widowhood, and
of her children, Robert had established himself as a respected Philadelphia physician, and Shippen was beginning to earn his national
reputation as an expert in constitutional law. (Shippen Lewis later
helped to represent the National Woman's Party during the ratification campaign.) Dora Lewis' entrée into Philadelphia society made her
invaluable as a fund raiser, and it was to Lewis that Paul turned immediately after leaving the NAWSA convention.[16]

With this core of dedicated feminists in place, the first task of the
Congressional Committee was to solicit volunteers and funds. The five
Committee members pooled their respective lists of contacts and inaugurated a campaign to accomplish both goals. Paul started with the
list of NAWSA's Washington, D.C. chapter members, provided by
the organization. This was to be its main contribution to the work of
the Committee. Unfortunately, the Washington chapter membership
list had been sadly neglected and most of the women still listed as
members had either moved from the area or long since died.[17] Soliciting volunteers became a door-to-door task. Members of the Committee called on college classmates, friends, acquaintances, friends of
friends, and women whom they had merely heard about from other
women. By the time the Congressional Committee held its first meet-

ing on January 2, 1913, at its new headquarters in the basement of
1420 F Street, Washington, DC, the core group had expanded to twice
its original size. It now included another Vassar graduate, Elsie M.
Hill, the daughter of the congressman from Connecticut; Elizabeth
Kent, the former Congressional Committee chairwoman who had re-
linquished her seat when Paul took over; Helen Gardener, a journalist
working in the Washington area; Emma Gillette, a lawyer and one of
the founders of the National College of Law; Florence Etheridge, a
government employee working for the Bureau of Indian Affairs; and
aging feminist Belva Lockwood, then eighty-three years old, the lawyer who had run for President of the United States in 1884, who sat
in on the meeting mainly as a gesture in order to provide encouragement to the new group.[18]

From the moment that she assumed command of NAWSA's Congressional Committee, Alice Paul knew that the focus of its efforts had
to be the federal government, if they were going to succeed. Congress
would have to pass a federal amendment before it could be submitted
to the states for ratification. But even more crucial to the success of
federal suffragism was the support of the single most important figure
in the government: the President of the United States.

Ever since Theodore Roosevelt had changed the concept of the office dramatically with his much-publicized view of the presidency as
a "bully pulpit," which could provide strong leadership of both party
and nation, the office had taken on a new significance. Alice Paul was
one of the first to recognize the importance of this development. Paul
believed that lobbying for national political reforms was futile if the
President could not be persuaded to support those reforms. Win the
President and you win the battle.[19]

There were two good reasons, then, for scheduling the great Washington suffrage parade for March 3, 1913, the day before Woodrow
Wilson's inauguration. Large crowds were expected to arrive in Washington to view the ceremonial transfer of power symbolized by the
inauguration. Woman suffragists could count on an audience of substantial size, which would justify the newspaper coverage and publicity they hoped to receive. But more to the point, the parade would
send an unmistakable message to the new President. The suffragists
were putting Wilson on notice that they were a group to be reckoned

with. Furthermore, the suffragists intended to negotiate directly with the President and the Congress. They were moving the battle out of the front parlors of Boise and the street corners of Boston and Evanston. The arena henceforth would be Washington.

Response to the Congressional Committee's call to suffragists to mobilize in Washington for the parade came swiftly and forcefully. With less than two months from their initial meeting on January 2 to organize, finance, and carry the parade off, the results were spectacular. The five-member Congressional Committee and its handful of volunteers made up in enthusiasm and hard work what they lacked in numbers. The Committee's first task was to launch its fund-raising drive under the NAWSA letterhead, which served both to raise money necessary to finance the parade and to publicize the event in suffrage circles throughout the country. They succeeded in both efforts.[20]

The Committee devised a method whereby individual groups would, in effect, sponsor their own participation in the parade. All traveling and lodging expenses, plus additional expenses associated with special entries such as floats, were the responsibility of the sponsoring unit.[21] Funds solicited by the Committee were used for publicizing the parade and the federal amendment, and for providing the overall coordination necessary for success. At the same time, the Committee could concentrate on stabilizing its Washington operations and establishing a national support network.

The logistics of the parade seemed, at times, overwhelming. Each day seemed to present a new crisis which threatened to undermine everything that had already been accomplished. The more successful the Committee was in securing volunteers, the more differences in personalities had to be contended with, although for the most part a spirit of cooperation prevailed in each instance. There were, however, two potentially serious problems that had to be dealt with. The first involved a contingent of black women from Howard University, who had volunteered to sponsor and march in the college section of the parade. Elsie Hill reported to Paul that some white marchers had threatened to withdraw from the parade rather than march with blacks. It was a difficult situation.

Paul could easily have refused the Howard women permission to participate and ended the matter immediately. Racism, both openly

virulent and covert, prevailed throughout the land in 1913. Even
Theodore Roosevelt, the Progressive candidate for President in the
election of 1912, conducted a "Lily White" campaign in order to woo
southern voters. And the newly elected Wilson administration, as the
country would shortly witness, felt no constraints in embarking on a
path that would institutionalize significant and widespread segregation
in federal government agencies.[22] Like professional politicians, most
suffrage leaders saw a real danger in alienating white legislators, voters, and real or potential supporters of their cause. Thus, the social
climate that encouraged and fostered discriminatory behavior in society in general, dictated, with few exceptions, that blacks were not to
be encouraged to speak at or attend suffrage meetings in most sections
of the country.[23] All of these considerations were taken seriously and
discussed at the Congressional Committee headquarters.

Moreover, Paul herself was not immune to racist feelings. Indeed,
among some of her co-workers and critics alike, she had a reputation
for particularly noticeable prejudicial tendencies.[24] How accurate these
observations were is open to question. Paul could, on the one hand,
speak quite frankly about her desire to find a secluded home where
there were still "some American people."[25] On the other hand, as in
the case of the Howard women, she avoided what to others was an
obvious solution in favor of finding an acceptable solution. The problem in this case was resolved to everyone's satisfaction. Paul found cooperative contingents of prosuffrage male marchers who agreed to act
as a protective wedge for the Howard women by placing the female
marchers in the middle of the male line of march.[26] In this way peace
was preserved among both the white women who had threatened to
quit the parade and the black women who wanted to march.

The second problem that arose involved the safety of all the parade
participants, and proved to be much more serious than the first. A
month before the parade was scheduled, Major Richard Sylvester, the
Superintendent of Police of the District of Columbia, tried to persuade Alice Paul that the suffrage parade ought not to be held before
the inauguration. The crowds, predicted Sylvester, would be too unruly. Paul, of course, had no intention of postponing or canceling the
parade, and insisted on the date already selected and planned on. But
she worried over Sylvester's dire predictions and repeatedly pressed

him for whatever information he was privy to that led him to fear for the safety of the marchers. She "bombarded" him with repeated requests to provide adequate additional police protection, but in all instances was met with stern rejection.[27]

In all, some 8,000 marchers participated, along with twenty-six floats, ten bands, and five squadrons of cavalry with six chariots.[28] Marching units were divided into six sections. Women from other nations marched in the first unit. Clearly, the organizers perceived their movement not simply as one concerned with voting rights for American women, but as an integrated world-wide effort to secure equality for all women, regardless of their cultural identity or national origin.[29] The second unit was more a tableau than a simple line of marchers. The colorful costumes worn by the marchers, and the accompanying floats and bands were, altogether, an effort to represent the progress that had been made by suffragists since the first women's rights convention in Seneca Falls in 1848. This was followed immediately by contingents of marchers representing a wide variety of occupations and professions which women currently practiced. The fourth unit, the local, state, and national governments' contingent, also had a strong turnout of marchers participating. Unaffiliated volunteer marchers and male supporters of suffrage comprised the fifth unit. Among those participating in this unit were the women from Howard, about whom such a row had been made, and people such as Oswald Garrison Villard, the publisher of the *New York Evening Post*, and Senators Miles Poindexter and George Chamberlain, both staunch supporters of the cause.[30] The last and largest of the units was the state delegates' contingent.

The Congressional Committee planned its parade route up Pennsylvania Avenue past the Treasury Building, where the suffragists were to stage what they advertised as an "ongoing allegorical tableau," and on past the White House to the Elipse.[31] Two days before the parade, on Saturday, March 1, Congress passed a special resolution ordering Superintendent Sylvester to prohibit all ordinary traffic along the parade route, and to "prevent any interference with the suffrage marchers."[32] But the increasing hostility from the police convinced Paul that they would be useless should an emergency arise. Sylvester refused to discuss the matter of additional police protection, insisting that it was a problem for the War Department and not the Police Department.

Despite the fact that the War Department seemed equally inclined to do nothing, Paul made one last-ditch effort on March 2 to secure additional protection.

Paul enlisted the support of Elizabeth Seldin White Rogers, the sister-in-law of the outgoing Secretary of War, Henry L. Stimson. Paul and Elizabeth Rogers appealed to Stimson in person and asked that he assign military personnel to help keep order. Stimson sympathized with their plight but responded that his hands were tied by the law. Paul and Rogers were somewhat disappointed at the outcome of the meeting, although not terribly surprised. After reconsideration, however, Henry Stimson chose to bend the law, and ordered the Fifteenth Cavalry from Fort Myer, Maryland, to bivouac on the western perimeter of Washington. The horse soldiers were instructed to be prepared to move into the city on a moment's notice, should trouble develop.[33]

The fears of the Congressional Committee were well founded. When Woodrow Wilson arrived at Union Station on Monday afternoon, he was not greeted by the enthusiastic crowds that he expected. Instead, the streets of Washington were deserted, prompting one of Wilson's party to inquire, "Where are the people?" "Over on the Avenue watching the suffrage parade," he was told.[34] Indeed, it seemed as though everyone in Washington was on Pennsylvania Avenue. Over half a million people gathered along the parade route. "As far as the eye could see, Pennsylvania Avenue, from building line to building line was packed. No such crowd had been seen there in sixteen years."[35] Rowdies began hurling insults at the marchers as they progressed along the Avenue. The police, as Paul had feared, seemed indifferent to the increasing boldness of the ill-behaved in the audience. Thus encouraged, the troublemakers were joined by other spectators who began to push—and carry others with them by force of the momentum created—out into the line of march. Within a half-hour it was virtually impossible to distinguish the crowd from the marchers. The situation quickly deteriorated into a near-riot as spectators combined their heckling with pushing and shoving incidents.

The police, when not actually assisting the rioters, stood idly by, leaving the marchers to defend themselves. Genevieve Stone, the wife of Congressman Claudius U. Stone, reported that her pleas for help from nearby policemen only prompted the terse response from one, that if "my wife were where you are, I'd break her head."[36] Later, at the Senate inquiry into the affair, Senator Miles Poindexter testified that he personally had taken the badge numbers of twenty-two officers, including two sergeants, who had not lifted a finger to restore order.[37] Alice Paul claimed that the "Boy Scouts of Philadelphia were the only ones who did any effective police work." She related angrily how one hapless youngster who, instead of receiving assistance from the police when he tried to hold back the crowds, was rewarded with a thump on the head that sent the boy sprawling to the ground. At last, the Fifteenth Cavalry, summoned from their bivouac on the western perimeter, rode in to restore order. In all, 175 calls for ambulances were sent out, and over 200 persons were treated for mostly minor injuries at local hospitals.[38]

Woodrow Wilson, of course, had nothing to do with the parade or the ensuing riot. Those who cared to ponder his arrival during such a mêlé over women's rights, however, might have wondered if it would set the tone for the new administration. In any case, a special investigating committee of the Senate convened on March 6 to hear four days of testimony that confirmed reports of police malfeasance. Despite an editorial in the *Washington Post* which chided the public for over-reacting, and dismissed the riot as an "occasional isolated piece of rudeness," the investigating committee found a good deal to criticize in the behavior of the officials concerned. They placed the blame squarely on the shoulders of Major Sylvester, a condemnation that cost him his position as Superintendent of Police.[39]

The Congressional Committee staged the suffrage parade for two reasons: to focus attention upon the federal amendment, and to generate enthusiasm among both suffragists and the general public. But they could not have anticipated the extent of the publicity that resulted. Nor could they have predicted the special Senate investigation even though they had been fearful of a potentially unruly crowd, and therefore not too surprised at the turn of events. Nonetheless, they were prepared to take full advantage of the outcome. Paul stirred public opinion against the authorities even more when she asserted, in an interview, that the top police and civilian officials had conspired to promote trouble for the suffragists. "There is no question that the police had the tip from some power higher up to let the rough characters . . . try to break up our parade."[40] Whether Paul's claim had merit was less important than the impression it left on the readers of the *Washington Post* and other publications that picked up the story, as well as the Senate committee scheduled to meet the following day.[41]

The parade and its aftermath greatly benefited the suffrage movement and enhanced the reputation of the Congressional Committee. For one thing, contributions to the Committee increased markedly and included a gift of $1,000 from the editor of the *Washington Post*.[42] This gift, along with other donations and the sale of tickets to various parade-connected activities, allowed the Congressional Committee to meet fully their parade expenses, which amounted to $13,750.[43] But more important, the press coverage stirred vigorous new interest in the work of Paul's Committee. Alva Belmont was only one of many persons who contacted Paul to volunteer her assistance to the Congressional Committee.[44] Moreover, the response extended well beyond the Washington–New York corridor. "[I] stand in readiness to . . . render any aid possible to the cause so dear to my heart. . . . At present we are only a struggling band of women, but we see victory already crowning our efforts," wrote one enthusiastic resident of Atlanta, Georgia.[45]

Not all the feedback was positive. Frederick Sullens, the editor of the *Jackson* [Miss.] *Daily News*, observed that, "walking is splendid exercise, but it has nothing to do with a woman's ability to determine whether a law is wise or unwise."[46] Nor was the connection between the activities of the Congressional Committee and the British suffragettes lost on some critics. When Senator William A. Clark was asked to support a subsequent suffrage parade, he refused, alluding to the foolishness of the British women, and noting that, in his view, the parade on March 3 "amply demonstrated that they [American suffragists] are unworthy of enjoying any greater rights than they now possess."[47] Such criticism, of course, made NAWSA leaders somewhat nervous, but for the time being, they said nothing. Suffrage was on the front pages, the wave of publicity had been almost entirely sympathetic, and the government was paying attention to the issue. If all the NAWSA leaders were not totally enthralled with the parade or the near-riot it caused, or the few expressions of unhappiness voiced by some critics, they could not deny that Paul and her Committee had accomplished much in such a short time. So, for the moment, they chose not to rein in the Committee members or otherwise to express discontent with Paul's stewardship of the Committee.

CHAPTER 3

Conflict Within: Independence from NAWSA

Within days of the suffrage parade, on March 17, 1913, the Congressional Committee organized its first delegation to the White House. The delegates included Alice Paul, Ida Husted Harper, the current editor of *The History of Woman Suffrage*, and Genevieve Stone, the congressman's wife who had been verbally assaulted during the parade.[1] Paul secured the appointment for the delegation in order to ask Wilson to include suffrage in the agenda which he was preparing to present to Congress when it convened for a special session on April 7.

Much to their amusement, Wilson, the former teacher, reverted to schoolroom procedure, seating the women in a semicircle facing his own chair, which was in the middle.[2] The President told the delegates that suffrage was an issue that had never been brought to his attention before and he therefore had no opinion on its merits. He needed time, he said, to gather information since the matter was entirely new to him. It was not an accurate response. Although suffrage was an issue about which Wilson knew very little, he exaggerated when he claimed never to have heard of it. During the campaign of 1912, when asked to state his views on suffrage, Wilson responded, "Ladies, this is a very arguable question, and my mind is in the middle of the argument."[3]

Wilson's earliest public responses to questions about suffrage were handled in standard political fashion. The dimensions that the suffrage issue would assume during his tenure in office were not yet apparent, either to him or to anyone else with the possible exception of Alice Paul and Lucy Burns. But for the moment, suffrage was still a minor irritant to be "handled" with as little disruption as possible. Attitudes regarding votes for women were a reflection of prevailing attitudes about women's role in society. Consequently, the answers provided to women who broached the subject were often superficial at best, and were intended to pacify rather than inform.

The meeting with Wilson did convince the members of the Congressional Committee that a great deal remained to be done to move suffrage from its low-priority status to an issue of paramount concern that politicians, regardless of their personal inclinations, could not afford to ignore. For the proponents of the federal amendment, the urgency of the situation could not be overstated: "Until women vote, every piece of legislation undertaken by the Administration is an act of injustice to them. All laws affect the interests of women and should not be enacted and put into execution without the cooperation and consent of women."[4]

Both Paul and Burns knew very quickly that they needed a national organization whose focus would be a federal amendment. The small size of the Congressional Committee saddled its members with far too great a handicap. Five people could not at the same time do all the work to promote a federal amendment and raise the money to finance their activities. The difficult task of fund raising already was complicated by misunderstandings. NAWSA members across the country to whom the Congressional Committee appealed for funds, frequently confused the purpose of the appeal. These women, for the most part, did not distinguish between money to be used for federal work and money ear-marked for state campaigns. Thus, requests for donations for the support of federal work were often answered by direct contributions to the NAWSA treasury, rather than the Congressional Committee treasury. All donations made directly to the NAWSA treasury, of course, remained with NAWSA, regardless of the donor's intent.

For a variety of good reasons, then, Paul realized that the task of securing both money and volunteers would be infinitely easier if their committee, while still a part of NAWSA, operated as a distinct entity whose sole function would be to promote federal amendment work. The new Congressional Committee would be "permanent and could continue to carry on the federal work as long as the necessity for doing so remained, while the life of the [old Congressional] committee, of course, could be terminated at any time by the Association." Paul and Dora Lewis discussed the matter with Anna Howard Shaw and Mary Ware Dennett at the NAWSA headquarters in New York in March 1913. Both NAWSA officers "approved heartily" of the plan. Dennett even suggested a name for the new organization: the Congressional Workers Union of NAWSA. They called themselves the Congressional Union of NAWSA for a short time, until Shaw informed them that they could not use "NAWSA" in their name. Thus, in April of 1913, the Congressional Union for Woman Suffrage was founded and existed side-by-side with the Congressional Committee.[5]

From the start, the Congressional Union made it clear that there were fundamental differences between its approach toward suffrage and that of the more traditional organizations. Unlike NAWSA's, the Union's first membership drive was not an attempt to enlist great numbers of people who counted themselves as suffrage supporters but intended to remain inactive. Rather, the Union selectivity sought out women who were committed to a federal amendment and who were willing to work actively toward that end. At the same time, the Union did not perceive its task as propaganda work. In Paul's view, suffrage had long since passed the propaganda stage. "It is a subject infinitely more familiar to voters than the tariff, the currency, or conservation," *The Suffragist* pointed out, referring to the political issues currently holding center stage. "Therefore we declare that suffrage . . . has reached its political stage."[6] The Union solicited only members who believed that suffrage was *the* fundamental issue, the one that by its nature had to supercede all other contemporary political issues.[7] At the same time, the Union had no desire or intention to remove itself from under the NAWSA umbrella. Although its focus was a federal amendment, Paul and Burns made it clear that a spirit of cooperation among all suffragists was essential, regardless of which aspect of work they might be involved in. "The [Congressional Union] hopes that no women will for a single moment relax their efforts to win suffrage by a state measure."[8]

The leaders of the Congressional Union possessed an optimism frequently lacking in suffrage leaders. To be sure, active suffragists were dedicated women who worked willingly and tirelessly, but in 1913 they still often thought in terms of life-long struggles. In an effort to dampen Alice Paul's optimism about the potential for securing a federal amendment fairly quickly, Carrie Chapman Catt reiterated her belief that suffrage was a long-term struggle. "When you have more experience," Catt warned the younger woman, "you'll know it's a much longer fight than you have any idea of."[9] Paul not only believed that a federal amendment was possible in the short run, but she also understood well the psychological advantage of maintaining the optimism that generated her belief. When the president of NAWSA's Ohio chapter accused the Union of "madness" in insisting that a federal amendment could be passed during the current session of Congress, Union member Doris Stevens responded that the Congressional Union knew that the amendment would fail but saw no harm in asking for it anyway. On reviewing a copy of Stevens' letter, Paul admonished her subordinate roundly. "You must never say that again and never put it on paper. You see, we *can* get it this session if enough women care sufficiently to demand it now."[10] Neither Paul nor the Congressional Union ever abandoned the belief that they could succeed. The more united suffragists were, the quicker the goals could be realized. "Success can be ours if suffragists stand shoulder to shoulder behind the federal amendment."[11]

Given the differences in philosophies and methods, both sides, in retrospect, ought to have expected a difficult, if not impossible, relationship. Certainly, a subtle undercurrent of unease was present ever since Paul and Burns first approached NAWSA in 1912, and were initially rejected. But since they were all pursuing in theory the same goal, internal conflicts were, for the most part, ignored. Still, the relationship hit snags early on that ultimately proved to be only the forerunners of eventual dissolution.

Shortly after its formation, the Congressional Union applied to NAWSA for auxiliary status. During the discussions with Shaw and Dennett, the latter suggested to Alice Paul that such an application would be appropriate. However, NAWSA delayed their response for several months, primarily because a NAWSA officer, Laura Clay, had objections to the Congressional Union. Clay was the chairwoman of NAWSA's Membership Committee. In order to gain acceptance as a NAWSA auxiliary, the Union had to submit a certified list of 300 members already enrolled. Because many of the 300 came from cities and states other than Washington, D.C., Clay defined the group as a national organization. As such, Clay questioned whether NAWSA would be able to "control" the Union. In fact, it was a good question and one that was pointing to the heart of the matter—the whole issue of the intentions of the Congressional Union. For the time, it was not an issue that Paul wanted to deal with. She assured Clay that the Congressional Union would be as bound by NAWSA policy as any other affiliate. Nevertheless, Clay remained adamant that the Membership Committee could not act on their application.[12] The matter was kicked back to Shaw and Dennett, the sponsors of the request. Despite Clay's continued objections, Shaw and Dennett helped to secure the recognition of the Congressional Union as a NAWSA auxiliary. They informed Paul of the decision in November 1913, and it seemed at the time that the conflict had ended amicably.[13]

Alice Paul did not suspend activity while the membership disagreement was being settled. By the end of 1913, the Congressional Committee/Congressional Union, whose executive boards were identical, managed to compile an enviable record of achievement. NAWSA held its annual convention in Washington in early December that year. The Congressional Union played host and served as principal financial backer for the convention. Paul read her report of the Congressional Committee and Congressional Union, noting that it was almost impossible to disassociate the two groups since their work overlapped to such a great extent. With notable exceptions, no one at the convention was particularly disturbed by the melding.

The Congressional Committee/Congressional Union had concentrated much of its efforts on legislative work with Congress. On April 7, 1913, Paul reported, Senate Joint Resolution I, which called for passage of a federal suffrage amendment, was introduced in Congress by Senator George E. Chamberlain of Oregon and Representative Frank W. Mondell of Wyoming. The Senate referred the bill to the Senate

Woman Suffrage Committee, a standing—albeit often just barely—committee since 1877.[14] The House had no woman suffrage committee to which it could refer the proposed legislation. On May 14, 1913, the Senate Woman Suffrage Committee, which had recently received majority status, voted to issue a favorable report to the Senate. The report, issued on June 13, was unanimous. The Senate set aside July 31, 1913, for full discussion of the resolution on the floor, and, on that date, twenty-three Senators spoke in favor of the federal amendment, while only three Senators rose to oppose the measure.[15] Again, on September 18, Senator Wesley M. Jones of Washington, spoke on behalf of suffrage, and Senator Henry Fountain Ashurst of Arizona, announced that he would press the measure to a vote at the earliest possible moment. In the House, in the meantime, the issue was still before the Judiciary Committee, but three separate resolutions urging creation of a House Woman Suffrage Committee had been introduced and were then under consideration by the Rules Committee.[16]

Congress took no steps more positive than consideration and discussion of the issue, but that in itself was a victory for women. The last time that suffrage had been discussed in either house of Congress was in the Senate in 1878. It had never been an issue before both houses of Congress simultaneously. The Congressional Committee/Congressional Union could claim the entire credit through its tireless effort to focus attention on suffrage. In addition to the suffrage parade in Washington the previous March, the Congressional Committee coordinated an assembly of one woman from every congressional district in the country, on April 7, 1913, to coincide with the opening of the special session of Congress. The women, carrying petitions and resolutions from their districts, met at the Capitol and proceeded to seek out their congressmen and senators in order to lobby on behalf of suffrage.[17]

When the Senate placed suffrage on its agenda agenda for July 31, the Congressional Committee/Congressional Union immediately set to work to persuade the senators that suffrage had nationwide support. A series of pilgrimages, organized around the country, proceeded to Washington. Along the way, they gathered as many signatures as they could. A Congressional Union escort met the pilgrims on July 31 and accompanied them through the streets of Washington to the Capitol.

The organizers shrewdly assigned several members of the Senate Woman Suffrage Committee to the lead car. At the Capitol, the suffragists presented to the Senate a petition signed by more than 250,000 supporters.[18]

The work of the Congressional Committee/Congressional Union was not limited to Congress. Following the first deputation to Wilson on March 17, three more were arranged. In April, a delegation from the College Equal Suffrage League met with the President, and in June, the National Council of Women Voters sent their representatives to the White House. On November 17, 1913, seventy-five New Jersey women asked Wilson to take up suffrage during the regular session of Congress. On that occasion Wilson reported that, only the day before, he had spoken to several members of Congress about a House suffrage committee.[19] Less than a month later, on December 8, 1913, another delegation led by NAWSA's Anna Howard Shaw left the White House cheered by Wilson's noncommittal observation that the formation of a House Woman Suffrage Committee would be a good thing.[20]

Perhaps the most ambitious endeavor undertaken by the Union in the months following its organization was the launching of its own publication, *The Suffragist*. The weekly news magazine, intended to reach a national audience to keep it informed of the status of the federal amendment, began publication on November 15, 1913. Paul and Burns chose Rheta Childe Dorr as the first editor. There were few women who matched Dorr's background or her credentials as a journalist. The writer-feminist had defied her parents at the age of twelve to hear Stanton and Anthony speak on woman suffrage. In the years since, she established herself as a respected journalist and acquired a husband and a child of her own. But, after several years of marriage, Dorr left her conservative businessman husband, John Pixley Dorr. With her son Julian, Dorr relocated in New York City in order to pursue her career in earnest. Her job as a columnist for the New York *Evening Post* brought her into contact with people such as Charlotte Perkins Gilman, Florence Kelley, and Lillian D. Wald. Committed to suffrage and the elimination of the double standard, Dorr developed a concern for the plight of working women and children that led to her appointment as chairwoman of the General Federation of Women's Clubs' Committee on the Industrial Conditions of Women and Children. Along with the Women's Trade Union League and the Association of Social Settlements, Dorr helped to persuade Congress to undertake, through the Bureau of Labor, the first official investigation of working women. In 1906, Dorr resigned from the *Evening Post* to travel in Europe where she did free-lance writing. There, Dorr met the Pankhursts and, like many of her American suffrage colleagues, became committed to militant suffragism. So sympathetic was she to the Pankhursts that Dorr, in 1914, helped Emmeline to organize material for her autobiography, *My Own Story*.

Dorr agreed to edit *The Suffragist* and used her considerable talents to make the publication financially self-sufficient. She also applied rather new publicity techniques to help fulfill the primary purpose of the publication, which was to keep the suffrage issue before the public and Congress. Dorr arranged press conferences in order to confront directly Wilson and other public officials, asking provocative questions calculated to generate the kind of responses that made good press, and that other publications could pick up on.[21] In an effort to prove its legitimacy as a reliable source of information, Paul repeatedly stressed that *The Suffragist* was not a propaganda paper. Under Dorr's apt tutelage, the publication claimed 1,200 paid subscribers by December 1913, and enough advertising revenues to cover the costs of production.[22]

The remaining activities activities engaged in by the Congressional Committee/Congressional Union included organizing campaigns in New Jersey, Long Island, Rhode Island, Delaware, Maryland, and North Carolina (the first ever suffrage organization in that state). The Union organized the Men's League for Woman Suffrage as well. General Anson Mills took the post as temporary chairman, and a substantial portion of the membership was made up of prosuffrage congressmen. In addition, the Union printed and distributed over 120,000 pieces of literature, and conducted a number of fundraising events. Paul reported that, as of December 1913, the Union had over 1,000 dues-paying members who could be counted upon to donate time and money over and above the membership dues of twenty-five cents per person.[23]

Soliciting funds was an ongoing occupation for the Union members, not only in the first year but for the entire existence of the organization. Since much of their revenue came from donations, and because they hoped to establish a dependable monthly operating fund, both the Congressional Union, and later the National Woman's Party, employed the technique of securing monthly pledges from women of means. This was not always as easy as it seemed it ought to be for, as one woman explained, "I don't see five dollars in cash from one month to another, and if my husband doesn't approve of what I write in my checkbook, he either won't pay it or I don't do it again." She wrote the checks, but her husband signed them, she explained, adding, "I could never give you a monthly pledge because he doesn't approve of what you are doing." [24]

Not all women had this problem, of course. Alva Belmont controlled her own purse strings and eventually donated hundreds of thousands of dollars to suffrage. [25] Louisine Havemeyer, the widow of Henry Osborne Havemeyer, the former head of the American Sugar Refining Company, also had a fortune at her command. Havemeyer, in addition to her suffrage commitment, engaged in philanthropic work and was a generous collector and patron of the arts. As a young woman, while living in Paris in a *pension* and attending boarding school with the granddaughter of Lucretia Mott's (one of the principals, along with Stanton and Anthony, in the Seneca Falls Convention of 1848) Havemeyer met the American artist, Mary Cassatt. Havemeyer became an instant and enthusiastic convert to impressionism. Cassatt introduced Havemeyer to her circle of friends which included Courbet, Degas, and Monet. Havemeyer, in turn, introduced the impressionists and their paintings to America. Over the years, Havemeyer acquired a modern art collection that included several Cassatts and was valued in the millions of dollars. Eventually, she bequeathed her collection to the Metropolitan Museum in New York and, with this act, transformed this institution into the foremost museum of modern art in the country. [26]

Havemeyer's interest in suffrage extended back to her childhood when she became aware of her mother's interest in and friendship with the "pioneers of the movement." Later, Henry Havemeyer encouraged his young wife to support suffrage. "If a woman does not know how to vote, she'd better get busy and learn," he told her. Havemeyer was interested in the Union from the start and her social prominence, her name, and her "salty speech" made her an invaluable speaker and a favorite with the crowds. She donated generously to the cause. The only time that Havemeyer consented to a public showing of her art collection, she did so for the benefit of Alice Paul and the Congressional Union.[27]

Most women did not have fortunes to spend as they wished. Fortunately, some of those, like Elizabeth Kent, the former chairwoman of the Congressional Committee, had the support of their husbands. Elizabeth Kent agreed to contribute to the Union as generously as the Kents' pocketbook would allow each month;. But she also undertook the important task of gathering together a permanent committee of donors who would assume responsibility for paying the rent on the headquarters. They later became the Committee of Two Hundred, which remained equal to the task of raising ever greater sums of money, all under Kent's watchful direction.[28]

Those not as fortunate as Belmont, Havemeyer, and Kent were forced to employ creative measures in order to gain at least the semblance of economic freedom. Some used the "charging a hat or coat" method to obtain spending money. By this method, women charged an item that a shrewd shopkeeper would bill to the woman's husband, while giving the customer cash instead of the merchandise—for a modest fee.[29] Pledges and spontaneous donations became the mainstay of the Congressional Union and the National Woman's Party. By the end of 1913, the Union had raised a total of $25,343.88. Paul had more than fulfilled her agreement with NAWSA to raise her own operating funds and had managed to cover all operating expenses for the year.[30]

With such encouraging results to report to the constituents of the NAWSA convention, the members of the Congressional Committee/Congressional Union executive board justifiably expected some praise. And indeed, the "convention received the report with enthusiastic applause, giving three cheers and rising to its feet to show its appreciation."[31] Almost before the cheers subsided, however, it became apparent that there was trouble in the offing with NAWSA leaders. In truth, the Congressional Committee/Congressional Union had anticipated trouble. Paul and Mary Ritter Beard analyzed the problem as a clash of political ideologies which pitted the advocates of a federal amendment against the proponents of state rights.[32] Rather than shy away from possible confrontation, the members of the Congressional Committee/Congressional Union advertised their commitment to a federal amendment. They placed a conspicuously large sign behind the speaker's podium, which read, "We Demand An Amendment To The Constitution of the United States Enfranchising Women."[33]

This attitude, claimed Carrie Chapman Catt, revealed to many of the delegates "a dark conspiracy to capture the entire 'National' for the militant enterprise."[34] Catt's allegations were extreme. Paul never pretended to be committed to anything other than a federal amendment. Her advocacy of that position could hardly have come as a surprise. Moreover, the response of the rank and file to Paul's report was not consistent with fears of "conspiracy" on the part of Paul and her colleagues.

Following Paul's report, Catt tried to enforce separation of the Congressional Committee and the Congressional Union. She moved that only that portion of the report dealing with the work of the Congressional Committee be accepted and entered into the minutes. Catt wasted little time in making her point. "I want to inquire what has happened to the National American Woman Suffrage Association. It seems to me that there is something called the Congressional Union which is running the whole campaign on Congress."[35] Catt then launched into a discussion of finances. Why, she wanted to know, did the Congressional Committee not have a budget allowance from NAWSA? What was the purpose of organizing the Congressional Union? By what authority did the Congressional Committee/Congressional Union raise over $25,000 and not forward one penny to the national treasury when that was standard operating procedure for all affiliates? Did not the Congressional Union misrepresent itself by using NAWSA stationery in its fund-raising campaign? The questions came fast and furious as everyone in the now-hushed hall watched the unfolding drama.[36] Katherine Dexter McCormick of Boston, NAWSA's national treasurer, at once seconded Catt's motion and sentiments. McCormick, less subtle than Catt, revealed her dislike of the younger group as she adamantly insisted that NAWSA could not—and should not—tolerate such a state of affairs which bordered on insubordination.[37]

organizing efforts, in the eyes of the NAWSA people, was that federal work superceded state work. Since many NAWSA members, particularly Southerners like Laura Clay, believed that suffrage was a states' rights issue and not the concern of the federal government, their discomfort was understandable. While NAWSA could applaud the accomplishments of the Congressional Committee/Congressional Union, they also strongly desired the federal amendment proponents to confine their work to Washington, and to stay out of the states.[43]

A concomitant concern of many of the more conservative suffragists was the growing perception of a wholesale transfer of militant tactics from England by Paul and Burns. While parades, pageants, and deputations to government officials were acceptable, other tactics were viewed less benignly and created controversy within the women's movement. Many NAWSA leaders and members were nervous about the noises that the Congressional Committee/Congressional Union had already begun to make about holding the Democrats responsible for failure to enact a federal amendment.[44] As if to confirm NAWSA's suspicions, an editorial by Lucy Burns in the December 6, 1913, issue of *The Suffragist* clearly defined their position. "Rarely in the history of the country has a party been more powerful than the Democratic Party is today. . . . We ask the Democrats to take action now. Those who hold power are responsible not only for what they do but for what they do not do. Inaction establishes just as clear a record as does a policy of open hostility."[45] There could be little misunderstanding on this point. Consequently, NAWSA members objected heartily to the possibility that some long-standing friends of suffrage in the Democratic party might be lost to the cause if the militants carried out their threats to oppose all Democrats.[46]

This conflict at the 1913 convention was the first full-fledged clash between the *New Suffragists* and the older suffragists. Reaction to the Congressional Committee/Congressional Union activities on the part of NAWSA probably had as much to do with the perception that the militants were young upstarts who did not understand how things worked, as it did with the tactics themselves.[47] Even so, neither side seemed willing to make a break with the other. Both camps still professed to believe that a solution to the problem could be found.

By now, there was a blanket of confusion that those in the audience found disconcerting. In the end, because of the confusion, the delegates voted to adopt Catt's motion to accept that portion of Paul's report which concerned the Congressional Committee. It also directed Paul to submit a new report, which distinguished between the work of the Committee and the Union. At the same time, the NAWSA Board agreed that the Congressional Committee should be continued, albeit in "such a way as to remove further causes of embarrassment to the Association." Finally, the Board directed the NAWSA treasurer to include a Congressional Committee budget in appropriations for the next year. Under the new terms, there would be no legitimate reason for continuation of the Congressional Union. And, in a seemingly unrelated move, the delegates approved a motion to require all NAWSA auxiliaries to resign from the organization and submit new applications for readmission. NAWSA committee members identified the reasons for the necessity of such action as having to do with internal structure, and assured all auxiliaries that readmission would be strictly *pro forma*. Auxiliaries would never really be out of the organization.[48]

Immediately after the adjournment of the convention, on December 6, 1913, the leaders of NAWSA met with the Congressional Committee/Congressional Union members and presented them with an ultimatum which NAWSA believed to be both fair and in keeping with the resolution passed by the convention. Alice Paul could retain chairmanship of the Congressional Committee provided that she resign as chairwoman of the Congressional Union. In retrospect, the ultimatum seemed more intended to force the issue rather than to reach a fair compromise. Paul could not agree to the directive. NAWSA was already on record regarding federal suffragism. By declaring that the Committee could not engage in activities deemed "embarrassing" to NAWSA, the leadership was taking a stand on the side of the states' rights advocates. If any meaningful federal work was to be carried out in the future, it would have to be under the auspices of the Congressional Union. To resign from the Union now would, in Paul's view, mean abandoning the federal amendment. Paul therefore declined to accept a second year as chairwoman of the Congressional Committee. NAWSA next offered the chair of the Committee to Lucy Burns and added, as a concession, that Paul would be allowed to remain on the Board. If NAWSA leaders thought that Burns was any less resolute than Paul in her attitude toward federal work, they were mistaken. And if they thought that Burns would be lured by an opportunity to rise in the ranks of the NAWSA organization, they were equally mistaken. Burns also refused the chairmanship of the Congressional Committee. With the restrictions placed upon the Committee, both Paul and Burns concluded that it had been rendered ineffective. In these circumstances, they found little to agree upon with NAWSA representatives and, although they did agree to meet again, the first meeting ended in a failure to reconcile their differences.[49]

On December 11, 1913, NAWSA and Congressional Union members met once again, with Lucy Burns representing Alice Paul. NAWSA now offered two alternative plans for Burns and Paul to consider. Both alternatives were intended to curtail severely their ability to work effectively for a federal amendment by insisting that Burns and Paul refrain from organizing in the states.[50] In substance, neither of the alternatives offered anything more than the first set of conditions proposed five days earlier. Burns would only agree that there was further room for negotiation within the plans presented by NAWSA. Clearly, however, Burns was not happy with the proposals, and once again the meeting adjourned with no commitments or concessions by either side.[51] NAWSA then left the entire matter in the hands of Ruth Hanna McCormick, who harbored little sympathy for the members of the Congressional Union. It was probably no surprise to anyone that subsequent meetings between the Congressional Union and NAWSA proved to be fruitless.

Shortly after the New Year, by January 5, 1914, the conflict went public. Newspapers carried reports of the accusations made by NAWSA members that the Congressional Union had solicited funds under false pretenses. The "liberal financial support" that had "poured in" to the Congressional Union, claimed "prominent Washington suffragists," was solicited in such a way as to be "hopelessly confusing" to women who thought they were supporting the work of the Association.[52] Such strongly suggestive reports of malfeasance were the final straw. Gradually, more and more reports filtered back to Paul, reports which indicated that the allegations of misconduct had reached a wide audience.[53] Furthermore, if NAWSA leaders did not really believe that Paul had misappropriated funds, as Carrie Chapman Catt admitted much later in recounting her version of the incident, they nevertheless refused publicly to deny the stories. On the contrary, NAWSA sanctimoniously suggested that Alice Paul and the Congressional Union deserved the bad publicity they were getting.[54]

For Paul, both NAWSA's behavior and its imperious demands were too great a price to pay for continued association with it. The Congressional Union would not agree, said Paul, to "surrender its right to decide how lobbyists, the organization, its press bureau . . . should operate."[55] One week later, on January 12, 1914, members and supporters of the Congressional Union publicly demonstrated their allegiance to and faith in Paul's leadership. Elizabeth Kent opened her home to over 400 suffragists who gathered to urge that the work of the Union be continued. Assisted by Belle LaFollette, the wife of Senator Robert M. LaFollette, Ellen Hale, the daughter of Edward Everett Hale, and Mrs. John Jay White, a prominent member of New York society, Kent raised nearly $10,000 for the Union. And, in a vote-of-confidence gesture, the group presented Alice Paul with a silver cup in recognition of her successful year's work just ended. Their support was clear and Paul responded by announcing her intention to proceed as scheduled. The Congressional Union, said Paul, "will make a vigorous campaign against the Democratic candidates for Congress in close districts as the responsibility for the failure of the legislation should be placed on the Democratic Party."[56]

In the face of all this, Paul was still reluctant to take the final step that would sever for once and all relations with NAWSA. She admitted that the relationship between the Union and NAWSA was damaged to the point where they could not continue on their old footing, but hope persisted that NAWSA would relent. In December 1913, Paul had applied to NAWSA for the readmission of the Union as an auxiliary member in accordance with the terms of the convention of 1913.[57] As an auxiliary, the Union was going through what should have been strictly a *pro forma* procedure in order to retain its status. While some observers might have questioned Paul's reasons for reapplication, even through the bitterest of the conflict with NAWSA she maintained that the two organizations could work together for the same cause.

Despite her disagreement with NAWSA and her refusal to abandon federal work, Paul did not want to start an independent organization that would act as a rival to NAWSA. The leaders of NAWSA, however, felt differently. Anna Howard Shaw originally had approved the formation of the Union and its admission as a NAWSA auxiliary. Now, however, she agreed with Laura Clay that the Union posed a threat to NAWSA and perhaps the entire suffrage movement. Shaw took advantage of the Union's request for readmission with such alacrity that it seems altogether possible that NAWSA changed its constitution for the very purpose of flushing out dissidents. Shaw compared the Union to "Judas Iscariot" and predicted dire consequences for NAWSA if the Union were to be readmitted.[58] Shaw also sent a memorandum to NAWSA's general membership urging them to support the repudiation of the Union's application. The National Executive Council of NAWSA subsequently sustained Shaw and turned down the Union application by a vote of fifty-four to twenty-four.[59]

Once again, in the face of open hostility, Paul asked to meet with NAWSA. This meeting, held in Washington on February 12, 1914, was to be their last.[60] The meeting opened with a discussion of the parade which the Union had already scheduled for the following May, but it was soon clear that there were serious impediments to any real effort to cooperate. On the one hand, NAWSA representatives were confident that the Union could not long survive as an independent organization; on the other hand, the Union representatives were confident that the break with NAWSA would insure the forcible pursuit of a federal amendment.[61] No agreement could be reached.[62]

Despite dire predictions from political analysts who said that dissension in the ranks of the women's movement would do irreparable harm to the suffrage cause, Alice Paul pursued the only course she believed open to her.[63] She wasted little time in making good her threat to wage an anti-Democratic party campaign. At the first national strategy meeting held by the now-independent Congressional Union for Woman Suffrage, in the summer of 1914, the militants mapped out their campaign.

CHAPTER 4

Taking on the Democrats

Marble House, a two million dollar "cottage" commissioned by Alva Vanderbilt Belmont in the 1890s as part of her campaign to gain acceptance into New York high society, stood in a row of magnificent mansions on the Atlantic coast in Newport, Rhode Island. In the summer heat of August 1914, representatives of the Congressional Union traveled to Newport to meet at Belmont's monument to wealth. If the Union delegates worried over developments in Europe that had only recently plunged half the world into a long-expected catastrophic war, they made little mention of this fact. They had in mind to wage a different kind of war. Alice Paul's intention was to map out a strategy that would pit the suffragists against the Democratic party in the elections of 1914.

Only one of the delegates who gathered at Marble House experienced a sense of discomfort at accepting Belmont's invitation to meet in this bastion of wealth and privilege. Mary Ritter Beard, although she encouraged the purpose of the conference, refused, as she said, "to do the Newport stunt." She confided to Alice Paul, "I shall probably be the only one who, for labor attachments, feels that participation in the Newport plans is inadvisable."[1] Paul assured Beard that the gathering would not be "particularly plutocratic," but Beard remained steadfast in her resolve to stay away from Newport. She did advise Paul to be aware of the situation and to use it to good advantage.[2]

"Newport and money stand in the popular mind for one and the same thing and you might just as well play them up together in the press reports of the conference and get all the help possible from the combination. There is no advantage in having Congressmen against whom we propose to wage war to get an impression that we went into Newport and ate in Child's Restaurant and brought away no money. Let them think we invaded the seats of the mighty and brought away a war chest." Beard, moreover, graciously refused to condemn her colleagues who did go to Newport even if she would not. "I just don't feel like making that play, invaluable to success as it is, especially since so many of you are brave enough to do it well alone. I think I am a pure coward in this."[3]

It was neither the first nor the last time that Paul had to contend with perceptions that she and her organization were elitist and authoritarian. Immediately following the break with NAWSA in February 1914, dissidents within the Union complained about the structure of the organization. They charged that the process for choosing leaders was undemocratic, and they felt cut off from decision-making.[4] It was a bothersome complaint. Neither Paul nor Lucy Burns was inclined to try to change the structure of the Union, and Paul in particular feared the consequences of creating an "immense debating society" that would destroy the Union's effectiveness. For, while the cause she was espousing was equality for women, Paul had no conflict with, in her view, the reality that centralization—thus authority—was necessary to be effective. With the backing of her Executive Committee, Paul maintained that it was absolutely crucial to have a small, centralized leadership cadre which could make and implement policy without waiting for consent or approval from the rank and file.[5] For Paul, it was the ability to act quickly that would make the Union an effective organization. In her mind, there was no confusion between advocating equality in a democratic society and supporting the unilateral authority that would best achieve the goal. Nevertheless, she solicited advice and suggestions from the critics, partially out of politeness, and partially to placate the critics. "We would be most grateful for any constructive plan which you can lay before us."[6]

Edith Houghton Hooker of Baltimore, as ardent a suffragist as her sister, Katharine Houghton Hepburn, and a staunch believer in the

Congressional Union, did suggest a solution to the dilemma, to Lucy Burns.[7] Hooker proposed that the Union adopt a constitution which would allow a National Advisory Council which, in turn, would elect the Executive Committee and provide for the election by the rank and file of state chairpersons who would have voting privileges at Congressional Union conventions. Since the Executive Committee would ultimately be responsible for appointing the national council, Hooker's solution was less than perfect. Nevertheless, it seemed to allay the misgivings of the critics and, at the same time, retained the integrity of the leadership and guaranteed the functioning of the organization.[8]

Over the course of the next several months, a new constitution was drawn up. It provided that each state branch elect a state chairwoman, who would then appoint the members of her state committee. The state chairwomen were eligible to vote at all national conventions and were responsible also for electing the Executive Committee. Nominees for the Executive Committee were selected by former members of the Executive Committee, subject to approval by the National Advisory Council. The Executive Committee chose a chairwoman from among its members, and they also appointed a National Advisory Council, composed of prominent and influential women who held no other official position in the Congressional Union. The direction of the Congressional Union remained solely in the hands of the Executive Committee.[9]

Hooker's proposal proved valuable for reasons that went beyond soothing the critics. Establishing a National Advisory Council provided an opportunity to enlist the visible support of prominent women who enjoyed national reputations in a variety of fields and thus were immediately identifiable to potential supporters of the Congressional Union who might otherwise question the legitimacy of the organization. In addition, it was an instrument by which to enlist wealthy women who were attracted to the Union but who generally did not wish to take an active role in the day-to-day operation of the organization. Such women, it was hoped, could provide badly needed funds, both through their own contributions and by soliciting support from their friends. By the end of its first year, the Congressional Union had put together a stellar Advisory Council which included Helen Keller, Phoebe Hearst, Charlotte Perkins Gilman, Florence Kelley, Olympia

CONGRESSIONAL UNION ORGANIZATION (1914)

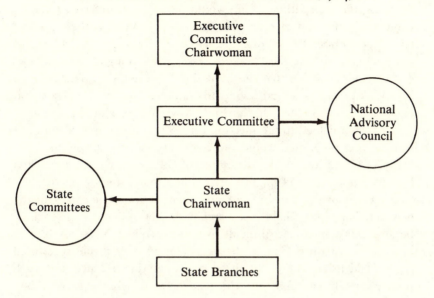

Brown, Abigail Scott Dunniway, and Harriot Stanton Blatch.[10] It was not a group accustomed to rubber-stamping anyone's decisions, even Alice Paul's. Much to everyone's consternation, however, even this exemplary group could not eliminate entirely persistent criticisms of authoritarianism. Such criticisms, of course, were generally directed at Paul. When Charlotte Whitney resigned from the Advisory Council, it was "because the Congressional Union is an autocratic organization with its controls entirely in the hands of one woman."[11]

Such criticisms at times seemed endless. But Paul steadfastly refused to enter into any agreement that would hamstring the Executive Committee so long as she and it were making progress toward the goal of securing a federal amendment. If there were those who disagreed with the way that the Congressional Union was run, they had a right to resign and join an organization in which they would be more philosophically comfortable. "I do not see how you can possibly belong to an organization with whose policy you are not in sympathy," she wrote to one critic. She suggested that, in the circumstances, the woman might want to consider resigning her membership.[12]

Needless to say, criticism came from outside as well as in, but for different reasons. Although she would have much preferred to cooperate with other suffrage groups, especially NAWSA, there seemed few opportunities to do so. Anna Howard Shaw, in particular, lost few occasions to take the Union to task for one thing or another. Despite Shaw's assertion that she wanted to "ignore their existence," the NAWSA president seized upon rumors about the Union with suspicious alacrity.[13] Indeed, her attitude toward Paul and the Congressional Union helped to produce the very consequence that Shaw most feared—that the Union would succeed in attracting to its organization many NAWSA members. A number of suffragists who were excited by and supported the Congressional Union found themselves torn between their loyalty to NAWSA and their desire to be a part of the new activism. Many held memberships in both organizations, which became more and more difficult over time. When NAWSA leaders like Shaw and Ruth Hanna McCormick aired their displeasure to all who would listen, the possibilities for cooperation lessened with each passing day. In an effort to circumvent the seemingly inevitable, Abby Scott Baker, Marie Forest, and Elizabeth Loud, all NAWSA members who eventually went to work for the Congressional Union, appealed to Shaw to "unite us on a platform broad enough to hold all suffragists, or to enable us to work . . . sustaining each other . . . and the great work." They also tried to assure Shaw that the rumors that Alice Paul intended to "smash" NAWSA were patently false. "Miss Paul is not trying to break down the National Association. We know this is true, for if she had so wished, she could have taken hundreds away from it [NAWSA] here in Washington."[14] The trio swore that no antagonism toward NAWSA came from Paul or other Union officers, adding that any assertions to the contrary were lies.[15]

Shaw and her NAWSA colleagues over-reacted to the multitude of rumors that rippled through suffrage circles. But Paul decided early on to remain silent. She believed little could be gained by answering the barrage of attacks leveled against her. "It seems to me better that we should not make any reply to these public attacks, as a reply simply prolongs the discussion."[16] Thus, the personal attacks went unanswered by both Paul and the Congressional Union, while mediators continued to seek a common ground upon which the two groups could cooperate.

A peremptory action taken by Ruth Hanna McCormick, early in March 1914, in her capacity as chairwoman of NAWSA's Congressional Committee, made the search for common ground even more elusive. Paul, who had returned to Moorestown for a much-needed rest, received an urgent note from Lucy Burns informing her that McCormick had, without warning, endorsed a new suffrage amendment on NAWSA's behalf. The Shafroth–Palmer legislation had been introduced in Congress on March 2, 1914.[17] In essence, the new legislation, which became popularly known as the Shafroth amendment, intended to make suffrage strictly a states' rights issue. The legislation provided that whenever 8 percent of the voters in a state, who had voted in the previous election, consented by petition, suffrage would be placed on the state ballot as a referendum item. The rationale behind the measure was that congressmen who supported suffrage, but adhered to a states' rights principle, would find the Shafroth amendment more acceptable than a federal amendment. Moreover, since many states required action by the legislature in order to amend the state constitution, the new proposal theoretically provided a way to circumvent this process, thus presumably making it easier for the voters to secure woman suffrage in their state.[18]

Paul returned to Washington at once. She asked to meet with NAWSA leaders in order to discuss the situation, hoping to persuade them to denounce the Shafroth amendment. Anne Howard Shaw, Jane Addams, Mary Ware Dennett, and Katherine Dexter McCormick of NAWSA, met with Paul, Lucy Burns, Dora Lewis, Elizabeth Kent, and Mary Beard, for a series of discussions that lasted two days. It quickly became obvious to the women from the Congressional Union that Ruth Hanna McCormick had acted upon the advice of her father's (Mark Hanna) political cronies. They convinced McCormick that Congress would never approve the Anthony amendment, and if it did, that the states would never ratify it. It also became painfully clear to all present that McCormick had acted upon her own initiative, without consulting the NAWSA Board. McCormick simply presented NAWSA with a *fait accompli*. In the end, NAWSA could only comment lamely that "Mrs. McCormick has all these positions and friends in Congress who know so much about it all and think it the best thing to do, and have already introduced it." No amount of reasoning could persuade them otherwise. Even the sympathetic Jane Addams could not change the situation. NAWSA's stubborn refusal to comply with *any* request, regardless of its merits, that emanated from the Congressional Union, forced NAWSA into the position of having to support McCormick's actions even though some of its own Board members questioned the value of the Shafroth amendment. The Union members might have guessed from the beginning of the conference that the situation was hopeless when, at the start of the discussions, Katherine Dexter McCormick turned her chair so that she sat with her back to Paul and her colleagues and remained that way for the entire two days.[19]

With NAWSA thus committed to the Shafroth amendment, the Congressional Union saw its own role as that of fighting to keep the Anthony amendment alive and in the forefront of the suffrage struggle. And, in the circumstance, the Union, in one of its few public retorts to date, took aim at NAWSA for perpetuating the charges of authoritarianism leveled against the new group. In an article in *The Suffragist*, which detailed the Union's objections to the Shafroth amendment, editor Rheta Childe Dorr noted—perhaps with some amusement over the irony of the situation—that the "action of the National American Association in introducing the new amendment without consultation with the body of the Association savors a bit of autocracy."[20]

While the Congressional Union generally did refrain from engaging in public arguments with NAWSA, Paul believed that it was imperative that they make their position absolutely clear on anything that struck so close to matters critical to the movement. With one stroke, Paul managed to dismiss both the Shafroth amendment and NAWSA when she responded to an inquiry about the Congressional Union's position on the matter. "We are not antagonistic to the new resolution at all, and think that if some initiative and referendum society were to press it, it might be a helpful thing," she noted. "We feel, however, that we must concentrate upon one amendment or another as otherwise one will be used by congressmen against the other."[21]

To be sure, the Congressional Union was not alone in its opposition to the Shafroth amendment. Many of NAWSA's rank and file were confused, angry, or both at the new and unexpected departure. At the Mississippi Valley Conference held in March 1914, and sponsored in part by NAWSA, a resolution endorsing the Anthony amendment "was signed by practically every official present, with the exception of a few who seemed afraid if they did so, they would lose the help of the National in their campaigns." [22]

With NAWSA's rank and file in such disarray over the Shafroth amendment, Dr. Shaw felt compelled to issue a long detailed statement explaining its position. Characteristically, Shaw refused to admit that support of the two amendments—which NAWSA claimed—was inconsistent, and placed the blame for internal conflicts squarely at the doorstep of the Congressional Union. Shaw reiterated the states' rights rationale proffered by Ruth Hanna McCormick, and ended with an appeal for loyalty from NAWSA members and a slap at the Congressional Union. "If the Union would stop trying to create false impressions . . . there would be less difficulty. . . . [The] main purpose [of the Congressional Union] is to create a disturbance. . . . To cooperate with an association which is outside the National Association . . . seems to me lacking in that sort of loyalty which gives courage and strength to an organization." [23] It would have been difficult for Paul and the Congressional Union to create a falser impression or to provoke a bigger disturbance among the NAWSA members than did the actions of its own Executive Board.

NAWSA's decision regarding the Shafroth amendment did not, of itself, determine the course of the Congressional Union. The Democrats had helped to cement the plans that eventually were approved at Marble House. Throughout the protracted break with NAWSA, and its establishment as an independent organization, the Congressional Union had not ignored its political program. Deputations and demonstrations continued with regularity, beginning with a delegation of 400 working women who met with President Wilson on February 2, 1914. [24] Led by Rose Schneiderman of the National Women's Trade Union League, Melinda Scott of the New York Women's Trade Union League, Rose Winslow, a textile worker from Pennsylvania, and Margaret Henchey, a laundry worker, the women heard Wilson intone, "Until this party, as such, has considered a matter of this very supreme importance and taken its position, I am not at liberty to speak for it."[25] Wilson did not have long to wait for the party to make its views clear. The following day, February 3rd, the Democratic House Caucus met for the sole purpose of announcing its stand on woman suffrage. Representative John Baker of California proposed that the caucus vote to establish a House Committee on Woman Suffrage. An antisuffragist, J. Thomas Heflin of Alabama, immediately proposed a substitute resolution which declared suffrage a states' rights issue and not a federal issue. The caucus voted 123 to 57 to accept Heflin's resolution.[26] Lest there was any uncertainty regarding the party's position, Representative Oscar W. Underwood of Alabama, a powerful member of the Democratic party, clarified things further in a speech in the House: "I not only said I was opposed to it [suffrage amendment], but I said the party on this side of the chamber was opposed to it, and the party that has control of the legislation in Congress certainly has the right openly and above board to say that it will not support a measure if it is not in accordance with its principles."[27]

The reaction from NAWSA was predictable. Rather than take aim at the Democrats, NAWSA leveled its guns at the Congressional Union. It was unwise in the first place, spokeswomen asserted, to force the issue by demanding that the Democratic Caucus meet and take a stand on suffrage. The older suffragists claimed that "five years of good suffrage work has been undone by this action."[28] As Alice Paul pointed out, however, forcing the Democrats to take a stand benefited suffrage regardless of whether the stand was for or against establishing a House Committee on Woman Suffrage. If the Democrats had reported favorably, the suffrage issue would have been advanced; if, as they did, the Democrats reported negatively, it would prove that the party indeed had to be held accountable for its refusal to support suffrage. Whether or not her suffrage colleagues entirely agreed with the strategy, Paul was accurate on one count. "We can draw the support of women with greater ease," she noted, "from a party which shows a weak hand on suffrage, than from one which hides its opposition behind silence."[29]

Despite the defeat in the House, NAWSA urged the Senate to bring the issue to an early vote. The Union preferred that the Senate not vote upon the Anthony amendment until after May 2, 1914. On that date, a series of demonstrations, which the Union had been organizing for several months, were to take place. If the vote were delayed until after the second of May, *The Suffragist* pointed out, the demonstrations might help to persuade uncommitted senators to vote for the amendment.[30] Once again the Congressional Union found itself at loggerheads with NAWSA over strategy.

The Suffragist reported that NAWSA was urging an early Senate vote knowing full well that the amendment could not possibly pass. The chairman of the Senate Committee on Woman Suffrage, Senator Charles S. Thomas of Colorado, publicly acknowledged that the measure would fail if brought to an early vote. The Congressional Union provided a reason for NAWSA's peculiar early-vote stance: defeat of the Anthony amendment would clear the way for action on the Shafroth amendment. An editorial in *The Suffragist* which analyzed the situation, noted that ultimately it would be the Democrats and not NAWSA who would have to bear responsibility for defeat of the amendment. But in its view, NAWSA made it much easier for the Democrats.[31]

Despite the best efforts of the Union to delay the vote, NAWSA won out. On March 19, 1914, for the first time in twenty-seven years, the Senate voted on a federal woman suffrage amendment. As expected, the amendment failed by a vote of 35 yeas to 34 nays—far less a majority than the required two-thirds necessary for passage.[32] An overwhelming majority of the votes against passage were cast by southern Democrats. By their actions in agreeing to the early vote and then failing to support the amendment, the Democrats had once again demonstrated their opposition to suffrage.

As it turned out, the Congressional Union was correct in supposing that the demonstrations on May 2, held simultaneously in cities and towns across the nation, would have some positive effect on members of Congress. Union organizers had gone to almost every state in the nation to coordinate the event which drew together practically all suffrage organizations in the country. The purpose of the demonstrations was to demand passage of the Anthony amendment, and even NAWSA, after assurances that they were not to promote the Union, agreed to participate. The Congressional Union readily admitted that without NAWSA's participation, the demonstrations would not have been nearly as successful.[33] The response to the demonstrations ought

to have given pause to all suffragists regarding the value of cooperation. Three days after the demonstrations, on May 5, the House Judiciary Committee reported out the Mondell Resolution (Anthony
amendment) without recommendation. It was as far as the Rules
Committee could bring itself to go, but it marked nevertheless the first
time that a suffrage measure had been out of committee in the House.[34]

The amendment next went to the Rules Committee, which was
charged with allocating time on the House calendar for consideration
and debate. Once again, the Democrats demonstrated their hostility
to the suffrage amendment by holding it up in the Rules Committee.
The Congressional Union sent a series of deputations to members of
the Committee, finally extracting a promise that they would convene
on July 1. On June 30, Alice Paul sent a delegation from the General
Federation of Women's Clubs (GFWC) to call upon Woodrow Wilson. The President received them in the East Room. The women urged
Wilson to use his influence to secure prompt action by the Rules
Committee. Rheta Childe Dorr, acting as spokeswoman for the deputation, presented Wilson with a resolution passed by the GFWC several weeks earlier. Wilson told the group that he was still bound by
his party's platform and that, in any case, he, too, believed that suffrage was a matter that ought to be decided by the states and not the
federal government.[35]

July 1 came and went with no convening of the Rules Committee.
No explanation was provided for the women who had gathered at the
Capitol. However, the suffragists were assured that the Committee
would meet, without fail, one month hence.[36] A month later, the Rules
Committee again filed to convene. It was not until August 28, the day
before the meeting at Marble House, that the Committee finally met.
The members voted to report favorably on a bill providing for greater
self-government for the Philippines. Their work for the day accomplished, the Committee promptly adjourned.[37]

While the Rules Committee was voting to report the Philippine bill,
members of the Congressional Union were en route to Newport. The
news of the Rules Committee's failure to act on woman suffrage while
voting favorably on self-government in the Philippines, only strength-
ened their resolve. The ladies of Marble House were now determined
to deal boldly with their Democratic adversaries.

Lucy Burns spoke first to the assembled delegates. Outlining the accomplishments of the Congressional Union in the preceding several months, Burns followed up with an analysis of the workings of Congress and set the stage for Alice Paul. Before beginning, Paul requested that the members of the press withdraw. She then pledged to secrecy the delegates present, asking that no one tip the hand on the Congressional Union prematurely—that is, before such time as all phases of the plan were ready to be implemented.[38] Paul then launched into a discussion of the function of political parties in American politics. She announced that the primary task of the Congressional Union in the weeks to come was to "convince the dominant party, and all other parties, that opposition to suffrage is inexpedient." Paul submitted for the delegates' approval, the Executive Board's plan to wage political war against the Democrats in the nine western states where women were already enfranchised. "The time has come," Paul said, "when we can really go into *national* politics and use the nearly four million votes that we have to win the vote for the rest of the women in the country. Our fight is a political one. . . . The question is whether we are good enough politicians to take four million votes and organize them and use them."[39] It was a rhetorical question. The only answer, as far as Paul was concerned, was a resounding "Yes!"

In the course of her talk, Paul anticipated every possible objection to the proposed campaign. She might just as well have announced that she was answering charges and accusations raised by NAWSA, for she addressed all the accusations leveled at the Union by NAWSA, including the charge that the policy was a partisan one. "This policy is absolutely non-partisan," Paul asserted. "It calls upon women to lay aside all party affiliations and put suffrage before their party."[40] Answering the objection that opposing prosuffrage Democrats would prove counterproductive to the cause, Paul pointed out that all congressional candidates in full suffrage states were, by definition, prosuffrage. She admitted that the "political leaders will be aroused to a high pitch of indignation," but she insisted that the more concerned were the political leaders, the better it would be for suffrage. To those who accused them of fomenting militant action, Paul answered: "It is militant only in the sense that it is strong, positive, and energetic." Finally, analyzing the effect that the Union's anti-Democratic campaign would have on other political parties, Paul noted, "when once the political parties are made to realize that opposition to suffrage means their defeat, when once it is shown that suffragists can actually affect the results of a national election, our fight will be won."[41]

It was a masterful speech. Paul's plan, simply stated, was that the Congressional Union would undertake to organize the nine full-suffrage states, and vigorously campaign against all Democratic candidates in those states. The Advisory Council gave their overwhelming approval. "The way you and Lucy Burns with your program swept us all completely into the movement is something I was very much impressed with," Katherine Houghton Hepburn later confided to Paul.[42] Florence Kelley of the National Consumers' League concurred. "I do not see how there could possibly be a more statesman-like proposal than that which has been made this afternoon."[43]

The meeting at Marble House marked a new departure in the history of woman suffrage in the United States. For the first time, enfranchised women would be able to help their unenfranchised sisters in purely political fashion by disavowing party commitment in favor of sex solidarity. Certainly, the Congressional Union entertained no false hopes about the ease with which this could be accomplished. From the start, a major goal in 1914, in addition to defeating as many Democratic candidates as possible, was to convince politicians of all parties that women could be mobilized as a voting bloc, to further the best interests of the sex and to the detriment of those parties or individuals who opposed suffrage. The candidates in 1916 would be much less certain of their ground, where women were concerned, if it could be demonstrated that the Congressional Union was successful in laying the foundation for a potentially powerful special interest group.

With the Congressional Union press department functioning smoothly, the media did its part in declaring the Marble House meeting an important departure for women. The New York *Tribune* noted that Marble House "marked the entrance of women into the arena of practical politics. . . . At Newport, for the first time was launched a national movement of women armed to fight with political weapons for their rights."[44] The press department was, of course, careful to divulge only what Paul wanted revealed at the moment.

Within two weeks of the Marble House gathering, the Union had begun to implement its plan. Two organizers were sent into each of the nine western states where women held the vote and in Nevada, to assist in the referendum campaign at the request of NAWSA's Nevada manager, Anne Martin. One woman was responsible for opening and operating the headquarters, which involved attending to the press, distributing literature, and arranging speaking tours. The other organizer stumped the state, speaking on behalf of both the federal amendment and the Congressional Union, urging women to vote against the Democratic candidates in their districts as a matter of honor on behalf of women not yet enfranchised.[45]

An essential element of success in the field was choosing the right women to present the case of the Congressional Union. Alice Paul had spent several weeks culling her organization for women with the right combinations of independence, motivation, managerial and organizational skills, and public-speaking talent with style and flair.[46] The organizers had to be politically astute, creative, tactful, and hard as nails to remain in the field. In addition to raising their own expenses as far as possible, to endure everything from automobile breakdowns in remote, uninhabited rural areas, to frequently primitive accommodations, and weather conditions which ranged from blistering desert heat to blizzard-like snowstorms and freezing temperatures. Living conditions (substantially unchanged between 1914 and 1916) were graphically described two years later by organizer Sara Bard Field. Field, organizing in Nevada, found herself stranded in a small town with one run-down hotel, which she described as "one big spittoon with all the cooking odors in the state for two generations collected within its walls."[47] Needless to say, the organizers also had to endure the antipathy of the Democratic party and the pro-Democratic press in the nine suffrage states and in Nevada.[48]

Paul selected Lucy Burns and Rose Winslow, a fiery and riveting speaker for both the suffrage and the labor cause, to organize California. In Denver, Doris Stevens, a young woman with journalistic experience and ample reserves of sheer nerve who was noted in suffrage circles both for her radical views and her stunning appearance, teamed up with Ruth Noyes, whose demeanor was much quieter, but who possessed unflagging energy. Josephine Casey, a labor organizer with a reputation as a no-holds-barred speaker, was enlisted to organize Arizona with Jane Pincus, who was an effective fund-raiser. Lola Trax and Edna Latimer, both of whom had helped to organize Maryland's Just Government League, were dispatched to Kansas. The press secretary of the Congressional Union, Jessie Hardy Stubbs, organized Oregon with the help of Virginia Arnold, whose mild-mannered personality was a disarming cloak for a single-minded persistence. In Washington state, Margaret Faye Whittemore and Anne McCue, both of Philadelphia, conducted the campaign, while the founder of the Wage Earner's League of Minneapolis, Gertrude Hunter, established her headquarters in Cheyenne, Wyoming. In Utah, it was Elsie Lancaster, whose placid exterior belied a spine of steel, who carried the banner. And finally, in Idaho, the chairwoman of the Norwalk (Connecticut) Suffrage League, Helena Hill Weed, took a six-week furlough from home and children to open headquarters in Boise.[49]

Most of the field organizers were unmarried. Those who were married, like Helena Hill Weed, were able to spend extended periods away from home. Regardless of their status, however, the work required sacrifices. For some, such as Rose Winslow and Josephine Casey, it meant giving up their jobs without the luxury of family financial support to fall back upon. Organizers in 1914 were not, as a rule, paid salaries by the Congressional Union, although the organization did provide expenses if that was necessary.[50] In unusual cases, such as that of Weed, a widow with small children who had enormous debts incurred by her spendthrift husband, small salaries were paid.[51]

The reception that greeted the organizers varied from state to state, but almost all of the women shared the common experience of incurring the ridicule, if not the wrath, of the Democratic establishment—both politicians and press. Citizen response was less predictable. In Phoenix, Jane Pincus found organizing the women of Arizona a frustrating experience for the most part. In mid-October, however, Pincus reported that "the one woman in Phoenix and almost in the state, who has to take the initial step before the rest do anything, came down to our office."[52] For Pincus, her entire effort in the state seemed to be directed at attracting this one individual. In California, by contrast, Lucy Burns reported many visitors to the Congressional Union headquarters on Stockton Street, just around the corner from San Francisco's busy main thoroughfare, Market Street. Reflecting on the "frightful prices" they had to pay for rent, Burns noted that "if the women here, however, would only give me the money they are willing to spend on luncheons and dinners I will get along admirably."[53] In Kansas, Edna Latimer found the reception encouraging. On reaching Dodge City, for example, she was informed that local residents were holding a political meeting "out on the prairie," and Latimer was asked to speak at the gathering. She arrived at an isolated schoolhouse at eleven o'clock at night to find 300 people waiting to hear her talk about suffrage. At five o'clock the next morning, while waiting for a freight train that would take her on to Topeka, a man walked up to Latimer and said, "My wife was at your meeting yesterday . . . and I thought I would tell you that I have voted the Democratic ticket for forty years, but I have voted for it for the last time."[54] The exchange must surely have lightened the load of her grueling schedule.

While the citizens of suffrage states received the organizers with varying degrees of enthusiasm, politicians were much less ambivalent.[55] The *Republican Herald* of Salt Lake City, Utah, reported that W. R. Wallace, the "Democratic generalissimo and his gang of political mannikins" threatened to "advertise Miss [Elsie] Lancaster the country over by means of the Associated Press as being in league with 'sinister' influences in Utah."[56] And the *Seattle Sunday Times*, a Democratic newspaper, reported that Democratic candidate for the Senate, Judge W. W. Black, showed up at the Union headquarters in Seattle, in order to express his "fatherly concern for the two young women suffrage leaders." He suggested that they "go home and wage a campaign for female suffrage, and let the Democratic congressional candidates . . . alone."[57]

Several incumbent candidates expressed their displeasure in the halls of Congress. Representative Carl Hayden and Senator Marcus Aurelius Thomas Smith of Arizona, first attempted to placate the Congressional Union organizers in their state early in October 1914. They sent telegrams to the Democratic chariman of the state convention in session at Phoenix. Hayden and Smith announced that they would be willing to support a federal amendment—a departure from their previously held state-rights positions—and instructed the chairman to include a plank in the platform advocating support of the Anthony amendment. Jane Pincus remarked wryly, but with a great deal of satisfaction, that "every candidate who was running, even for state or county offices, felt it necessary to declare that he had always believed in woman suffrage, that his mother had believed in woman suffrage, and that his grandmother believed in it."[58] While it was a measure of their effectiveness, the Congressional Union made it clear that the Hayden–Smith declaration, admirable though it was, would not deter the suffragists from their path. Hayden then took to the floor of the House of Representatives and, for two hours, delivered a diatribe against the Congressional Union, Jane Pincus, Alice Paul, and whomever else he could think of. Not only did these women *not* represent the majority of women, accused the irate congressman, but anti-Democratic appeals were an insult to the women voters.[59]

Shortly after the campaign in Kansas opened, a Democratic congressman, Dudley Doolittle, visited the Congressional Union's national headquarters and urged the organization to withdraw from his home state. When he was denied, Doolittle railed at their obstinence in a scathing speech delivered from the floor of the House. The Union, Doolittle assured his colleagues, did not have the support of the nation's suffragists.[60]

Newspaper opposition to the anti-Democrats campaign developed just as swiftly as that from the politicians. "Monday afternoon, they [the Congressional Union] desecrated a charitable gathering of the Ladies Hospital Aide Society," reported the Cheyenne *Wyoming Leader* in an article criticizing organizer Gertrude Hunter's presence. "If it was nothing more than the harmless effort . . . to earn some Congressional coin, it might be overlooked, and these two women, with fatherly tenderness, told to go back home. But it involves an insult to the intelligent citizenship of this state."[61] In Colorado, the *Fountain Herald* invited its readers to invite Doris Stevens to "leave the state at once."[62] And, just as quickly as the Democratic newspapers printed their stories excoriating the Congressional Union, the Republican newspapers sprang to the defense of the suffragists, although it is questionable how motivated were the publishers by a sense of justice for the women or the cause. The *Cheyenne Tribune* took the *Cheyenne Leader* to task for attacking the Union. The *Tribune*, in a series of articles, defended the "two highly educated and cultured women who were sent to Wyoming."[63] The *Jewel City* [Kansas] *Republican* gleefully reported one benefit of Lola Trax's arrival in Kansas: "She threw the Democratic editors into fits. They have just been having one fit after another all over the state."[64]

By election day, November 3, 1914, the Congressional Union had accomplished its major goals. It had made suffrage a major issue in the states where anti-Democratic campaigns were waged. The campaigns, moreover, achieved prominence not only locally, but nationally as well, both through the press and through the efforts of beleaguered congressmen to denounce their tormentors. In addition, the Union attracted a number of prominent opponents, but even this anticipated development served a function. Whether the Congressional Union was being praised or damned, its presence was felt and suffrage was on everyone's lips.

In the entire field of candidates in the ten states in question, the Union campaigned vigorously against forty-three Democrats running for House and Senate seats, and offices of governor. Only twenty of these candidates were elected to office. The Congressional Union refrained from making extravagant claims about its role in the defeat of the twenty-three Democrats. Many of the Democratic candidates may well have lost regardless of the Union's campaign against them. In the election of 1912, the split between the Republicans and the Progressives benefited all Democrats. In 1914, however, the Progressives returned wholesale to the ranks of the Republican party. This, in combination with the traditional loss incurred by the incumbent party in off-year elections, undoubtedly accounted for substantial losses suffered by the Democratic party nationwide. Nevertheless, the Union could claim that its campaigns had aided in the defeat of the twenty-three Democrats in varying degrees, with little fear of being held up to ridicule by disbelieving analysts.

The Congressional Union did claim full credit for five Democratic losses. In Kansas, George A. Neeley's defeat was considered a "veritable triumph" for the Union. Neeley's election has been conceded because the opposition was hopelessly divided between the Republican, Charles Curtis, and the Progressive, Victor Murdoch. In the end, Neeley lost by a hair. He garnered 34.8 percent of the vote (175,929), to Curtis' 35.5 percent (180,823). Murdoch pulled 116,755 votes, or 22.9 percent of the total.[65] Colorado Representative Harry Seldomridge's 22,000 vote plurality of two years earlier evaporated in 1914. Seldomridge had polled fully 44.5 percent of the votes cast in 1912, outdistancing his opponent by two-to-one. In 1914, Seldomridge's percentage decreased to 42 percent, while his Republican opponent, Charles H. Timberlake, pulled in 46 percent of the votes cast.[66] Seldomridge's constituents attributed his loss to the campaign conducted by the Congressional Union, although the ex-congressman refused to concede that the suffragists played any significant part in his defeat.[67]

The hard-working Congressional Union organizers were also gratified by the defeat of James H. Moyle, Democratic senatorial candidate in Utah, especially since the *New York World*, among others, had predicted that Moyle would be an easy winner. And in Idaho, the loss of James Hawley, Democratic senatorial candidate, to his Republican opponent James H. Brady, similarly produced gratification within the Congressional Union. Shortly before the election, a scandal had broken out in Idaho, which involved Republican state office-holders. Helena Hill Weed noted that the women in the state were "aroused as they never have been before to the power they hold as voting women. . . . This scandal will eventually help them to realize their power and responsibility in national affairs."[68] Weed's task was made doubly difficult because the Republican party was under fire due to the embezzlement of state funds by the Republican state treasurer. It was a perfect opportunity for the Democrats to capitalize on the situation and capture the Senate seat. The Union campaigned tirelessly against Hawley. His loss by a mere 6,000 votes allowed the suffragists to claim the Idaho Senate race as one of their successes.[69] In the northwest states, the Union claimed responsibility for the loss of Democrat A. F. Flegel, to Republican Clifton N. McArthur, in Oregon's third congressional district, along with Roscoe Drumheller's defeat in Washington's fourth congressional district.[70]

In a number of other races, the Union took advantage of the diminished pluralities of several candidates in order to enhance further its own reputation as a spoiler. These races included that of Senator Smith of Arizona, whose election was in question for nearly a week, Representative Edward Keating of Colorado, and Senator Charles S. Thomas, also of Colorado, whose 45,000 vote plurality in 1912 was reduced to just over 3,000 votes in 1914. Thomas, for one, readily confessed that the Congressional Union had given him the "fight of his life."[71]

Postelection analysis reported in the newspapers across the country tended to support the claims of the Congressional Union. In this way, the newspapers helped to shape the perceptions people held regarding the effectiveness of the Congressional Union campaign. The headline in a Denver newspaper reporting on Senator Thomas' reelection, read: "Man Who Betrayed Colorado Interests and Double-Crossed Woman Suffrage Retains Job By Less Than One Thousand Votes." And a lengthy article syndicated by the Newspaper Enterprise Association noted that the Democrats were only just beginning to consider seriously the importance of the Union's campaign. "The Democratic campaign committee in Colorado acknowledged the power of the women's influence when it devoted its last campaign circular, issued on the eve of the election, entirely to the women's campaign." The article went on to say that the Oregon Democratic state committee exhibited similar concern with its last appeal to the voters for the reelection of Senator George Earle Chamberlain—a plea for the support of women voters. "The importance of the situation will be more fully realized by the Democratic polls when they understand that this wonderful fight which the women made this time was the result of a very short campaign, by only two women organizers in each state, with very little money. . . . with two years more . . . the women can absolutely assure a Democratic defeat.[72]

The Congressional Union's campaign in the West, therefore, was not the dismal failure that the antisuffragists, and even NAWSA, claimed.[73] A most gratified Alice Paul confided to Mary Beard that the Union had succeeded beyond her "fondest hopes."[74] The campaign had begun with a characteristic burst of energy and a flourish that became a Union trademark, with the organizers departing Washington on a "suffrage train" bedecked with purple, white, and gold banners. It ended with all the organizers in "the last stage of exhaustion."[75] Beyond the political benefits deriving from the efforts of the women, the organization had grown markedly in members, money, and importance, both in the suffrage movement and in the women's movement. If the Congressional Union needed further confirmation that politically and tactically it was on the right track, the news brought back by a deputation to the chairman of the House Rules Committee, on December 9, 1914, erased all lingering doubts. Elizabeth Kent and Helen Hamilton Gardener called on Chairman Robert L. Henry as soon as he arrived in Washington after the election recess. Henry wasted little time in assuring the suffragists that the Rules Committee would report favorably on House Resolution 514, which would provide time on the House calendar to debate suffrage and vote on the amendment. Henry attributed the earlier difficulty in getting the report out, to vague and unidentified—but apparently effective—"sinister influences." Once again, a "sinister" force had reared its ugly head in the campaign of 1914, although presumably it was not the same sinister force with which Elsa Lancaster was in league, in Kansas.[76]

CHAPTER 5

The Widening Rift with NAWSA

If, by the end of 1914, the campaign-weary organizers were looking forward to a rest, they must have been disappointed. Alice Paul already had a new project in mind that would keep everyone busy. At a meeting of the National Advisory Council on March 31, 1915, Paul proposed the next logical step in their effort to secure a federal amendment. It was now time to organize in all those states where the Congressional Union did not already have a branch. The purpose for organizing in the states was not to lobby for state suffrage. NAWSA was doing everything that could be done on that level; there would be little advantage in duplicating those efforts. The purpose of organizing the states was to continue what the campaign of 1914 had begun—to make suffrage a national issue and to create a nationwide demand for passage of the amendment.[1] Paul hoped that the organizing process would proceed quickly and planned to culminate the drive with the first national convention of women voters, to be held at the Panama-Pacific Exposition in San Francisco, in September 1915. "We want to make woman suffrage the dominant political issue from the moment Congress reconvenes," Paul told the Advisory Committee. "We want to have Congress open in the middle of a veritable suffrage cyclone."[2]

The relationship between the Congressional Union and NAWSA

had not improved in the intervening months since the election. NAWSA leaders were still convinced that the Union's intention was to take over NAWSA. Paul, Burns, and Mary Beard did discuss the possibility of attending the annual NAWSA convention with as many Congressional Union supporters as they could muster, but not with the intention of capturing the organization. Rather, they sought to lobby NAWSA members to vote to support a federal suffrage amendment. In the end, Paul decided that it was wiser to concentrate on other matters, since there seemed little chance of persuading the majority of NAWSA delegates to oppose their leaders on the federal amendment issue.[3] The events of the NAWSA convention proved the wisdom of her decision.

Ruth Hanna McCormick and Antoinette Funk presented a masterful argument on behalf of the Shafroth amendment but even so, delegates were not overwhelmingly in favor of that amendment. The rank and file wanted desperately to return to support of the Anthony amendment, but the leadership stubbornly insisted on supporting the Shafroth amendment. So bitterly was the Shafroth measure opposed that Jane Addams refused to continue to serve as vice-president, and would not even agree to accept the title of honorary vice-president.[4] But even in the face of this opposition, the delegates refused to stage an open revolt and consented instead to support the Shafroth amendment through their re-election of Dr. Shaw as the president of NAWSA.[5]

There were so few areas of agreement between the two organizations that it was hardly surprising when NAWSA objected to the Congressional Union organizing in all the states, particularly since that had been one of the original disagreements before the split occurred. Even more of a problem, however, were the votes on the suffrage issue which were scheduled to take place in 1915 in several states, in most of which NAWSA was deeply involved. The conservative suffragists took a dim view of anyone who threatened to bring instability into even a losing battle. Not all NAWSA members in positions of leadership agreed with this view, however.

It was quite clear to Anne Martin of Nevada, who was running the 1914 NAWSA referendum campaign in that state, that her superiors objected heartily when the Congressional Union "lent" Martin one of their organizers, Mabel Vernon. When Martin and Senator Key Pitt-man got into a public argument over the merits of the Anthony versus the Shafroth amendments, Anna Howard Shaw fired off an angry letter in which she accused Martin of being a dupe of the Congressional Union and of Mabel Vernon. "I thought it must have been the action of the Congressional Union for, if there is any possible way of making a political blunder, the Congressional Union has a facility for finding how to do it. When I learned that Miss Vernon was with you, I could not help feeling that the influence of the Congressional Union had something to do with your issuing this document."[6] A month later, Martin still had not regained Shaw's good graces. Raising the Pittman issue yet one more time, Shaw remarked, "I must frankly state that I have not much regard for your judgement."[7] Shaw's displeasure reached a peak in September when she let Martin have it with both barrels. "There has never been any financial correspondence with you that you have ever gotten straight or have kept straight, and I frankly confess I am pretty tired of your constant quibbling." The "quibbling" Shaw referred to concerned an inquiry which Martin made regarding the allocation of funds to cover the expenses of a NAWSA speaker who was coming to Nevada.[8] Shaw apparently forgot and forgave when the Nevada referendum campaign ended in success, although there were no apologies forthcoming regarding Martin's judgment.

By 1915, NAWSA was every bit as resistant to the Congressional Union's intention to organize state branches. Even Harriot Stanton Blatch raised objections to Alice Paul's plans concerning New York state organization work. Paul had made it clear on numerous occasions that she had no intention of jeopardizing the state campaigns.[9] Nevertheless, misunderstandings regarding Paul's intentions did persist. Blatch insisted that Paul had discouraged suffragists from supporting state campaigns by declaring that the current efforts were hopeless and had further sworn to "use all her influence privately to prevent women in New York from giving their time or money to the referendum campaign."[10] Actually, Paul had discussed the situation at a Union meeting in Washington the previous December. She said then that it was a waste of time and money to mount state campaigns that clearly had no chance of success; she had not, however, included New York, Massachusetts, or Pennsylvania as hopeless states. At the same time, she made it clear that her preference was indeed for all suffragists to put their efforts fully behind the federal amendment. "The only question is whether all the suffrage sentiment in the unenfranchised states are focussed behind it, whether we dissipate our energies into innumerable state campaigns, or whether we all stand absolutely shoulder to shoulder back of this [federal] amendment."[11] The statement was very different from the one attributed to Paul by Blatch when she tried to prevent the Congressional Union from establishing a New York branch prior to the referendum.[12]

Blatch's interpretation of Paul's position may have been the result of a simple misunderstanding. Carrie Chapman Catt's attempts to interfere with Paul's plans were clearly deceitful. Catt, at the time the president of NAWSA's New York state affiliate, asked Paul to hold off organizing in New York until after the referendum. Otherwise, she predicted, the Congressional Union would attract only "disgruntled suffragists here and there," and the "really efficient ones" would resent the Union's participation in New York affairs. Promising that the field would be free after the vote should New York reject woman suffrage, Catt suggested with apparent good-will that Paul could do well to concentrate, in the meantime, on those states where no referenda faced the public. "Why not work there *now*," Catt urged Alice Paul. And she added that such a course of action would "give us the chance to think of you as allies and not as competitors."[13]

Paul's response was immediate and agreeable. Although she had doubts about the expectations for success of the state referendum, the chance to bury the hatchet with NAWSA was a welcome opportunity. She told Catt that the New York office had not been opened for the immediate purpose of full-fledged organization in that state. Instead, the New York office was to be considered a headquarters from which to direct the Union's national work. Paul further noted that there was no difference of opinion as to the course of action that the Union ought to pursue in the states in which there were active campaigns pending. "I need hardly tell you that we are deeply interested in the success of the New York campaign and wish its success as ardently as even you can do." The Congressional Union, concluded Paul, would not be carrying on organization work in referenda states.[14]

Within a week of their correspondence, however, Catt was berating

Harriot Taylor Upton, the president of the Ohio Woman Suffrage Association, for inviting both NAWSA and the Congressional Union to set up offices in that state. The Ohio Association, said Catt, had "lost its senses." Catt predicted that the rank and file would be incapable of deciding the merits of two organizations whose tactics were so different. It seemed clear that more than a concern for the peace of mind of the rank and file motivated Catt. "If I were in your place . . . I would have said to that Committee, I insist upon your fortifying the state of Ohio against the Congressional Union."[15] Ohio, it should be noted, was not engaged in a state referendum campaign in 1915.

One month later, Catt professed to be indignent that Alice Paul had broken her pledge "against further mischief." Catt's anger was not a consequence of the Union organizing suffragists in New York, for, as Paul had promised, they were not doing organization work in the state. Catt was angry because the Congressional Union was conducting routine business (as Paul had told Catt in April she intended to do), such as talking about the issue of a federal amendment with the congressmen from New York.[16] Catt's charges were ludicrous and a clear effort to undermine Paul's integrity. Paul calmly responded to the charges and included copies not only of the previous correspondence between Catt and Paul, but Catt's letter to Harriet Upton—which Upton had passed along to Paul, for her information. "[Y]ou may not have these letters accessible," Paul wrote to Catt, graciously suggesting that Catt's memory may have been at fault.[17] If Catt was embarrassed to be confronted with the written proof of her duplicity, she contained her embarrassment well.

NAWSA's persistence in portraying the Congressional Union as consciously engaged in activity harmful to suffrage produced a variety of responses to the organizing efforts of Paul and her colleagues in the states. Caroline Katzenstein of the Philadelphia Equal Franchise Society believed that her support of the Congressional Union had to be kept as quiet as possible for the good of the cause. "I make the request as a sacrifice because I like very much to be classed with the CU workers and never hesitate to let my allegiance be known, but there is so much opposition from a few of the Equal Franchise Society members . . . that it may handicap my work if I am made conspicuous."[18] A rumor that made the rounds of the Equal Franchise Society and helped to resolve Katzenstein's dilemma, only reinforced the negative feelings harbored by some toward the Congressional Union. Union supporters, it was alleged, "attacked" President Wilson in the course of attempting to secure a meeting with him. The willingness of critics to believe this rumor helped to persuade Katzenstein that she could not, in good conscience, continue to maintain a low profile. As Katzenstein well knew, the alleged attackers had not even seen Wilson, never mind attacked him. The suffragists, of whom Katzenstein had been one, were from Philadelphia and, after Wilson sent word that he would not see the ladies, the delegation left Washington immediately to return to Philadelphia.[19] Following the defeat of the Pennsylvania referendum, therefore, Katzenstein shed the constraints which she had previously felt bound by. "I gave the best that was in me to the state work . . . but I do not hesitate now to say that the federal work is the special undertaking now before us."[20]

Clara Ueland of the Minneapolis Woman Suffrage Association, a NAWSA affiliate, became more and more disenchanted with the parent organization. "It is no secret that we are a good deal alienated. . . . We do not at all believe in the Shafroth amendment and we do not believe in the campaign of criticism which the National is waging publicly against the Congressional Union. It seems to us both unfair and unworthy." Ueland went on to say that she did not consider the Union to be militant since, in her view, sending delegates to the President and to congressmen was an "entirely legitimate method." Although Ueland, like a great many other suffragists, felt inadequate to judge the expediency of the Congressional Union's anti-Democratic campaign in 1914, she nevertheless believed that the Union had "already advanced the sentiment for the Federal Amendment."[21] For those reasons, Ueland reported that although the Minneapolis Woman Suffrage Association would continue to remain a NAWSA affiliate, it would also welcome the Congressional Union's efforts on behalf of a federal amendment in Minnesota.[22]

In Nevada, Dr. Shaw reiterated the by-then widespread charge of Congressional Union "treachery" which, she claimed, had resulted in retrenched opposition from individuals who were on the verge of announcing their support for woman suffrage.[23] By this time, the members of the Congressional Union were less reluctant to answer back.

"[News]papers and individuals that talk in such a puerile manner do not deserve to be taken seriously," Eunice Brannan and Elizabeth Rogers wrote to the Executive Committee. "Supporters as childish as that are not really converted in the least. They will always find an excuse."[24] Shaw attempted to persuade the Nevada Women's Civic League (formerly the Nevada Equal Franchise Society), to enroll as a full-fledged NAWSA affiliate.[25] Like the Minnesota association, the Nevada women hoped that they could work with both organizations. Thus they continued to walk a tightrope in order not to antagonize NAWSA unduly and at the same time, to maintain a relationship with the Congressional Union.

Another event fueled NAWSA's growing distrust of its rival. The Woman's Political Union of Connecticut following yet one more suffrage defeat at the hands of the Hartford legislature in 1915, voted unanimously to apply for affiliation with the Congressional Union. The Union, it proclaimed, "[is] striving to bring about the only practical method for obtaining woman suffrage by working for the passage of the . . . amendment to the Federal Constitution."[26]

While other sections of the country periodically witnessed defections to the Union, the South proved least troublesome for NAWSA. The race question was inextricably bound up with the suffrage issue in that section of the country. This problem in the South eclipsed by far the difficulties that suffragists in other sections of the country faced from antisuffrage, special interest groups, and from the Roman Catholic Church.[27] Since many Southerners sympathetic to these groups also opposed suffrage for racial reasons, organizing in the South was a truly formidable task. Nevertheless, even in this stronghold of conservatism and racism, the Congressional Union heard from an occasional supporter willing to put all other considerations aside for the sake of suffrage. "The Congressional Union, to me, means the freeing of over eight million women of my sunny South who would never be freed if we have to wait for the vote by way of the states," wrote one woman who had finally determined to abandon the states' rights principle.[28] Such evidence of support was relatively rare, however, as southern women were no less immune to cultural and social mores than were southern men.

Despite the persistent attacks from NAWSA, and opposition by those unable to overcome their fear of militancy, or who clung to the principle of state rights, the Congressional Union made remarkable progress throughout 1915. A growing number of suffragists no longer considered loyalty to NAWSA more important than pursuing the most direct means of achieving suffrage. By the end of the year, the Union had succeeded in organizing branches in nineteen states and had the cooperation or total support of existing suffrage groups in several other states including the full-suffrage states which, by that time, numbered eleven.[29]

Most of the branches were located in cities, for it was in the cities that one was likely to find educated women, working women, and those who had been involved in the politics of progressivism and were less likely to succumb to propaganda against militancy and radicalism. It would take an additional year-and-a-half for the Congressional Union to establish affiliates in the remaining states. But the progress was more than satisfactory. With affiliates and members in key cities across the nation, the Congressional Union could now believe it had a substantial base from which to work for the federal amendment.[30]

Plans for the women voters' convention at the Panama-Pacific Exposition proceeded apace with the state organizing efforts. Alice Paul went to extraordinary lengths to create a spectacular event that was certain to attract nationwide attention. The setting matched the event. The Exposition Committee had chosen the Presidio, a military compound on San Francisco Bay, as the site of the fair. Clusters of pale pink buildings with red roofs, which reflected an array of architectural styles from Greek to Spanish, housed the exhibits. Appropriately called the Jewel City, the exposition attracted thousands of visitors daily, all of whom were eager to be entertained, educated, and bedazzled by the collected wonders of the modern world. A favorite of the crowds was a Ford Motor Company assembly line, where fascinated spectators could actually watch the production of twenty-five Model T Fords each day.[31] The crowds quickly came to be on the lookout for activities of the woman suffragists as well, for they too staged some breathtaking events. Hazel Hunkins, a young Californian, for example, took an airplane ride above the Bay and the city and dropped thousands of leaflets advertising suffrage. For most of the spectators fortunate enough to catch her act, it was the first time they had seen a real airplane. For

Hazel, it was a first airplane ride, and although she was a hardy and daring soul, she probably would have passed up the opportunity to fly, had it not been for Alice Paul urging her on. Fortunately for Hunkins, the Congressional Union, and suffrage, her pilot and his biplane were both up to the challenge.[32]

When they were not watching Model *T*'s, or flying suffragists, or exploring the "Joy Zone," an amusement strip carefully monitored by the local Purity League, visitors to the Exposition could stroll over to the Education Building where the Congressional Union had managed to secure one of the hard-to-come-by booths. Visitors there were asked to sign a gigantic petition which, along with others collected from around the country, would be presented to Congress.

The women voters' convention convened on September 4. Discussions during the three days of meetings focused on ways in which the women in the western states could best use their political power to further the federal amendment. On the final day of the convention, September 6, a public meeting featured representatives from the suffrage states, Alaska, and enfranchised nations. Exposition officials had proclaimed the day "Congressional Union for Woman Suffrage Day."[33] Among the speakers were Helen Keller and her teacher, Annie Sullivan Macey; the evangelist, Billy Sunday; former President Theodore Roosevelt; the actress, Mabel Talliaferro; and Italian educator, Maria Montessori.[34] There was, in short, someone for everyone. As one of its final acts, the convention adopted resolutions which advocated support for the Anthony amendment, and conveyed greetings to the eastern states whose voters would shortly consider suffrage referenda.[35]

Paul chose Sara Bard Field to deliver to Congress the 18,000-foot-long petition which contained more than 500,000 signatures. Field, one of the more popular suffrage-circuit speakers, at first insisted that she had to remain in California to complete work on a book. Personal commitments were not legitimate excuses for Paul, and she insisted that Field make the trip. Actually, Field was more concerned about the hazards that lay ahead for anyone making a three-thousand mile cross-country car trip. Although the automobile, named the *Suffrage Flier*, was in reasonably good condition, road conditions and service facilities were still fairly primitive. "How shall I cope," Field wanted to know, "if something happens to the car?" The notion that Field might run into problems while crossing the desert or some other equally deserted and potentially lethal area, did not seem to faze Paul. "Oh," she shrugged, "you'll just find some man to help you out."[36] In Kansas, Field did run into exactly the kind of car trouble she had feared. She found herself and the car nearly immersed in muddy waters and unable to move forward or backward. The intrepid Sara finally abandoned the safety of the car along with the hope that she could stay dry, in order to go for help. She slipped into the hip-deep mud, pulled herself to dry land, and then trudged to the nearest farm house where, at midnight, she woke the startled occupants.[37]

The Congressional Union's press department as well as the national press kept readers apprised of Field's progress, and the emissary from San Francisco was well received in Reno, Salt Lake City, Chicago, Detroit, Cleveland, and Boston. At times, while the reception was warm, the city officials were less than enthusiastic about her cause. Reporting on one stop, Field said, "The Mayor quite flustered me with his speech." With good humor, she described the official's address. "He said so many things about women—for instance that woman was a Muse that soared; that she was the poetry of our existence; and something about the sun, moon, and stars. Then he added," said Field, pausing with perfect timing, "that he didn't think women ought to be allowed to vote."[38] It was just such an ability to turn negative remarks about suffrage into humorous anecdotes that won over more than one non-receptive crowd for Field, and made her so popular with the public.

Field arrived in Washington amidst much fanfare by the welcoming committee, in December 1915. Arrangements were made to deliver the petition to Congress and to meet with Woodrow Wilson at a reception in the East Room of the White House.[39] Wilson remarked on the influence of the women suffragists in collecting such a mammoth list of petitioners and said that he would remain in close contact with the Congress on the issue. However, he continued to insist that he was bound by his party's platform.[40] Even so, Wilson seemed to have moved somewhat on the suffrage issue. Between the time when Field left San Francisco and the time when she stood in the East Room, Wilson had, without warning, announced his decision to vote for suffrage in New Jersey.[41] There were several explanations for his action.

The President, whose first wife had died in 1914, was also about to announce his forthcoming marriage to Edith Bolling Galt. Several members of his official family feared that Wilson's remarriage might generate ill-will among the women voters in the West. At the same time, suffrage itself had become a much more respectable proposition. At least two of Wilson's daughters, Margaret and Jessie, were suffragists, and Jessie had participated in several Congressional Union activities. Margaret, on one occasion, asked her father's closest advisor, Colonel Edward M. House, to intercede with Wilson in order to persuade him to support a federal amendment.[42]

Then too, Wilson was not the only member of his administration to take the step. His secretary, Joseph P. Tumulty, and Secretary of War Lindley M. Garrison, also voted for suffrage in New Jersey. At the same time, Secretary of the Treasury William Gibbs McAdoo, Wilson's son-in-law, and Secretary of Commerce William C. Redfield voted for suffrage in New York State. In Pennsylvania, Secretary of Labor William B. Wilson also supported the suffrage referendum.[43]

Wilson's decision, at least in part, was influenced by women suffragists. It is entirely possible that he was referring to the Congressional Union's Women Voters' Convention in San Francisco when he candidly remarked: "I know of no body of persons comparable to a body of ladies for creating an atmosphere of opinion. I have myself in part yielded to the influence of that atmosphere for it took me a long time to observe how I was going to vote in New Jersey."[44] His evolution, gradual though it was, moved Wilson from an opponent of suffrage, in the years before he was elected President, to one who was indifferent to the issue, to a state-rights advocate. This shift in the President's stance encouraged federal suffragists to believe that he could be further persuaded to lend even greater support to the suffrage cause.[45]

At the convention, Dr. Shaw stepped down as president of NAWSA. In her farewell speech, Shaw observed that the cause of most difficulties that NAWSA had encountered was the "failure to recognize the obligation which loyalty demands. . . . It is unquestionably the duty of the members of an organization, when, after in convention assembled certain measures are voted and certain duties laid upon its offices, to uphold the officers in the performance of those duties, and to aid in every reasonable way to carry out the will of the association."[46] The speech provided an interesting parallel to Wilson's oft-cited reasons for not supporting a federal amendment: he could do nothing without the assent of his party.

Carrie Chapman Catt was unanimously elected to replace the departing Anna Howard Shaw.[47] At the same time, NAWSA quietly dropped its support of the Shafroth amendment, thus reestablishing its traditional, if lackluster, support of the Anthony amendment. Catt, with her own agenda in mind, maneuvered behind the scenes to eliminate the Shafroth amendment with as little fuss as possible. The new President of NAWSA, was, after all, an experienced and canny politician. Without the Shafroth amendment, a source of conflict between the leadership and the rank and file had been eliminated. NAWSA's renouncement of the Shafroth amendment did not mean that the organization was ready to withdraw from state campaigns. It continued to insist that the surest road to suffrage was through concentration on state work.[48] But within a year, Catt announced her "Winning Plan." The plan called for enfranchised states to petition Congress on behalf of a federal amendment, selective referendum campaigns, and state-by-state agitation in the South.[49] If either Catt or Paul took conscious note of the similarities between the "Winning Plan" and the Congressional Union program, neither brought it up in public. It was auspicious enough for the suffrage movement that, for the first time, both suffrage factions now made Woodrow Wilson the focus of their efforts. Paul, with the threat of electoral reprisal, intended to force Wilson, if necessary, to support the federal amendment. Catt hoped to educate him and thereby enlist his support.

NAWSA's new allegiance to the Anthony amendment and the election of a new president led some of the younger suffragists to believe that the time was ripe for a reconciliation between NAWSA and the Congressional Union. Zona Gale, a novelist, poet, and playwright from Wisconsin—who, some years later, won a Pulitzer Prize for the dramatization of her novel, *Miss Lulu Betts*—initiated the attempted reconciliation.[50] Gale, the Vice President of the Wisconsin Woman Suffrage Association, was also a staunch friend of the Congressional Union. She approached Alice Paul about a meeting with NAWSA people, a suggestion which Paul believed was worth pursuing. At NAWSA's national convention, Gale spoke to the Executive Board, with the result that the two groups were to meet at the Willard Hotel in Washington on December 17, 1915.

Two days earlier, on December 15, both NAWSA and the Congressional Union testified before the Senate Committee on Woman Suffrage and the House Judiciary Committee. Each side used the occasion to appeal for support of the Anthony amendment and to defend their differing strategies. The Senate hearings passed uneventfully. At the Judiciary Committee hearings on December 16, 1915, Catt testified, with good humor, that it was her observation that "when a man believes in woman suffrage, it is a national question and when he does not believe in it he says it is a question for the states."[51] When Alice Paul took her turn to testify, however, the hearings quickly heated to the boiling point. It was the first time since the election of 1914 that members of the Congress had an opportunity to confront the notorious Alice Paul and the Congressional Union. The primary concern among the Democrats on the Judiciary Committee was what Paul planned to do in 1916—whether she intended to repeat her 1914 campaign against Democratic candidates. Again and again that question, or a variation of it, was fired at Paul. She was a match for them, however, and quite as skilled in fielding the questions as they were in asking them. When asked if it was true that the Republicans had sought out the services of the Congressional Union for the next election, Paul responded, "We are greatly gratified by this tribute to our value." When Congressman Joseph Taggert of Kansas asserted that the Union had not defeated a single Democrat in 1914, Paul inquired politely, but pointedly, "Why, then, are you so stirred up over our campaign?" But when the Congressional Union was accused of having a blacklist of potential Democratic targets, the congressional courtesy traditionally shown among members suddenly evaporated. "This inquiry is absolutely unfair and improper," Congressman Volstead complained. "It is cheap politics and I have gotten awfully tired listening to it."[52]

Having weathered one hostile set of inquisitors, Paul and her colleagues prepared to do so again at the Willard Hotel. NAWSA officials included Carrie Chapman Catt, Ruth Hanna McCormick, Katherine Dexter McCormick, and Antoinette Funk. Paul was accompanied by Lucy Burns, Dora Lewis, and Anne Martin. Wasting little time, NAWSA proposed that the Congressional Union become an affiliate

of NAWSA once again, and suggested a program of frequent communication between the two groups in any case. Paul did desire open
lines of communication, for nothing could be gained by refusing to
talk to NAWSA and to keep them apprised, when possible, of Union
activities. She did question the price that the Union would have to
pay in order to become an affiliate. After some discussion, NAWSA
laid down its terms: renunciation of the anti-Democratic party campaign and a promise that the Congressional Union would refrain from
entering political campaigns in the future. In addition, NAWSA wanted
Paul's promise that the Congressional Union would stay out of states
where existing suffrage organizations, i.e., NAWSA affiliates, were
already operating. With such demands, there was little room for bar-
gaining. NAWSA wanted everything and was prepared to give nothing. The meeting ended abruptly when Catt, looking squarely at Paul,
rose from her chair and declared, "All I wish to say is, I will fight you
to the last ditch."[53] The attempted reconciliation thus ended in failure
and marked the last such effort. It was also the last time that Paul and
Catt confronted each other directly.[54]

For the Congressional Union, its first full year as an independent
organization had been highly successful. Membership was up to nearly
4,500; it had raised more than $50,000, most of which had been used
to finance the state organizing efforts; it had established a credible record with woman suffragists across the nation and with politicians on
both sides of the issue. Moreover, despite Paul's early protestations,
The Suffragist had proven to be a valuable propaganda weapon and its
circulation increased dramatically. Finally, the Congressional Union
had succeeded in avoiding the roadblocks erected by NAWSA without doing damage either to the Union or the suffrage movement.[55] By
almost any measure, the suffrage movement had benefited greatly from
the Union's efforts. For the first time, a President of the United States
had voted for suffrage in a state referendum. In the short space of two
years, the locus of the struggle had shifted from the states to the national level. It was an irreversible trend and marked a distinct turning
point in the suffrage struggle. From 1916 on, and despite NAWSA's
claims to the contrary, the fight would be waged almost exclusively
on the national level, with the President, the Congress, and the major
political parties all very much involved.

CHAPTER 6

The Founding of the National Woman's Party and the Campaign of 1916

With a successful year of organizing ended, and buoyed by the prospects for the ensuing year, Alice Paul revealed her plans for the months ahead. The Executive Committee called a meeting of the Advisory Council and the state and national officers on April 8 and 9, 1916. The meeting was held at Cameron House, the Union's new headquarters. Cameron House, commonly referred to as the Little White House, and located across Pennsylvania Avenue from the real White House, had become the headquarters for the Congressional Union in January 1916. By April, it was well-settled into by the organization. While not as grand or imposing as Marble House, where Paul had announced the anti-Democratic campaign of 1914, Cameron House nevertheless served a similar purpose, as the members of the Advisory Council gathered to hear about the next step in Paul's plans.

Paul proposed to organize a woman's political party which, she believed, would serve as the balance of power in the national election which promised to be closely contended. "The state of Nevada was won by only forty votes in the last Senatorial election," Paul pointed out.[1] "In Utah, it was a week before the campaign was decided. In Colorado, the same. Going back over a period of twenty years, it would have been necessary to have changed only nine per cent of the total vote in the Presidential elections in order to have thrown the election to the other Party. This gives a position of wonderful power, a position that we have never held before and that we cannot hold again for at least four years, and which we may not hold then."[2] The delegates at the conference in April 1916 needed little convincing to give their blessing to the new program.

The Congressional Union lobby in Washington, directed by Nevada's Anne Martin and assisted by Maud Younger, the "Millionaire Waitress" from San Francisco, had labored furiously for three months in an attempt to persuade the House Judiciary Committee to report out the suffrage amendment. Alice Paul could not have asked for two more dedicated workers. Martin's experience as a NAWSA coordinator in Nevada during the referendum there was invaluable for her new task. Maud Younger earned her nickname when she single-handedly organized the Waitress's Union in San Francisco. Like many progressives of her time, Younger did not let her family wealth and status blind her to the plight of the poor and disadvantaged. She gradually focused her concern on working women and, in 1911, was influential in getting California's eight-hour workday law for women passed. Although she was always a suffrage advocate, Maud did not get involved in the movement until 1914. Thereafter she devoted almost all of her time to suffrage and worked with the Congressional Union and then the National Woman's Party. By 1915, Maud Younger was Alice Paul's key Washington lobbyist, and she had amassed a card index file which provided an instant reference on every congressman and senator in Congress, as well as prominent administration figures. Maud Younger's card index became legendary in Congressional Union—and congressional—circles.[3]

Despite the efforts of Martin and Younger, the Democrats remained adamant about refusing to consider an amendment until the following December—after the national elections. The committee chairman did promise Martin and Younger that his committee would meet to consider the suffrage issue if the lobbyists could assemble a majority of the committee. With such an incentive, and after much cajoling, corraling, and steam-rolling, the lobbyists succeeded in persuading a majority of the committee to meet at an agreed upon day and time. All of Martin and Younger's hard work came to naught when the committee met. In a closed meeting, pro-amendment congressmen were stymied when a motion was immediately made to shelve *all* constitutional amendment proposals for an indefinite period of time. This master stroke at once created chaos within the committee, as members were forced to either accept or reject a whole range of pending amendements on such issues as marriage, divorce, and prohibition. This, as the authors of the scheme well knew, was impossible. The committee adjourned, after an angry two hours, with no action taken on anything. Once again, the Democrats, who controlled the committee, had delayed dealing with the suffrage amendment and, in the process, had convinced the Congressional Union members that the Democratic party was contemptuous of the issue.[4] When, therefore, Alice Paul called for a convention of women voters to meet at the Blackstone Theatre in Chicago on June 5, 6 and 7, 1916, for the purpose of organizing the National Woman's Party (NWP), the delegates gave their unstinting support.

Membership in the NWP was to be limited to enfranchised women, and its sole purpose would be to promote the federal amendment.[5] In preparation for the Chicago convention, Paul sent a delegation of twenty-three organizers to tour the western states on a train dubbed the *Suffrage Special*. The timing of the western swing and the convention were important, as Lucy Burns explained, because the Union was in its "strongest position before a national election & ought to put on the pressure now—no wait till Congress has adjourned."[6]

Plans for the western trip had been under way for several weeks prior to the April 9 departure, with the groundwork for the emissaries' visits laid down by the state chapter members. By now, the Union expected some efforts to undermine their activities by NAWSA, regardless of circumstance, and they were not disappointed in this instance. "With two representatives of 'the National' in Laramie County throwing all the cold water they possibly can, we are keeping the newspapers in the quiet little town of Cheyenne busy," Wyoming organizer Margery Ross reported back to Washington. The conflict served Alice Paul's purposes well, however, for as Ross noted, "Incidentally, we are awakening these Cheyenne women who have, to be frank with you, gone to sleep."[7]

The *Suffrage Special* left Washington amidst a flurry of pageantry and publicity. For more than a month, the emissaries from the East lived and worked in the train, in cramped quarters, but with sustained good humor. "If you Washington ladies could peep into the Suffrage Special at any hour of any day when nine typewriters are pounding away and Press reports and resolutions are being written and literature being folded and counted and membership cards listed and the Business Manager receiving money . . . you would realize that this is no place for the graceful letter writer!" Ella Reigel wrote in response to pleas for the news from California.[8] Several days later, in Sacramento, Reigel noted, "My charges are busy and happy—not too much coddled— and so far no broken heads!"[9] The four-week tour met with enthusiastic response from women voters and a great deal of attendant publicity as well.[10]

As a consequence of the successful western tour, more than 1,500 women delegates from the suffrage states arrived at the Blackstone Theatre on June 6, eager to participate in the historic event. They believed success was within their grasp in the 1916 election since, they reasoned, less than nine per cent of the total vote in the suffrage states would be enough to deflect the election away from the Democrats.[11] The delegates quickly established a set of rules to govern the NWP. First, the party nucleus would be composed of Congressional Union members. Second, the party would remain independent and would not align itself, officially or unofficially, with any existing political party. Third, the only plank in the party's platform would be a resolution calling for immediate passage of the Anthony amendment. Fourth, the party would be organized along the same lines as the Congressional Union, with a chairwoman, two vice-chairwomen, and an Executive Committee composed of the officers, state chairwomen, and the chairwoman of the Congressional Union. Fifth, all state chairwomen would autmotically become members of the Executive Committee of the Congressional Union.[12] It was as simply organized and—theoretically—as much as a single-issue political party as its founders could conceive. The convention delegates, therefore, quickly disposed of the major business at hand, voted to accept the proposal to establish the

National Woman's Party, and elected Anne Martin chairwoman, and Alice Paul one of the two vice-chairwomen.[13]

The three-day convention received maximum press coverage, in part because Chicago was already flooded with reporters who were assigned to the Republican and Progressive party conventions. Indeed, as Inez Haynes Irwin said, the NWP convention was a "god-send" since the press was relieved of the chore of ferreting out preconvention stories that would keep both their editors and their readers satisfied. The NWP delegates were only too happy to help out their friends in the press with detailed information of the proceedings.

Alice Paul extended invitations to representatives of all the major parties, to address the NWP convention. Even this served as grist for the media's mill. Ida Tarbell, the famous muckraking journalist who had exposed the Standard Oil monopoly in the pages of *McClure's Magazine*, covered the convention for the *New York World*. Tarbell described with amusement the dispatch with which the women handled the male politicians. She reported:

'We do not ask you here to tell us what we can do for your Parties, but what your Parties can do for us,' Miss Martin told the speakers in a tone of exultant sweetness which sent a cheer from shore to shore of the human sea which filled the house. Another thing the gentlemen must have noticed—used as they are to the same game—and that was, that no amount of eloquence made the faintest scratch on the rock-ribbed determination of the women. The one and only thing they wanted to know . . . was whether or not they proposed to support the amendment, . . . Was it, yes or no?[14]

The NWP convention closed on the day that the Republican and Progressive party conventions convened with a "Suffrage First" luncheon, which turned into a standing-room-only affair. The speakers at the luncheon, who included Crystal Eastman, Rheta Childe Dorr, and Helen Keller, were only slightly less exuberant than their audiences. In spite of the lack of elbow room, the audience managed to cheer and clap wildly, so caught up were they by the feeling of solidarity that pervaded the room.[15]

In the months ahead, the NWP became almost a casebook example of Charles A. Beard's description of the purpose and function of third parties in a two-party system: "By agitation and by the use of marginal votes in close campaigns, minorities are able to force the gradual acceptance of some or all of their leading doctrines by one or the other of the great parties, and through inevitable competition between these parties, to educate the whole nation into accepting ideas that were once abhorrent."[16] In the meantime, the NWP would immediately have an opportunity to agitate the major parties.

Members of the NWP appeared before the resolutions committees of each of the parties in an effort to persuade them to support federal suffragism. For the first time, both major parties included suffrage planks in their party platforms, although neither one endorsed a federal amendment. The Republican delegates accepted their committee's resolution with little argument, probably because they were only too happy to cooperate with potential allies against their November adversaries. When the Democrats opened their convention in St. Louis on June 14, the NWP advised the resolutions committee that unless the Democrats, as the party in power, supported the Anthony amendment, the NWP intended to campaign against them in the West.[17] Not only were the Democrats unwilling to endorse federal suffragism, some of them did not wish to endorse suffrage at all. The suffrage plank, consequently, was brought to a floor fight—the only issue so debated at the convention.[18] The minority favored no plank at all and preferred that the states be left to their own devices regarding suffrage. Senator Thomas James Walsh of Montana, speaking on behalf of the states' rights plank, noted the advisability of including a suffrage plank of some sort since women voters had the power to defeat the President and to give the Senate majority to the Republicans.[19] In its follow-up analysis, the *New York Times* concurred with Walsh: "Whatever the more conservative suffragists think or say . . . the radical wing which calls itself the Woman's Party . . . offer[s] facts and figures to prove that they have an organized vote which can be swung in any direction they want . . . Whether the hand that ruled the Democratic convention today, rocks the cradle in its hours of recreation . . . it can certainly add up a column of figures in a convincing manner."[20] The minority plank was subsequently defeated and the Democrats, too, included a suffrage plank based on state rights in their party platform, which, observers agreed, had been largely written by Woodrow Wilson. And, while the Republicans and Democrats could bring themselves only to endorse suffrage while refusing to support a federal amendment, the

Progressives, Socialists, and Prohibitionist parties all came out une-quivocally for a federal woman suffrage amendment.[21]

NAWSA could not have been happier at the turn of events since it had lobbied simply for recognition of the principle of woman suffrage and not for support of a federal amendment.[22] In NAWSA's eyes, the NWP had suffered a defeat. The NWP, although it was disappointed, certainly did not consider itself defeated. For one thing, it had re-ceived enormous amounts of publicity. There were few areas in the country where people remained unaware of the new political party composed entirely of women. Thus it had succeeded in large measure in making the "National Woman's Party convention in Chicago dom-inate the suffrage world, so that it seem[ed] to the public and to the politicians assembled there that the whole agitation [was] really on be-half of the national amendment."[23] The NWP also managed to secure support from quarters that previously had questioned its effectiveness. The *New Republic*, for example, had, in 1914, jailed NAWSA's "ra-tional" and "thoughtful" approach as the best hope for success.[24] Now, the journal believed, "the time has undoubtedly come for NAWSA to revive their tactics. . . . The political power of the woman voter must be brought to bear on Washington now. . . . If the National Associ-ation cannot see its way to harvest this field, they should leave the field clear for the Congressional Union [i.e., NWP]."[25] Finally, Charles A. Beard, in a letter to Carrie Chapman Catt, expressed the view of many who believed that "all that was got at Chicago and St. Louis was got only because the politicians were afraid of the impending dan-ger created by the Congressional Union and the Woman's Party, namely that western women would not be non-partisan when the freedom of their sisters was at stake."[26]

Immediately following the conventions, the NWP began to put pressure on Republican nominee Charles Evans Hughes. Earlier that year, in May 1916, Paul and Harriot Stanton Blatch had secured Theodore Roosevelt's support for the federal amendment.[27] Now, Paul sought to enlist Roosevelt's assistance to help persuade Hughes to come out for the amendment. Discussions with Roosevelt at Oyster Bay confirmed Paul's impression of Hughes' state of mind: the former President believed Hughes was ready to commit himself to the federal amendment. It was simply a matter of the proper timing.[28] Paul inaugurated a campaign calculated to help convince Hughes that the time was now. State NWP and Union officials were encouraged not only to write letters but to "flood Hughes with telegrams from every possible source."[29] In addition, Paul dispatched Anne Martin and Abby Scott Baker to track down Hughes on the campaign trail in order to make a personal appeal.[30]

The lobbying effort paid off handsomely. On August 1, Hughes, departing from his party's campaign platform, endorsed the federal amendment. His reasons for doing so, as he himself admitted, were to many people more eyebrow-raising than the fact that he was supporting federal suffragism at all. Hughes readily conceded that women should have the vote. That, he felt, was no longer at issue. What was at issue was the impact that suffrage agitation of the sort engaged in by the NWP would have on national politics. "Facts should be squarely met. We shall have a constantly intensified effort and a distinct feminist movement constantly perfecting its organization to the subversion of normal political issues. We shall have a struggle increase in bitterness . . . inimical to our welfare. . . . It seems to me that in the interest of the public life of this country, the contest should be ended promptly."[31]

Hughes' endorsement of the federal amendment was an important victory for suffragists. For the first time, a major party's presidential candidate had publicly stood up for federal suffragism. On such a momentous occasion, Paul debated whether or not to break policy and endorse Hughes straight out. She decided against such a step in order to retain her organization's independence. Besides, publicly allying herself and the NWP with the Republicans would give the Democrats an opportunity to turn the issue into a partisan one. The NWP, therefore, would not endorse Hughes' candidacy, but it applauded vigorously his endorsement.[32] Not only did they have Hughes' support, but the Republican's action would almost certainly require some response from the Democrats. But if Paul hoped that Wilson would follow Hughes' lead, those hopes were short-lived. Carrie Chapman Catt, who apparently had the same thought, approached Wilson about announcing in favor of federal suffragism, particularly since his opponent now had the clear edge on the issue. Wilson declined. "If I should change my personal attitude now I should seem to the country like nothing better than an angler for votes."[33]

With Wilson obviously committed to the states' rights principle, in accordance with his party platform—his standard excuse for refusing to take up federal suffragism—Alice Paul called a meeting for August 10, 11, and 12, to take place in Colorado Springs. She had in mind to map out the role the NWP would play in the upcoming elections. The decision of the conference would be greatly influenced, Paul noted, by the record of the Democratic party when the women met on the tenth of August.[34] With her usual eye toward maximum publicity, Paul chose August 10 to convene the meeting because of the automobile races, scheduled for that time, celebrating the opening of the new road up Pike's Peak. "There will probably be large numbers of people there at the time," Paul explained.[35]

There were few delegates, if any, who arrived at the Antlers Hotel in Colorado Springs who were seriously in doubt as to the outcome of the conference. The Democrats had done next to nothing in recent months to suggest that their position on suffrage would change. The conference, then, was not concerned with whether the NWP ought to be involved. Discussions revolved instead around organizations, tactics, and issues. Wilson, of course, would be the primary target. As the leader of his party, Wilson symbolized the control which the Democrats exercised over all political and legislative matters. The issue of states' rights was to be handled in as straightforward a manner as possible, pointing out that since thirty-six states had to ratify a federal amendment, each state legislature could indeed be responsive to the needs and desires of its constituents by ratifying or failing to ratify when the time came. A federal amendment, secured under the terms of the Constitution, could in no way be construed as an infringement of states' rights.[36]

With state leaders thus armed with guidelines and instructions, the NWP inaugurated its campaign of 1916. In many ways it was a replay of 1914, with two organizers again assigned to each suffrage state, with essentially the same responsibilities as the organizers had in 1914. Alice Paul dispatched her most effective organizers—women who had proven their skills as managers, fund-raisers, and especially as public speakers with "crowd pleaser" reputations. Doris Stevens, Sara Bard Field, Maud Younger, Elsie Hill, Anne Martin, and Mabel Vernon, all agreed to spend another fall enduring the rigors of the campaign trail.[37]

Longtime members who had not organized in 1914, but who demonstrated valuable organizing and speaking skills, were also enlisted. Perhaps the most noticeable of this group was Inez Milholland Boissevain, a lawyer and feminist who had graduated from Vassar and New York University. It was Inez who had led the suffrage parade, in flowing white robes and riding a white horse, in Washington in 1913. Her photograph, taken during the parade, became one of the memorable images that people associated with the event. It was not unusual to see her name accompanied by adjectives such as "brilliant" and "beautiful," for she was both. Inez' political beliefs led her to champion a number of feminist and radical causes. She was, for a time, part of the bohemian-radical group that dominated Greenwich Village in the early twentieth century—a group that included Crystal Eastman and her brother Max. Inez and Max Eastman, the editor of *The Masses*, had a short-lived romance that ended when she married Eugen Jan Boissevain, a Dutch entrepreneur. Following her marriage, Inez traveled to Europe with Guglielmo Marconi, another longtime admirer, in order to report on the war in Europe. Her pacifist articles earned Inez an invitation to leave Italy, where she was based, tendered by the Italian government. Within months, she was back in Europe, this time on Henry Ford's Peace Ship. On her return to the United States, Inez became more actively involved in suffrage, offering her services as a speaker throughout the West. So great was her reputation, that the success of political rallies sometimes hinged entirely on Inez' agreement to be the featured speaker.[38]

In addition to Inez Milholland, Alice Paul enlisted other promising and enthusiastic young women, a "second generation" of organizers to round out the contingent of seasoned organizers sent to the West.[39] Included in the second generation organizers, were Iris Calderhead, the daughter of a Kansas congressman; Hazel Hunkins Hallinan, the Vassar alumna who had taken the daring airplane ride over San Francisco; Lucy Branham, a Johns Hopkins graduate who had won a Carnegie medal for heroism after saving a man and woman from drowning in Florida; and Rebecca Hourwich Rehyer, who managed to squeeze in suffrage activities between her studies, first at Columbia and then at the University of Chicago, her marriage, and the birth of her first child.[40] This second generation of organizers tended to be younger than the first. In age, background, and education, the new organizers were very representative of the new members coming into the NWP. The NWP still attracted only a small percentage of the women joining suffrage organizations in 1916. But Paul needed all the volunteers she could get. The increase in membership permitted the NWP to engage not only in the political campaign in the suffrage states, but in increasingly active lobbying in Washington.[41]

Although the structure of the campaign of 1916 resembled that of 1914, there were new problems for Paul and the NWP. For one thing, 1916 was the organization's second political campaign effort. Democrats and antisuffragists were better prepared this time around. For another thing, 1914 was an off-year election featuring races for the Senate, the House, and state offices. In 1916, the Presidency was at stake. Local Democratic machines were even less willing to tolerate the organizers than they had been two years earlier. After distributing literature in Denver, for example, Elsie Hill was arrested and taken by "paddy wagon" to the local police station. In Colorado Springs, a banner whose legend demanded passage of the federal amendment was confiscated and held by the police authorities overnight, to the amusement of the suffragists who reported that their banner had been arrested and detained in a jail cell. In Chicago, 100 women stationed outside an auditorium where Wilson was scheduled to speak, were attacked by a mob. Their banners were torn down and the suffragists were pushed and shoved aside, with minor injuries sustained by some of the women in the process.[42] Iris Calderhead reported the increasing hostility of the Democrats in Arizona. Calderhead explained that the municipalities were largely controlled by the Democrats who could, and did, prohibit street meetings, advertising, poster and billboard notices, and most other forms of activity and advertising that the NWP engaged in.[43]

At the same time, the relationship between the NWP and the Republican party had to be carefully monitored. Paul did not want the NWP linked to the Republican party in an overt or official way. Yet,

it was clearly in the best interest of suffrage and the NWP, to promote votes for the GOP. "Our interest is in . . . the amendment and
not in . . Hughes, but it is vital to the success of the amendment
. . . that we secure the defeat of Wilson," Paul noted. Nevertheless,
she cautioned her lieutenants that it was paramount that the NWP remain distinct from all other political parties in order to maintain its
integrity among the voters. Furthermore, Paul believed that it was
tactically more effective to conduct a campaign of opposition *against*
Democrats rather than one of support *for* Republicans. Paul did not
want the burden of having to defend Republican policy.[44]

The Republicans, for their part, viewed the NWP as a useful ally
in the campaign, but they also maintained a patronizing attitude toward
the women. W. Y. Morgan, the director of the Republican National
Committee's publicity bureau, advised Kansas Republicans that the
NWP could be "helped without any injury to the Republican Party."[45]
In any event, the Republicans, while willing to make use of the NWP,
did not particularly feel comfortable with the idea of an independent
woman's political party. Offers of economic support from the Republicans to the NWP, which were declined in every instance, often came
with conditions attached. "The truth is that they are unwilling to give
us some money unless we will give up our independence and become
an annex of the GOP," reported Abby Scott Baker in disgust. "When
I am with the GOP's, I'd rather die than be one," she declared. But,
she added ruefully, "I feel the same way when I am with the Democrats, so I think I'll go into a convent."[46] Rumors that the NWP was
on the Republican payroll did not help their cause either. "Every indication that has ever been brought to my notice advances the theory
of the oft-repeated statement that the National Woman's Party is merely
an ally of the National Republican Committee," wrote the editor of
the *Nevada State Herald* to Mabel Vernon.[47]

Moreover, the Republicans were unwilling to take seriously the overall
campaign analysis provided by the NWP regarding the jeopardy in
which Republican candidates stood in the suffrage states. Doris Stevens reported to Alice Paul from California that the Republicans were
trailing Wilson in that state. Stevens believed that the GOP's difficulties had arisen in large part because the Hughes' people managed to
alienate governor Hiram W. Johnson, the powerful Progressive can-

didate for the United States Senate, whose support Hughes badly needed.[48] "I have taken your various letters with regard to the situation in California to the Republican headquarters," Paul told Stevens. "But I have seemed unable to even suggest to them that there is any possibility that California may not go to Hughes."[49] In Nevada, the political situation seemed more hopeful on the local level, but it was still bad for Hughes. "The great trouble is that the Republican state campaign committee is not putting up an active fight—not as active as the Democratic campaign committee," Anne Martin observed. She added that the Republicans were not even as active as the NWP.[50] Martin also reported to Paul on the state of affairs in Utah. "Utah is in a very critical state. The Democrats have never stood such a good chance of carrying the state. . . . The Republican organization rely on the fact that the Mormon Church is Republican. They tell me to rest easy. . . . Perhaps there is some mystic word that can be sent out but I think they had better get busy and send it out pretty quickly because the situation looks alarming to me."[51] Martin's exasperation over the seemingly casual attitude of the Republican party to its own plight was only too obvious. In the face of such fumbling on the part of the GOP, it was no wonder that NWP campaigners became frustrated. "The Republican Party is really so stupid," complained Abby Scott Baker. "Sometimes I despair of pulling them through."[52]

To be sure, the lackadaisical campaigning of the Republican party during the first weeks of the campaign was not the major stumbling block for the NWP. The major campaign issue in 1916 was the peace issue. As the war in Europe raged on, with the growing threat of United States involvement in the conflict, hardly a voter in the country remained neutral about the peace issue. The NWP attempted to counter the Democratic slogan, "He Kept Us Out Of War," with its own slogan, "He Kept Us Out Of Suffrage."[53] The two appeals placed women voters in a quandary of conscience. Where did their allegiance lie? Ought they to place their desire for equality first, or their desire for peace? Even the members of the NWP felt torn by the dilemma. Some, like pacifist Crystal Eastman, decided that she could not support an anti-Democratic campaign at such a crucial juncture in the nation's well-being. A Hughes Presidency, Eastman believed, would surely mean United States entry into the war. Eastman chose to campaign for Wilson and peace, rather than for suffrage.[54] As the campaign progressed, it became more and more apparent that most voters agreed with Eastman's sentiments. And, although suffrage was considered by most observers the main local and domestic issue in the suffrage states, peace was the overriding national foreign-policy issue.[55] While the NWP almost always attracted audiences sympathetic to suffrage, their audiences frequently had to admit that they could not and would not support Hughes' position on preparedness and the implications of that policy.[56]

The campaign for the NWP was, to say the least, an uphill battle and was so reflected by the pessimistic note struck in many of the organizers' reports. "The opposition is so strong that no matter how much we try or how many people we interview, we seem to make little progress," wrote Helen Heffernon, the Goldfield, Nevada organizer.[57] "Nothing but luck will carry the Republicans through [in Nevada]," concurred Abby Scott Baker.[58] "There is no doubt that the women in this state [Oregon] are strong for Wilson," concluded Margaret Whittemore.[59] In Montana, organizer Clara Louise Rowe, who had been organizing the state since early spring, lamented then that, "It's very uphill here in Montana. I sometimes wonder if it is worth all the money & effort, but Miss Burns [Lucy] said it was . . . so I suppose it is."[60] Her task did not grow any easier as time went on.

In the circumstances, Paul was asked to reconsider the campaign which the NWP had embarked upon with such high hopes. Despite the pessimistic predictions from the field, Paul refused to even consider withdrawing from the campaign in order to cut NWP losses. "No," she insisted, "if we withdraw the speakers from the campaign, we withdraw the issue from the campaign. We must make this such an important thing in national elections that the Democrats will not want to meet it again."[61]

For the organizers and speakers, the campaign was physically taxing as well as psychologically difficult. Although the NWP now paid its field organizers monthly salaries that ranged from $70 to $100 per month, still the stipend barely covered expenses, if they were frugal.[62] As in most things, Paul attempted to transfer imposed frugality into an advantage to be harvested. Organizers were cautioned by her to exercise conspicuous frugality, since "the more frugal you are, the greater the appeal you will make to people from whom you will have to collect money."[63]

The necessity to make do was inconvenient and the efforts to change hearts and minds was frustrating. But most organizers were not deterred and viewed the hardships as well worth the price for ultimate success. But the exhaustingly long hours and nearly impossible schedules began to take their toll. Paul herself had succumbed to exhaustion on several occasions over the course of her suffrage career. Ill health and frazzled nerves forced her into a hospital at one point early on.[64] In addition to her own health, she had to be aware of her changes, for each one lost to the campaign meant a significant diminishment of effort. Inquiring about the health of one organizer, Mabel Vernon commented, "Poor Alice Paul has been fairly desperate, I hear, because so many of the organizers have failed her on account of illness."[65] For some, the stress resulted in more than just a few days of being under the weather. Edna Latimer, after six weeks in Arizona, required a complete rest in a San Francisco sanitarium.[66] Most tragically, the vivacious and energetic Inez Milholland, so much in demand as a speaker, and who suffered from pernicious anemia, ignored the warnings of her father and her husband to conserve her strength. Milholland collapsed in the middle of a speech in Los Angeles, on October 22. Rushed to a local hospital, she received repeated transfusions over the course of the next several weeks as she alternately rallied and then failed. Her death on November 25, at the age of thirty, sent shock waves through suffrage circles.[67]

Throughout the campaign, the NWP had to contend with NAWSA, which, predictably, viewed the activities of the younger suffragists as detrimental to suffrage. To be sure, NAWSA's own strategy had changed in interesting ways. Carrie Chapman Catt was a much shrewder politician than Anna Howard Shaw had been. Catt also had a far greater facility for organization and management, as well as an eye for what had to be done to secure suffrage. NAWSA's convention of 1916, held in September of that year, was significant for good reason: Woodrow Wilson was the featured speaker, thanks in large measure to Carrie Chapman Catt's efforts.

Wilson had agreed to speak to the NAWSA convention the previous August, in response to Hughes' endorsement of the federal amendment. When the President walked out on to the stage on the evening of September 8, the convention gave him a thunderous welcome. For the first time, Wilson did not overtly champion the states' rights position, although neither did he endorse federal suffragism. "I have not come to fight anybody, *but with somebody.*" he declared. "We feel the tide; we rejoice in the strength of it; and we shall not quarrel in the long run as to the method of it."[68]

Not only was Wilson responding to Hughes' declaration, he was also making a bid for the votes of the former Bull Moose Progressives, Independents, and Agrarians who were disenchanted with his failure to pursue further domestic reform during the previous two years.[69] His attempts to correct the situation, beginning in 1916, included supporting several pieces of social legislation which, for a variety of reasons, he had previously rejected and failed to support. These included the Adamson Eight-Hour Day Law, the Keating–Owen Child Labor Act, the Rural Credits Act, and a Federal Workman's Compensation Act. Woodrow Wilson was, in most cases, an astute politician. As both Governor of New Jersey and as President of the United States, Wilson demonstrated time and again a great capacity to read his constituency and articulate the issues accordingly. Extending the franchise as an act of social justice, in line with his support of other social justice measures, was a matter of political expediency.[70]

At the same time, Wilson's speech to NAWSA was also evidence of his evolving position on the suffrage issue. Wilson, a Southerner by birth, subscribed wholeheartedly to views regarding women and their proper place commonly held by most Southerners. Indeed, as a very young man, he once stated that universal suffrage lay "at the foundation of every evil in this country."[71] While he had left that notion far behind him, at least as it applied to white males, Wilson had not yet accepted women as full citizens entitled to full equal rights, by the time he was elected President. But with three daughters of his own to contend with, and with his adoption of a states' rights position as his defense when questioned by suffragists regarding the issue, Wilson had succumbed to modest changes in his own beliefs that, when coupled with his perceptions of what was politically expedient, proved beneficial for suffrage. Whatever NAWSA delegates may have felt about his reasons for appearing at the convention, they were more than pleased with his speech. Anna Howard Shaw spoke for most of them when she declared, "We have waited *so* long, Mr. President! We have dared to hope that our release might come in your Administration and that yours would be the voice to pronounce the words to bring our freedom."[72]

With the implementation of Catt's "Winning Plan," which, like the NWP strategy, focused on federal suffragism, the two organizations technically were not that far apart. Yet, NAWSA's refusal to yield any quarter to the upstart NWP prevented a cooperative working relationship from developing. Thus, while the campaign of 1916 unfolded, the ever-present animosities surfaced and often revealed the deep-seated feelings of bitterness of some NAWSA people toward the NWP. "The situation in Chicago is extremely difficult," reported Abby Scott Baker, the NWP's national press chairwoman. "The animosity of Mrs. [Ruth Hanna] McCormick is almost unbelievable. She has broken up three meetings after they had been arranged for Mrs. [Louisine] Havemeyer, and we have reason to believe that she had [our] banners taken down in the town where she has her summer home."[73]

By election day, November 7, 1916, everyone was glad the campaign was over. Exhausted organizers waited in anticipation for the results. The race between Wilson and Hughes was one of the closest in American political history. In the last days of the campaign, some organizers detected movement away from Wilson and toward Hughes. In California, for example, the NWP organizer was told that "the street railway men are falling away [from Wilson], and the local labor leaders cannot get them back in line." The city editor of a Los Angeles daily—a Wilson supporter—expressed his fear that "it is the last swing. I am afraid the election will come on the crest of it. If it does, California will be lost to us."[74]

Suffragists notwithstanding, the war in Europe, not women's rights, weighed most heavily on the minds of Americans as they went to the polls on November 7. The election hung in the balance for some time as California slowly counted its votes. When the last vote had been counted, Wilson emerged victorious—although just barely—winning 277 electoral votes to Hughes' 254. Of the twelve suffrage states, Wilson won all but Oregon and Illinois, despite the NWP campaign. It is one of the ironies of the campaign that Wilson's narrow victory in

1916 was attributed to the women's vote—because of the peace issue. Women in California, with thirteen electoral votes and the election in the balance, voted disproportionately for Wilson, according to the *New York Times*. William Allen White observed that if women in Kansas had not voted for Wilson, "Kansas would have gone for Hughes." And analysts in Arizona, Idaho, Utah, and Washington credited women with swinging their combined eighteen electoral votes to the Democratic column.[75]

Many NWP organizers were disappointed and discouraged. They had hoped for a more obvious victory. But the campaign itself was far from a failure. Paul had stressed time and again the importance of "spread[ing] abroad the impression of a very active campaign on the part of women against Democrats."[76] The response of both the Republicans and the Democrats demonstrated the success of this strategy. The Republicans tried to capitalize on the NWP campaign; the Democrats tried to put a damper on it. Both parties attempted to win over women voters, and the Democrats, in particular, mounted a major effort toward this end.[77]

Then, too, Illinois, which did go for Hughes, was the only one of the twelve suffrage states where women's votes were counted separately from men's votes. In that state, Hughes won 52.6 percent of the overall vote. Women voters went for the Republican candidate by 55.3 percent, while only 49.9 percent of the male voters voted for Hughes.[78] In Illinois, it appears that women did indeed register a protest vote against Wilson.

Regardless of which party won in 1916, the NWP could not lose. As the *Wichita* [Kansas] *Eagle* observed, "When the Congress next meets, no matter whether Wilson or Hughes is elected, the women of the nation are going to have a powerful argument for national woman suffrage."[79] A *Ventura* [California] *Free Press* editorial noted that "the universal opinion of political leaders of all parties is that no new political party ever before made such a remarkable showing in a presidential campaign as has the National Woman's Party."[80] The Democrats, asserted the *New Republic*, owed their victory to women voters. "Yet but for women suffrage, to which he tepidly assents, Mr. Wilson would not have been continued in the White House. The balance of power, so far as Congress is concerned, and so far as rival parties are concerned, is conceivably in women's hands."[81]

Alice Paul had no intention of allowing the Democrats to forget to whom they owed their victory. Not that they were likely to forget. Vance C. McCormick, the chairman of the Democratic National Committee, in his own postelection analysis, noted the advisability of attending to the party's weak spots before the elections of 1918. "Our weakest spot is the suffrage situation," McCormick confided to a fellow committeeman. "We must get rid of the suffrage amendment before 1918 if we want to control the next Congress."[82] As the *San Francisco Examiner* noted, suffrage had ceased to be a "western vagary. Nothing that has 2,000,000 votes is ever vague to the politicians."[83]

CHAPTER 7

The Home-Front War: "A Poor Business"

On the morning of January 10, 1917, a strange sight greeted people on Pennsylvania Avenue near the White House. At 10:00 o'clock, a line of suffragists marching in single file emerged from Cameron House. The women carried banners of purple, white, and gold, some of which were emblazoned with the legend, "Mr. President—What Will you Do For woman Suffrage?" They crossed the Avenue and took up a silent vigil at the gate of the White House.[1] So began the most dramatic episode in the American campaign for woman suffrage—an episode that began as a peaceful, if highly visible, endeavor to persuade the President and the members of Congress to pass a federal suffrage amendment. It gradually evolved into a contest of wills between the leader of a nation finally plunged into a world war and the leader of an organization who refused to recognize the war as the paramount issue facing Americans, and particularly American women. Alice Paul and Woodrow Wilson were on a collision course—one that began benignly, revealed for those who cared to see the dark side of American government toward its own citizens, and culminated with the evolution of Woodrow Wilson from a states' rights advocate to a federal amendment evangelist who pleaded for passage of the amendment as a measure crucial to the successful prosecution of the war to make the world "safe for democracy."

Alice Paul had discussed with her lieutenants the possibility of conducting a picketing campaign in December 1916 and again in early January 1917. In New York, Harriot Stanton Blatch's Women's Political Union had already used that tactic at the State House in Albany. Blatch concluded months earlier that the time had come for new methods. In an interview with Woodrow Wilson, she minced no words in expressing her feelings. "I am sixty years old, Mr. President," she said. "I have worked all my life for suffrage, and I am determined that I will never again stand in the street corners of a great city appealing to every Tom, Dick, and Harry for the right of self-government."[2]

Although picketing, to some, seemed an extreme measure, Paul and Blatch knew that new methods had to be employed if the federal amendment was to be passed before the next presidential election. Paul gave Blatch a free hand to press the case before the National Executive Committee. "We can't organize bigger and more influential deputations," Blatch reasoned. "We can't organize bigger processions. We can't, women, do anything more in that line. We have got to take a new departure."[3] Although the Executive Committee was sympathetic to Blatch, the members needed further time to think about it, and they adjourned with no firm commitment one way or the other.[4]

Debate over the issue of picketing as a tactic ended abruptly on January 9, 1917. Earlier that day, some 300 women met with Woodrow Wilson to present resolutions passed on Christmas Day 1916, at a memorial service for Inez Milholland held in the Capitol. The resolutions, as in the past, dealt with a federal amendment. Wilson's response, under the circumstances, was galling to the assembled women. Although he did not explicitly dredge up yet one more time his commitment to the states' rights position, it was implicit in his response. "My personal action as a citizen, of course comes from no source but my own conviction, and there my position has been so frequently defined, and I hope so candidly defined . . . that I think nothing more is necessary to be said." The President then advised his audience that political change could only occur through the instrumentality of parties, and that women had to stir sufficient public opinion in order to spur action.[5] Wilson had cooly dismissed the participation of women suffragists in the last election. He spoke as though the NWP did not exist. As they proceeded back to Cameron House, the anger and disbelief that permeated the ranks of the suffragists filled them with a new resolve. It took little lobbying to persuade them, as Harriot Stanton Blatch said, "to stand beside the gateway where he [Wilson] must pass in and out, so that he can never fail to realize that there is a tremendous earnestness and insistence back of this measure."[6]

Having decided to proceed with the campaign, Paul now had to work out a strategy. A number of considerations had to be taken into account before they could go forward. After returning to Cameron House, the women spent the next several hours debating the structure of the campaign. Paul was concerned that the picketing campaign be perceived as both useful and effective. To begin something like picketing without reasonable assurance that the organization could sustain it over the long term could be counterproductive. She favored including members of both the NWP as well as the Congressional Union on the picket line. Acceptance of all volunteers to do picket duty might conceivably mean the difference between success and failure, in her view.[7] But Harriot Stanton Blatch and several other members of the Executive Committee viewed the picketing as an opportunity for women in the East to contribute to suffrage in as unique a way as women in the West had done during the election campaign. Western voters ought to continue exerting political pressure on Congress, where they could do the most good. Picketing, Blatch insisted, was the duty of the unenfranchised women of the East. Initially, then, members of the NWP were excluded from picketing duty. Within days, however, the headquarters staff received so many requests from women across the country—both voters and nonvoters—asking that they, too, be allowed to take their place among the picketers, that all restrictions, much to Alice Paul's relief, were dropped.[8]

To coordinate the picketing campaign, Paul turned to Mabel Vernon, who had done so exemplary a job during the 1916 campaign. It was Vernon who was responsible for seeing that enough picketers were on duty each day, beginning with the very first day, January 10. Vernon sent out a call for volunteers, the response to which was more than gratifying. During the eighteen months of picketing activity, in

1917 and 1918, thousands of women volunteered their services for picket line duty, ranging in time from one hour to days. "Of course we use every day some local people who volunteer for service for an hour or so," Paul later wrote to a colleague. "[Elizabeth] Kent . . . gives us two hours a week regularly. . . . A professor of sociology at Vassar College was in town recently one day for three hours. She picketed one hour out of the three, which showed real devotion."[9] Equally gratifying was the support extended from those who could not, for various reasons, participate in the picketing yet who wanted to demonstrate their solidarity with those who were on the line. "Don't give up the ship," wrote one supporter. "I approve every act of brave women who promote the cause of their sisters."[10] "The work is certainly a distinct service to every woman in America," wrote the North Dakota chairwoman. "There are thousands of women scattered over the country who are watching your achievements with pride and gratitude."[11] For many, their sheer distance from Washington prevented them from taking their turn on the line. For others, it was the responsibilities and constraints of motherhood that held them back. "If it were not for the fact that I have a young daughter . . . and no one to leave her with, I would be there with you," lamented one mother. "*I feel ashamed* to *have other women suffering* for *my cause*, and not be there to help them," she added.[12]

Some women, who were less sure of the effectiveness of such a campaign, nevertheless trusted Paul's judgment enough to continue their financial support of the organization. Josephine DuPont, of the Delaware DuPonts, acknowledged that she was "opposed to it [the picketing] as being sensational and undignified." However, she added, "my confidence in you [Paul] leads one to hope for better results than are apparent to the mere on-looker." She enclosed a check for $1,000 with her letter.[13] Similarly, Queene Coonley questioned the necessity for picketing. "It no doubt seems necessary to you but it is so unlovely that I could not feel that I want to support *that* effort." Nevertheless, she sent Paul $250 and pledged another $250 for the "congressional work and the federal amendment [which] I heartily support."[14] Not everyone who disagreed with the picketing campaign continued to offer financial support, of course. In response to a handwritten note from

Alice Paul appealing for funds, Mrs. Carle Sprague returned the letter with a terse note stating that she would not contribute one dime, since "I do not sympathize with your conduct."[15]

Others also objected to the picketing. The New York Times, unable to decide how to characterize the picketing, ended up referring to it as both "silly" and "monstrous." In an editorial condemning the picketing policy, the Times declared that it was such a female thing to do that it could "not even imagine the I.W.W. attempting it." The whole affair, for the editor of the Times, provided ample proof that women had no business involving themselves in politics. "That the female mind is inferior to the male need not be assumed," readers were loftily informed. "That there is something about it essentially different, and that this difference is of a kind and degree that with votes for women would constitute a political danger is or ought to be plain to everybody."[16] Most periodicals did not immediately find the picketing as offensive as did the New York Times. For many journalists, the picketing campaign was not an example of the inherent inferiority of women in political matters, and became a target of criticism only after the war became an issue.[17]

The National Association Opposed to Women's Suffrage took the opportunity to denounce both the picketing and the suffrage movement. " 'See us annoy the President!' the banners imply . . . 'We don't care what happens. We want our own way.' And that is very likely what the lighted match says when it carries the yellow banner into the powder magazines." They also claimed that the picketers were inviting a presidential assassination.[18] Although it was not clear whether the National Association Opposed to Women's Suffrage believed that a deranged picketer might attempt the assassination, its powder keg metaphor was, nevertheless, an apt one. Moreover, the fear of assassination came up again in May 1917, when a reporter, speaking with Alice Paul, claimed that some members of the administration were concerned about that possibility. When Paul inquired if the administration would be willing to make their fears public, the reporter said no. "The picketing will go on as usual," Paul replied.[19]

For his part, Wilson, at least in the early weeks, seemed to be the least disturbed by the picketing campaign. Often, as he passed through the White House gates, the President tipped his hat to the sentinels.

On one occasion, bitter weather prompted Wilson to extend an invitation to the picketers. "Hoover, go out there and ask those ladies if they won't come in and get warm, will you?" he asked the Head Usher. "And if they come, see that they have some hot tea and coffee." The aide returned quickly with their reply. "Excuse me, Mr. President, but they indignantly refused."[20]

Some members of his family, on the other hand, tended to be less sanguine than the President. Wilson's cousin, Helen Woodrow Bones, on hearing that Jessie Wilson was planning a suffrage meeting, wrote: "We are having an exhibition of suffrage idiocy just now—as you must have seen in the papers. . . . I wonder what they think it will do. They could stand there till time passed and eternity began and it would have no impression on W. W."[21] The President's second wife, Edith Bolling Wilson, found the behavior of the pickets reprehensible, and their constant presence outside the White House gates elicited only angry words from her.[22]

In order to impress upon the President, Congress, and the press and public the diversity of support both for the federal amendment and for the picketing campaign, Alice Paul and Mabel Vernon planned a series of special "days." The first was Maryland Day, when the picket line was composed entirely of volunteers from that state. This was followed by Pennsylvania Day, New York Day, Virginia Day, and New Jersey Day. Thirteen colleges were represented on College Day, and a variety of professional days, including Teachers' Day, also produced an ample number of appropriate volunteers. Theme days included Patriotic Day, Lincoln Day, and Labor Day. It was an effective strategy since it provided a constant source of press attention, thus keeping the issue before the nation.[23]

Before the United States entered the war, the picketers elicited more sympathy than derision from the public. Passers-by frequently stopped to provide words of encouragement and even material comforts such as mittens and hot bricks to stand on.[24] Even the White House guards came to look upon them as comrades. When the pickets arrived five minutes late one day, one guard told them, "I was kind of worried. We thought perhaps you weren't coming and we would have to hold down this place alone."[25] When, however, Alice Paul announced the NWP's "war policy," the public's attitude began to change markedly.

In the four-day period from January 31 to February 3, 1917, prospects for American involvement in the European war rose exponentially. Since the election of 1916, Wilson's major efforts had been directed toward attempting to negotiate peace among the belligerents. For a time, this appeared to hold some promise that the conflict in Europe could be settled and that the United States would be able to retain its status as a neutral. Abruptly, on January 31, all that changed. The German Ambassador hand delivered a note from his government which announced that it would undertake, beginning immediately, a campaign of unrestricted submarine warfare against all shipping, neutral and belligerent. After consulting with his advisors, cabinet, and members of Congress, Wilson reluctantly concluded that he had no other choice but to sever diplomatic relations with Germany, which he did on February 3, 1917.[26] To many observers, it was now merely a matter of time before an actual declaration of war. Others held the fleeting hope that war could still be averted. A consequence of the turn of events, however, was to force nearly everyone to confront the very real possibility, if not the probability, that the country would soon be engaged in the world war and to determine what their response should be. The nation's suffragists were no exception.

On February 8, Alice Paul sent a call for a convention to the state chairwomen of the NWP and the Congressional Union. The organization, she said, had to decide what position it would adopt in the event of war. They were alternately being advised to forego all suffrage activity in order to get behind the war effort, or to transform themselves into a peace society. Then, reminding the members of the purpose of the NWP and the Congressional Union, Paul made clear what she hoped would be the consensus of the convention. "Those who wish to work for preparedness, those who wish to work for peace, can do so through organizations for such purpose." But, she went on, "until the [NWP and Congressional Union Constitutions are] changed by action of a convention our organization is dedicated only to the enfranchisement of women." Paul's reasons for advocating this position struck at the heart of the problem, as she viewed it. "Never was it so urgent that women have a representation in government councils. The responsibility for the acts of our country belongs to women as much as men. We must do our part to see that war, which concerns women as seriously as men, shall not be entered upon without the consent of women." [27]

Most members of the NWP and Congressional Union agreed with Paul's assessment. "I am glad . . . that the . . . NWP . . . will continue to serve the nation as the means of political expression of the highest aims of the American women," a Philadelphia suffragist wrote in response to an appeal for support. [28] The staff of *The Suffragist* busied itself writing replies to women who communicated their endorsement. "We are glad to know you feel the stand the Congressional Union has taken . . . is the wise one. It seems to us that it is just the time for women to demand enfranchisement." [29]

By the time the convention was called to order on March 2, the question of the organization's war policy had already been settled. Florence Bayard Hilles, of Delaware, the daughter of Grover Cleveland's Secretary of State, voiced the opinion of the delegates. "We are composed of pacifists, militarists, Protestants, Catholics, Jews, Republicans, Democrats, Socialists, Progressives, Populists, and every other following. . . . If we for a moment divert our Party from the purpose of its organization, we not only weaken it, we destroy it. We must be considered an integral part of this country." [30] Accordingly, the convention passed the following resolution: "Be it resolved that the NWP, organized for the sole purpose of securing political liberty for women, shall continue to work for this purpose until it is accomplished, being unalterably convinced that in so doing the organization serves the highest interests of the country." [31]

At the convention the delegates also voted to amalgamate the NWP and the Congressional Union, a proposal that evoked some discussion because of a persistent residual feeling among many suffragists that unenfranchised women ought not officially to be a part of a partisan group, that is, a political party. Harriot Stanton Blatch, for one, believed that such a move would "lessen our political power." But the majority agreed with Alice Paul that the union of forces could only serve to strengthen their political goals. Paul argued:

All of us in the Congressional Union feel an affection for it. But that is no reason for continuing the organization. . . . Now that we have created the Woman's Party, we ought, it seems to me, to develop and make that the dominant suffrage factor in this country because that, through its name and associations, throws the emphasis more than does the Congressional Union on the political powers of women.[32]

It was an unsentimental end to an organization that had served its purpose well.

Following the vote to merge, the convention selected as officers of the NWP, Alice Paul, Chairwoman; Anne Martin, Vice-Chairwoman; and Mabel Vernon, Secretary. The Executive Board consisted of Lucy Burns, Alva Belmont, Eleanor Brannon, Matilda Gardner, Abby Scott Baker, Elizabeth Kent, Maud Younger, Doris Stevens, Florence Bayard Hilles, Edith Houghton Hooker, Allison Hopkins, and Dora Lewis.[33]

The convention concluded its business on March 4, 1917, the day before Wilson's public inauguration, with a massive demonstration at the White House. In some ways, it seemed a replay of the suffrage parade in 1913, but, four years later, there was less a holiday atmosphere and more an air of gritty determination among the suffragists. Intent on delivering their resolutions to Wilson, 1,000 suffragists, each carrying a purple, white, and gold banner, surrounded the White House. Guards were posted every fifty feet within the grounds, and all gates had been locked, making it impossible to gain entry. Nor would the guards, apparently under instruction from Wilson, agree to deliver the resolutions to either Wilson or his aides. In a driving, icy rain, the suffragists marched silently around the White House perimeter, attracting a large audience in the process, despite the inclement weather. Gilson Gardner, writing for the Scripps newspaper chain, wrote of the event:

A special committee . . . went to the west gates . . . but these gates for the first time in two decades were locked. . . . The delegation parlayed with the policemen and waited in the rain. They waited for a long time—which was typical of the attitude of the Administration. . . . Mr. Wilson from the first has kept the women waiting. It is a poor business—both for the women and for Wilson.[34]

At the same time that the NWP determined its war policy, NAWSA announced that it would support all of the administration's war policies. Although the NAWSA claimed that suffrage remained its primary concern, such an assertion was incompatible with its avowed support of all war measures, as events soon demonstrated. Woodrow Wilson declared war on April 6, 1917. Within hours, the Democratic caucus met and announced that, for the duration of the war and for six months thereafter, the Congress would act upon only those issues which Wilson determined to be emergency war measures. Suffrage was not an emergency war measure.[35] Under the circumstances, NAWSA's priorities were, at best, ambiguous. The decision of the Democratic Caucus placed the organization in a difficult situation.[36]

NAWSA's war policy was criticized for another important reason as well. Many suffragists, including Catt and Shaw, claimed to be pacifists and belonged to antiwar groups such as the Woman's Peace Party. Not only was NAWSA willing to commit the organization to support of the war, but it also felt compelled to persuade individuals to likewise forego their personal beliefs in order, as NAWSA believed, to demonstrate that women were loyal Americans first and foremost. It seemed unwilling to accept the idea that antiwar pacifists were acting in good conscience to promote the welfare of the country. It was a policy that lacked moral grounding. The decision by NAWSA leaders to jettison their pacifist beliefs in order to support the war as a way of demonstrating that women deserved the vote, seemed unnecessary to some. "To my mind, it [NAWSA] didn't need to do it and it is too evidently a bid for popular favor," one such critic noted.[37] The fact that both Carrie Chapman Catt and Anna Howard Shaw accepted appointments by President Wilson to serve on the Women's Committee of the Council on National Defense, did little to lessen the perception that the two NAWSA stalwarts were too eager to sacrifice principle for advantage. NAWSA member Edna B. Kearns declared that, "That 'Look at us, we don't picket—we help the country—please give us the vote' attitude disgusts me."[38] And another disgruntled critic of NAWSA policy concluded that "Nothing can excuse the Catt–Shaw crowd but their seventy years."[39]

The differing attitudes of the NWP and NAWSA became quite clear to Congresswoman Jeannette Rankin, a Republican from Montana and the first woman elected to the House of Representatives. Rankin was a life-long pacifist. Her commitment to a federal suffrage amendment was well known, and her commitment to pacifism was at least as strong and as well known. When it became clear that Rankin, as an act of conscience, could not vote in favor of the declaration of war, Carrie Chapman Catt and other NAWSA leaders exerted tremendous pressure on her to cast her vote for war. They argued that a negative vote would set woman suffrage back twenty years and perhaps even longer. It constituted moral blackmail and a weaker individual might have felt compelled to give in to the pressure. Not for nothing had Jeannette Rankin acquired a reputation in Montana as someone to be reckoned with. After the congresswoman cast her vote against entry into the war, Catt, exhibiting little sympathy for Rankin's predicament or admiration for her courage, expressed only anger and contempt for her.[40] Later, when Rankin ran for the Senate in 1918, Catt endorsed Rankin's opponent. Alice Paul, on the other hand, called on Rankin the night before the scheduled vote. She told Rankin that even though the NWP, as an organization, took no stand on the war, Paul, speaking for herself, wanted to let the congresswoman know that she supported Rankin's decision. Later, Rankin acknowledged that Paul's was "the only support I received from women in my vote."[41]

In the weeks following the declaration of war, the pickets continued their White House and Capitol vigil with little interference from Washington authorities. The banners carried by the pickets began to bear quotations from Wilson's various speeches, particularly those that most pointedly emphasized the disparity between his stated concern for democracy abroad and the lack of democracy that existed at home where women were concerned. A quotation lifted from Wilson's war message of April 2 became a standard banner slogan: "We shall fight for the things which we have always held nearest our hearts—for democracy, for the right of those who submit to authority to have a voice in their own governments.—President Wilson's War Message, April 2, 1917."

The device of quoting Wilson to make their point was intended by Alice Paul to be a source of embarrassment to the administration. Since the White House had become the center of diplomatic activity, with foreign emissaries crossing the picket line, it was effective, but hazardous. The public began to respond in an increasingly violent manner, frequently ripping the poles out of the hands of the women and destroying their banners. Such confrontations inevitably produced pushing and shoving matches, and, just as inevitably, some of the pickets sustained physical injury.[42] Although the district authorities became increasingly concerned over the "embarrassment" that the pickets were causing the President, they did nothing to disrupt the demonstrations until the end of June, just two days following what became known as the Russian Banner incident.

President Wilson had just sent Elihu Root and others to the new Russian Republic in an effort to persuade the Russians to stay in the war. In the course of a speech, Root stated that the United States was a country where "universal, direct, equal, and secret suffrage obtained."[43] Such misrepresentation of existing conditions outraged suffragists. When, on June 20, a delegation from the Russian Republic paid a return visit to Washington to continue talks about cooperation, Alice Paul stationed Lucy Burns and Dora Lewis outside the White House with an enormous banner addressed to the Russians. The banner conveyed in detail the anger that Root's falsehood had stirred. The printed message began:

President Wilson and Envoy Root are deceiving Russia. They say 'We are a democracy. Help us to win the war so that democracies may survive.' We women of America tell you that America is not a democracy. Twenty million women are denied the right to vote. President Wilson is the chief opponent of their national enfranchisement. Help us make this nation really free. Tell our government that it must liberate its people before it can claim free Russia as an ally.[44]

To the crowds gathered around the picketers, this sign was too much. As soon as the Russian delegation had entered the White House, people crowded in around the picketers and tore down the banner with such speed that one observer later commented, "One instant the banner was there, and the next there were only bare sticks."[45] A small disturbance ensued, during which the police did nothing to restore order.[46]

The incident was front page news the next morning. The *New York Times* claimed that "the Russians went by the gate so fast that it is doubtful if even those who read English were able to see the inscription on the banner."[47] In fact, the Russians did see and read the banner. Paul received a note from a member of the delegation, N.A. Nessaragof, in which he applauded the NWP for its courage "despite the angry crowd." Nessaragof urged Paul to continue pursuing her goal, despite the barriers placed in her way. "In Russia a different kind of oppressors did the very same thing the American police do now. Yet a real liberty was won at last, and there are not forces on earth which could deprive humanity of it."[48]

Such incidents clearly were embarrassing. They also provided marvelous copy for the nation's newspapers. Those unfamiliar with the NWP before the Russian delgation incident, could read all about it over breakfast. Whether or not people agreed with the NWP tactics, and most did not at that time, the newspapers provided a running account of the conflict. Anticipating the political and press reaction to the Russian banners, Alice Paul issued a press release of her own, which presented the NWP side of the story.

It is those who deny justice, and not those who demand it who embarrass the country in its international relations. . . . The responsibility . . . is with the government and not with the women of America, if the lack of democracy at home weakens government in its fight for democracy three thousand miles away.[49]

For both administration figures and district authorities, the situation was growing increasingly more disturbing. Hurried conferences between members of both agencies focused on possible solutions to their discomfort. Whether or not, as one NWP member later reported, discussions included consideration of a possible raid on NWP headquarters, the subject of arrests did receive serious thought. Major Raymond Pullman, the Chief of Police, subsequently called Alice Paul to warn her that further demonstrations would lead to arrests. Paul, who had taken the precaution of obtaining advice on the legality of picketing the White House, pointed out to Pullman that the women were protected under the terms of the Clayton Act. Pullman ended the conversation with the warning, "You will be arrested if you attempt to picket again."[50]

The threat of arrest added a new element to the picketing campaign. It was one thing to stand outside for a few hours holding a banner. It was quite another thing to go to jail for it. Paul, mindful of her own experiences in English prisons, advised her followers of the possible consequences. While she hoped that the response would be positive, she knew that each woman had to make up her own mind on the matter. Katherine Morey, a volunteer from Boston, expressed the sentiments of many, when she called Alice Paul. "We will have to have people *willing* to be arrested, and I will come down and I will be one," she said. Morey took the next train to Washington.[51]

Three days later, on June 22, Paul left Washington to attend a meeting in Pennsylvania. An undercurrent of tension permeated the gathering, for everyone was aware that the NWP had reached a critical crossroads. No one could predict what the authorities would do, and consequently preparations for the worst-case scenario had been made. At the same time, no one really believed that the police would move in and arrest picketers. When the telephone rang interrupting the meeting, therefore, discussion continued as Alice Paul, summoned by the housekeeper, went to answer the call. The women were "dumbfounded" when, on her return, Paul quietly informed them that her caller had been a reporter from one of the Washington newspapers. The worst—so they believed—had indeed happened. Lucy Burns and Katherine Morey had just been arrested in front of the White House by District police. During the ensuing discussion and spate of telephone calls, one thing became clear: their resolve to continue in spite of what had happened, had not weakened in the slightest. If the District authorities hoped that the arrests would be enough to crush the campaign, they were sadly disappointed, as Paul made clear in a subsequent telephone conversation with Major Pullman. "I feel that we *will* continue," she told him.[52] The decision to continue picketing despite the arrests and in the face of opposition from other suffragists unsympathetic to the NWP strategy, particularly since the country was at war, marked the beginning of real militancy in the suffrage campaign.

Between June 22 and June 26, police made twenty-seven more arrests. In all instances, the picketers were charged with obstruction of traffic, and released without penalty. On June 26, however, the women arrested were bound over for trial the following day. As the process of arrest, transportation to police headquarters, and release was not enough to deter the determined women, the authorities had no choice but to raise the ante. On June 27, six women were tried for obstructing traffic in a public place.[53] The suffragists were found guilty and fined $25.00. The judge noted that had they kept moving rather than standing still in front of the White House, they would not have been arrested. All six women on trial refused to pay the $25.00 fine, and were sentenced to three days in jail. They were confined to the District Jail "in six of the best cells with running water and bath facilities."[54] The sentences, according to the *New York Times*, were intentionally light because the authorities had heard rumors that the women planned to go on hunger strikes if imprisoned. "No one can starve to death in three days," observed the *Times*. The newspaper also noted, ominously, that police authorities intended to ask for heavier penalties if more arrests were made.[55]

The next series of arrests produced the same penalties. On July 14, however, sixteen women were arrested, tried, and sentenced to sixty days in Occoquan Workhouse in suburban Virginia.[56] The courtroom was filled with women, many of whom had never been in a courtroom, much less seen a trial. Their lack of intimidation was noteworthy, although they did not yet know what to expect. "Well, girls," observed Florence Bayard Hilles of Baltimore, whose father was Ambassador to Great Britain during the Cleveland Administration, "I've never seen but one court in my life and that was the Court of St. James. But I must say they are not very much alike."[57] A number of prominent men were also in the courtroom, including John A. H. Hopkins, a Progressive party leader and Wilson campaign coordinator from New Jersey, whose wife Allison Turnbull Hopkins was standing trial, Frederic Howe, Commissioner of Immigration in New York, Dudley Field Malone, Collector of the Port of New York, labor leader Frank Walsh, and conservationist Amos Pinchot.[58] Two of the women on trial acted as attorneys for the group. Doris Stevens of New York City and Anne Martin of Nevada, spoke on behalf of the others, although all the defendants had something to say in their own defense. And despite the best efforts of the prosecution, the suffragists succeeded in making politics the focus of the trial, rather than the traffic violation they were charged with. "We know full well that we stand here because the President of the United States refuses to give liberty to American women," New York society matron Elizabeth Rogers stated. "We believe, your Honor, that the wrong persons are before the bar in this Court." Matilda Hall Gardner of Washington D.C., was even more frank. "Even should I be sent to jail which, I could not, your

Honor, anticipate, I would be in jail because I obstructed traffic, but because I have offended politically, because I have demanded of this government freedom for women."[59] Each statement brought a round of applause from the packed courtroom. To most courtroom observers, the preponderance of evidence appeared to rest with the suffragists. The charge of obstructing traffic was little more than a pretext for removing an increadingly uncomfortable situation away from public view. Moreover, it was a charge that was arbitrarily as well as illegally imposed, as Alice Paul and her colleagues knew from consultation with their lawyers when they first began the picketing campaign. When District Court Judge Mullowney handed down the guilty verdict and sentenced the prisoners to sixty days in a workhouse, both defendants and spectators alike were stunned. It was a harsh and heavy-handed reaction on the part of the authorities.[60]

For the Wilson administration, events were quickly getting out of hand. Officially, Wilson ignored the whole affair, refusing to comment for the most part. George Creel, the Chairman of Wilson's Committee of Public Information, reaffirmed this nonrecognition policy in press releases to the public. Creel stated:

It is a fact that there remains in America one man who has known exactly the right attitude to take and maintain toward the pickets. A whimsical smile, slightly puckered at the roots by a sense of the ridiculous, a polite bow—and for the rest a complete ignoring of their existence. He happens to be the man around whom the little whirlwind whirls—the President of the United States.[61]

But, while the President could pretend to be able to ignore the situation publicly, he could not maintain the charade privately.

The same afternoon that the suffragists were found guilty and sentenced to Occoquan, Wilson met with an old friend and political ally, Dudley Field Malone. Malone called Wilson after leaving the courthouse and insisted on seeing the President immediately. He then took a cab directly to the White House. During the campaign of 1916, Malone had stumped the West for Wilson. Malone spent the campaign reassuring western voters that not only was Wilson sympathetic to suffrage, but that he would act favorably on it during his second term. By chance, Malone had witnessed the arrests on July 14 and was outraged over the treatment accorded the suffragists by both police and onlookers. His sense of commitment to suffrage as a consequence of the recent campaign prompted him to show up in District Court, unsolicited, in order to offer his services to the defendants. Malone felt obligated to make good on the promises that he had made on Wilson's behalf and with the President's knowledge in 1916.[62]

Malone reminded Wilson of the promises made to women in the West in the last campaign, and described the scene he had witnessed on July 14. Malone also told Wilson that in his opinion the trial was a travesty and the sentences meted out were unreasonably harsh and punitive. Wilson objected to having the actions of the district police laid at his doorstep. "Why do you come to me in this indignant fashion for things which have been done by the police officials of the city of Washington?" Wilson asked. " 'Mr. President," I said, "the treatment of these women is the result of carefully laid plans made by the District Commissioners.' " Malone's response was pointed, for the District Commissioners were appointed by the President. No action of the type taken against the suffragists would have occurred without the consent, if not the advice, of someone in the administration. Whether Wilson knew of the intentions of the District Commissioners beforehand, in Malone's view he could no longer plead ignorance regarding future treatment of the suffragists, either in the courts or at Occoquan. Wilson could no longer hope to be excused from complicity should the suffragists be accorded more of the "unnecessarily humiliating" treatment they had suffered at the hands of the authorities thus far.[63]

Following Malone's meeting with Wilson, rumors ran rife in Washington that he had tendered his resignation in protest. Malone did offer his resignation then because, as he informed Wilson, it was his intention to act as attorney for the suffragists in preparation of an appeal to a higher court. As a member of Wilson's administration, Malone felt that it would constitute conflict of interest to defend the prisoners against the administration. In the circumstances, Wilson asked Malone to reconsider his resignation tender. Malone could, Wilson said, pursue his defense of the suffragists and continue preparing their appeal. "Since you feel as you do I see no reason why you should not become their counsel and take this case up on appeal without resigning from the Administration."[64] Wilson asked Malone not to leave Washington without talking to him first.[65]

The day after Malone's meeting with Wilson, John Appleton Haven Hopkins asked to meet with the President. Not only had Hopkins co-ordinated the campaign for Wilson's re-election in New Jersey, but he and his wife Allison—now a convicted prisoner—had recently been dinner guests of the Wilsons at the White House. Hopkins was clearly distressed by the turn of events. "How would you like to have your wife sleep in a dirty workhouse next to prostitutes?" Hopkins report-edly asked the President.[66] Wilson professed to be "shocked" at the arrests and the severe sentences, saying he knew nothing about it. He asked Hopkins what could be done to relieve the situation. "The Pres-ident asked me for suggestions as to what might be done," Hopkins reported in an interview, "and I replied that in view of the seriousness of the present situation the only solution lay in immediate passage of the Susan B. Anthony amendment."[67] Hopkins' suggestion was not rejected out-of-hand by Wilson. Indeed, as the *New York Times* re-ported in its front page coverage, "the President discussed the possi-bility of treating the suffrage amendment as a war emergency mea-sure, and asked for data which would throw light on the question of whether it would be likely to pass Congress with the necessary ma-jority, if he should add it to the war emergency measures."[68]

On July 20, Wilson signed a pardon for all the suffrage prisoners confined to Occoquan. The pardon did not comment on the merits of the case. Dudley Field Malone correctly guessed that under the cir-cumstances, the suffragists might be thinking of refusing to accept the pardon. A trip out to Virginia confirmed his suspicions and, while he was entirely sympathetic to their position, he nevertheless pointed out that they had no choice in the matter. Malone recalled:

I advised them that as a matter of law no one could compel them to accept the pardon, but that as a matter of fact they would have to accept it, for the Attorney General would have them all put out of the institution bag and bag-gage. So as a solution of the difficulty and in view of the fact that the Presi-dent had said to me that their treatment was 'shocking' I made public the fol-lowing statement: "The President's pardon is an acknowledgement by him of the grave injustice that has been done.' This he never denied.[69]

Just in case Wilson did not fully understand the position of the suf-fragists, Allison Turnbull Hopkins made it clear to him in a terse let-ter. Although she had been released from prison, Hopkins wrote, she could not accept, in spirit or in good conscience, the pardon under

Wilson's terms. "In this case, which involves my fundamental constitutional rights, Mr. Hopkins and I do not desire your presidential benevolence, but American justice."[70] Hopkins noted that she would resume her picketing, a decision in which Alice Paul concurred. "We're very much obliged to the President for pardoning the pickets but we'll be picketing again next Monday. The President can pardon us again if we're arrested on Monday, and again and again, but . . . picketing will continue and sooner or later he will have to do something about it."[71]

CHAPTER 8

Politics, Prison, and Resolution

World War I, declared on April 7, 1917, formed the backdrop for a triangle that had been developing since Alice Paul left NAWSA in early 1914–a triangle consisting of the NWP, NAWSA, and Woodrow Wilson. Earlier, particularly during the anti-Democratic party campaigns, the relationship between the points of the triangle began to emerge. NAWSA, led by the politically canny Carrie Chapman Catt, struck a note of conciliatory cultivation with Wilson. By her criticism of the activities of Paul's NWP, Catt's NAWSA became, in Wilson's view particularly, the moderates, the representatives of real American womanhood. The intent may not have been conscious, but the effect was the same. Increasingly, compelled by events generated by the militants, Wilson made political concessions which he then attributed to the deserving nature of reasonable women, epitomized by the NAWSA suffragists. Thus, when Charles Evans Hughes was persuaded to endorse a federal amendment and Wilson felt compelled to respond in kind, he chose to make his announcement not to an NWP audience, but to a NAWSA audience, largely in an effort to undercut the influence and significance of the campaign against Democrats. (See chapter VII.) The war only served to emphasize this triangular relationship.

NAWSA took full advantage of the situation, assiduously cultivating friendships on Capitol Hill. Catt's lieutenant, Helen Hamilton Gardener, lost few opportunities to demonstrate that women, by their selflessness and patriotism, deserved full enfranchisement. Gardener was both persuasive and tactful, characteristics that made her an invaluable NAWSA liaison and brought even Wilson into her camp of admirers. A month after the declaration of war, and with the pickets still standing vigil at the White House gates, Gardener wrote to Wilson, asking him to assure Representative Edward W. Pou (D-N.C.), chairman of the House Rules Committee and a suffrage opponent, that he, Wilson, favored the creation of a House Woman Suffrage Committee. Wilson wrote to Pou on May 14 that he heartily approved "in this matter of very considerable consequence."[1] Faced with formidable congressional resistance, Gardener again appealed to Wilson for help. A word from Wilson to Representatives Carter Glass (D-Va.), and J. Thomas Heflin (D-Ala.), in particular, Gardener believed, would help stem the opposition. Wilson complied on June 13, and Heflin yielded. "After reading your letter several times, and thinking over the situation, I have concluded to follow your suggestion."[2] The Rules Committee was in no hurry to make a decision on the issue, however, partially because, by previous arrangement Congress had agreed to forego all matters not considered by the administration to be war measures. Gardener told Wilson, who was responsible for drawing up the list, that NAWSA "refrained from forcing the issue" because of Wilson's overwhelming task of war administration.[3] Wilson was free of pressure from NAWSA, but could, at his convenience, use NAWSA to explain actions which he took in reaction to the activities of the militants.

Had Woodrow Wilson kept a tighter rein on District authorities, he might well have avoided the suffrage crisis that worsened weekly in the middle months of 1917. It was a commonly held belief that Wilson had the final say regarding the suffragists. Moreover, District Commissioner Louis Brownlow discussed the situation with Wilson on at least one occasion, and noted that "Mr. Wilson did not want them [the suffragists] arrested, and I did not want to arrest them."[4] But, if Wilson and Brownlow made it known to their subordinates that they did not want further suffrage arrests, it made little impression.

Whatever their desires or instructions, for the next several months neither interfered when subsequent arrests and trials were conducted. The war, of course, played a crucial part in developments. In order to win total support for the war, the administration instituted the policy of "100% Americanism"—a policy that succeeded so well that both foolish and threatening actions were taken as a consequence. Sauerkraut, for example, was renamed Liberty cabbage, and German measles were henceforth called Liberty measles. German language teachers, in some cases, were reported to authorities by neighbors who were sure that their ability to speak German revealed seditious intentions.[5]

A perception developed among many people—promoted in good measure by some of the press coverage, in addition to the attitude struck by government authorities—that any dissent bordered on treason, regardless of ideology or cause. Newspapers such as the New York Times mixed anarchists, strikers, antiwar demonstrators, draft resisters, and suffragists, presenting them in such a way as to convey to their readers the implication that all dissent was equally meritless and harmful. And indeed, to some Americans—including the editors of the New York Times—no dissenter deserved differentiation.[6] The extent to which this perception filtered into the courtroom proceedings of the suffrage cases, was clearly revealed when, on July 17, Dudley Field Malone, defending the picketers, asserted their constitutional rights to "petition for redress" and criticized District Court Judge Alexander Mullowney for saying that the banners were seditious. Mullowney rebuked Malone soundly, retorting that he [Mullowney] had personally spoken with the United States Attorney about the banners. In June 1917, Congress passed the Espionage Act which, in part, prohibited false statements that obstructed the war effort or otherwise aided the enemy. "I know," Mullowney said, "the words on it are treasonous and seditious."[7] Since the banners to which Mullowney referred were inscribed with statements made by President Wilson, the authorities undoubtedly were in a quandary as to how to proceed. Prosecuting the women under the Espionage Act of 1917, as Judge Mullowney would have liked and undoubtedly had in mind when he consulted the United States Attorney, would have been difficult at best and probably highly embarrassing at the very least. Thus, Mullowney had to be content with stripping the women of their civil rights and liberties in order to coerce them into abandoning further picketing. But there was little doubt that treason was on the minds of some people.

Nevertheless, arrests and trials of otherwise conventional middle-class women did not sit entirely well with much of the press and public. Thus there was also a strong perception that the government over-reacted to the picketing, contradicting by its actions the intent of its wartime rhetoric. "Can't the disfranchised even ask for justice in a country so nobly going to the defense of oppressed nations?" asked the *Canton* (New York) *Advertiser*.[8] "It is ludicrous for Washington diplomats to pose as teachers of democracy to the people of benighted Russia which has admitted the women of their country to equal polit-ical and civil rights with men," observed a Florida newspaper.[9] The editor of another New York paper found even greater cause for con-cern: "The [suffrage] issue exists. It cannot be met by the denial of the right to public expression or even by the imprisonment of suffrage standard bearers. The fundamentals of our democratic institutions are at stake."[10]

Censure came from other quarters as well. Chief Justice Walter Clark of the North Carolina Supreme Court asserted that "the manhood of this country will never stand for war upon women." When asked by Secretary of War Newton D. Baker to go to France personally to nar-rate a propaganda film called "Damaged Goods," actor Richard Ben-nett tersely demanded, "Why should I work for democracy in Europe when our American women are denied democracy at home? If I am to fight for social hygiene in France, why not begin at Occoquan Workhouse?" asked Bennett, who had already heard of the unappeal-ing conditions in the prison.[11] Commissioner of Immigration Frederic C. Howe, who had sat through the first suffrage trials, noted dourly that "this is not the only time that truth has been on the scaffold." And Mary Beard's husband, Charles, fumed, "The government should be ashamed for arresting women who fight for liberty."[12] Criticism of this sort continued throughout the ensuing months.

Like the picketing issue, many citizens might have disagreed with such tactics, but they were more than a little concerned at the manner in which the situation was dealt with. Moreover, public focus on prison conditions that the suffragists encountered generated further discus-sion of the reasons for their imprisonment. Because of the extraordi-

nary amount of publicity given the picketers, attempts were made from
time to time, to censor or manage the news. "The truth is that as long
as they can get on the front page of the papers they will keep up their
pressure tactics," Mrs. Ellis Meredith, a member of the Democratic
National Committee's Woman's Bureau, advised Joseph Tumulty, the
President's secretary. "Mr. Creel [George Creel, Committee on Public
Information] tells me he can get the Associated Press and the other
two news organizations to suppress anything concerning them. . . .
It occurs to me that the newspapers of this city [Washington] would
respect the wishes of the President in this matter. . . . Dr. Anna
Howard Shaw has written to Mr. [William Gibbs] McAdoo . . . to
this effect."[13]

Arthur Brisbane, the editor of the *Washington Times*, also wrote to
Tumulty regarding the possibility of managing the picket story. Brisbane had consulted with the editor of the *Washington Star*, who proposed that the newspapers should "by a pact and agreement, refrain
from giving the suffragette ladies any publicity. He suggests, in fact,
nothing but the merest dull statement—nothing, as he puts it, 'to feed
their vanity.' " Brisbane went on to say that "what this paper intends
to do is whatever is desired by the President."[14] In response to Brisbane's inquiry, Wilson replied,

There is a great deal in what Mr. Brisbane says about entire silence on the
part of the newspapers possibly provoking the less sane of these women to
violent action. My own suggestion would be that nothing that they do should
be featured with headlines or put on the front page, but that a bare, colorless
chronicle of what they do should be all that was printed. That constitutes part
of the news, but it need not be made interesting reading.[15]

Brisbane also went directly to members of the NWP with a proposal
which he believed to be fair and equitable. The *Washington Times* would,
Brisbane promised, provide daily *back page* coverage of suffrage news
if the NWP would stop picketing and stop criticizing the administration. Paul and her colleagues met Brisbane's proposition with a mix-
ture of incredulity and amusement. And, although they declined his
offer, they did assure him that the NWP would continue to provide
the *Washington Times* with daily press releases for his use.[16] In any event,
suppressing the picket story proved to be a futile effort that was not
pursued with any great enthusiasm by the Wilson administration.

Pressure continued to bear down upon Wilson as the summer progressed. Confrontations between suffrage picketers and the crowds, gathered to observe the anticipated arrests, became rowdier and rowdier. There was a disturbing increase in the incidence of physical abuse directed at the suffragists, particularly when onlookers tried to relieve the women of their banners. In several instances, suffragists were dragged along the pavement as they fought to hold on to banners. Then too, more and more uniformed servicemen were taking on the role of defenders of the administration, and were frequently in the forefront of the mobs. Young boys, inspired by the examples of their elders, became a source of irritation for the suffragists, darting in and out of the picket line, ripping banners away, and ready with whatever name-calling they thought they could get away with. Except in very few instances, the assaults on the suffragists went unchecked. District policemen were notoriously derelict in their role as peacekeepers. For the most part the only time the police were actively involved was to arrest picketers.[17] Such obvious disinterest on the part of the authorities invited acts of greater violence. A bullet fired through a second floor window of Cameron House, alleged to have come from a serviceman's revolver, narrowly missed three suffragists in the building. As a consequence of this build-up in violence directed toward the suffragists, Congresswoman Jeannette Rankin later introduced a resolution calling for a congressional investigation into the involvement of United States armed services personnel in attacks upon the pickets.[18]

While this drama was unfolding over the course of the summer, NAWSA continued to cement its relationship with Wilson. A Periodic visitor to the White House, Helen Hamilton Gardener had been instructed by Carrie Chapman Catt to assure Wilson of NAWSA's continued support for his administration.[19]

In late August, in a published letter, Representative Charles A. Lindbergh (R-Minn.), charged Woodrow Wilson with responsibility for the denial of the picket's constitutional right to petition the government. In Lindbergh's view, Wilson possessed a position of leadership almost unprecedented in the history of the United States. All that was necessary to insure the safety of the pickets from police and crowd hostility, and to insure their fair treatment under law, Lindbergh believed, was one word of command from the President, one nod. "Yet you did not speak the word, you did not exercise the authority, and you withheld the nod." Lindbergh also decried the participation of American servicemen in the acts of hostility—a charge that prompted Wilson to issue stern warnings to members of the armed services regarding further incidents.[20] Lindbergh's letter condemning the administration appeared in newspapers across the country and further fueled the public controversy over the pickets.[21]

Immediately on the heels of the Lindbergh letter, Dudley Field Malone's public resignation produced still more shock waves. Following his meeting with Wilson on July, Malone had given the President what he considered adequate time to begin to take steps to amend the situation. By September, the former political ally and friend was convinced that no action would be forthcoming from the administration. Consequently, Malone submitted to Wilson a lengthy letter of resignation, carried the next day in the nation's newspapers. Malone wrote:

To me, Mr. President, as I urged upon you in Washington two months ago, this is not only a measure of justice and democracy, it is also an urgent war measure. . . . The whole country gladly acknowledges, Mr. President, that no vital piece of legislation has come through Congress these five years except by your brilliant and extraordinary leadership. . . . If the men of this country had been peacfully demanding for over half a century the political right or privilege to vote, and had been continuously ignored or met with evasion . . . you, Mr. President, as a lover of liberty, would be the first to comprehend and forgive . . . righteous indignation. . . . In every circumstance I have served you with the most respectful attention and unshadowed devotion. It is no small sacrifice for me now, as a member of your Administration, to sever our political relationship. But I think it is high time that the men in our generation, at some cost to themselves, stood up for the battle for the national enfranchisement of American women. So in order to effectively keep my promises made in the West . . . I hereby resign.[22]

The cumulative effect of the turbulent events of the summer and the extent to which those events generated negative publicity for the Wilson administration, was not lost on the Democrats in Congress. The Senate Woman Suffrage Committee, which had been sitting on the amendment for nearly six months while its chairman, Senator Andrieus Aristieus Jones (D-N.Mex.), prepared a "brilliant" report, suddenly decided to report it out.[23] On September 14, Senator Jones, responding to reports of ill-treatment of the suffrage prisoners (who followed the first group who had been pardoned), visited Occoquan to investigate conditions himself. The following day, September 15, his committee met and issued a brief but favorable report on the amendment.[24] Shortly thereafter, on September 24, four months after having begun debate on the creation of a House Committee on Woman Suffrage, came a breakthrough. The House voted to establish such a committee. For the first time, both branches of the Congress had standing Woman Suffrage Committees to take the issue under consideration. Perhaps more important than the announcement of the House Committee on Woman Suffrage, were statements made by chairman of the Rules Committee, Edward W. Pou. Waving Wilson's letter of May 14 overhead, Pou announced that the House would take up the suffrage issue as soon as "all current emergency war measures have been disposed of."[25] It was a startling announcement and it revealed how important were the pressures brought to bear on Wilson by friends such as J. A. H. Hopkins, with whom the issue of suffrage as a war measure was first raised during their dramatic meeting following Mrs. Hopkins' arrest and imprisonment. It is, of course, possible that Congressman Pou was acting on his own initiative in adding suffrage to the emergency war measures list, but it is much more likely that he did so on the advice and request of the President. It was a major step forward and bolstered the spirits of the suffragists, particularly those who were undergoing their ordeal by fire in the soon-to-be infamous Occoquan Workhouse.

News of the ill-treatment of the suffragists had been circulating since the first imprisonments. To be sure, the conditions under which the suffragists were imprisoned were not very different from the conditions that prisoners had to endure as a matter of course. And to be sure, few paid attention to the tribulations visited upon the prison population. When, however, the prison population included middle-class women of social standing and influence, the public and official Washington paid attention to complaints.

Because the pickets refused to be deterred by the threat of arrest or by the threat of imprisonment, longer and longer sentences were handed down, with confinement in Occoquan, a prison removed from Washington. When even this did not deter the suffragists, prison officials attempted to use psychological warfare to instill terror in the women.

Prison conditions in the District Jail were only bearable, despite reports that the suffragists occupied "the best cells, each fitted with running water and bath facilities."[26] At Occoquan, conditions were abysmal. Prison cells were small and dark, and the air fetid. Moreover, they were infested with a variety of animal life. Suffrage prisoner Julia Emory had to beat three rats in succession off her cot one night—a situation not uncommon in Occoquan. Alice Paul recalled that among the women imprisoned with her, "was one whose shrieks nightly filled the jail as the rats entered her cell."[27]

The Superintendent at Occoquan, Raymond Whittaker, lacked even the slightest sensitivity to the political ramifications of his treatment of the suffrage prisoners. Whatever his instructions—or lack of instructions—from administration and district authorities, Whittaker was bent on intimidating the suffragists. Prisoner Mary Winsor reported that during her stay, mail withheld from the suffragists.[28] A letter written to Natalie Gray from her mother, Susan H. Gray, was returned to Colorado Springs with the notation, "I consider this letter if admitted detrimental to the good discipline of the institution; same to be held up—Signed, Whittaker, Supt."[29] Pauline Adams of Norfolk, Virginia, arrested in September 1917, was not alone in her shock over the conditions that faced them at Occoquan. Adams, whose husband was a physician, focused her complaints on the lack of elementary sanitary practices, noting angrily that the prisoners were refused clothing changes and toothbrushes.[30] Prison cells were dank and dark, with fetid air, and the food was infested. In an ill-conceived effort to maintain spirits, one prisoner conducted a "contest," the winner of which would be the person who counted the greatest number of mealworms in her dinner dish. Even the hardiest of souls quickly turned queasy under the proliferation of mealworms.[31]

In addition to the abysmal facility conditions, authorities instituted a sustained program of physical intimidation. For one thing, Whittaker attempted to inflame racial tensions by playing on the prejudices of the suffragists. It was made clear to suffragists on several occasions that they were housed in the same wing with black male prisoners who were allowed to roam about freely.[32] It was a calculated effort to intimidate that was not generally successful except to the extent that it managed to create some vague uneasiness in some of the prisoners.[33]

On other occasions, black female prisoners were ordered by guards to force suffragists to participate in prison routine which they had refused to engage in. The black women acted under threat of punishment from their jailors and succeeded, by their presence and obvious intentions, to intimidate the suffragists into cooperation.[34] Such actions on the part of the prison authorities were heavy-handed, to be sure, but Whittaker acted with seeming impunity, which lent credence to the commonly held belief that District and administration authorities tolerated, if they did not initiate or approve, the conditions under which the suffragists were confined.

The most serious incidents occurred in October and November 1917. On October 20, Alice Paul was one of four suffragists arrested in front of the White House. Her trial presented an opportunity for the authorities to make an example of the well-known ringleader of the NWP. Paul was sentenced to seven months in Occoquan, the harshest sentence yet handed down.[35] On October 30, Paul and Rose Winslow, who was serving six months, began a hunger strike in order to "secure for [their] comrades treatment accorded political prisoners in every civilized country but our own."[36] The decision to commence the hunger strike followed several weeks of effort to gain recognition as political prisoners.[37] Lucy Burns engineered the campaign to achieve political prisoner status from her own prison cell in Occoquan where she had been confined since her arrest in September. According to one account, Lucy began the petition under the noses of the prison officials before they knew what was going on and before they had time to place her in solitary confinement in the hopes that separation from her colleagues would mean an end to the "plot," as the authorities referred to it. Burns' confinement in solitary served only to flame the fires of resolve, and the petition was passed along from inmate to inmate until all the suffragists had had a hand in refining it and all had signed it.[38] The petition, smuggled out of prison and sent to the Commissioners of the District of Columbia, stated in part that the suffragists had "taken this stand as a matter of principle after careful consideration, and from it we shall not recede."[39] It was a predictably futile effort, for the only response was to place each of the signers in silitary confinement.[40] The next logical step was to commence a hunger strike.

"From the moment we undertook the hunger strike," Paul later recalled, "a policy of unremitting intimidation began. One authority after another, high and low, in and out of prison, came to attempt to force me to break the hunger strike. 'You will be taken to a very unpleasant place if you don't stop this,' was a favorite threat of the prison officials, as they would hint vaguely of the psychopathic ward, and St. Elizabeth's, the Government insane asylum. They alternately bullied and hinted."[41] After a week of threats, prison officials began force feeding Paul and Winslow. For three weeks, they were force fed three times daily. In addition, in an effort to disrupt the hunger strike, extraordinary measures were taken against Paul. She was separated from the other prisoners and later transferred to the prison psychopathic ward in the District Jail. She was allowed no visitors, including her lawyer Dudley Field Malone, nor was she allowed to receive mail or other messages. At the District Jail, the door was removed from her room and a matron charged with keeping an eye on Paul woke her every hour throughout the night with a bright flashlight, which made sleep impossible for more than a few minutes at a time. The windows in her room were boarded up with no explanation. Paul admitted:

At night, in the early morning, all through the day there were cries and shrieks and moans from the patients. It was terrifying. One particularly meloncholy moan used to keep up hour after hour with the regularity of a heart beat. I said to myself, 'Now I have to endure this. I have got to live through this somehow. I'll pretend these moans are the noise of an elevated train, beginning faintly in the distance and getting louder as it comes nearer.' Such childish devices were helpful to me.[42]

Prison psychiatrists interviewed her on several occasions and it was made clear to her that one signature on an admission form was all that was necessary to have her committed to an insane asylum. A great deal of emphasis was placed on getting Paul to talk about her feelings toward Woodrow Wilson. The psychiatrists wanted to know if Paul regarded the President as a personal enemy.[43] Paranoia and persecution complex, after all, were sufficient diagnoses for admission to St. Elizabeth's. Interviews by prison psychiatrists were at least interesting, if threatening. The District Jail head physician was another matter. "I believe I have never in my life before feared anything or any human being," Paul said. "But I confess I was afraid of Dr. Gannon, the jail physician. I dreaded the hour of his visit. 'I will show you who rules this place. You think you do. But I will show you that you are wrong.' "[44] While all of this was going on, Malone worked furiously to find out where Paul was incarcerated, for no one save Rose Winslow knew for a period of about ten days where she was. The constant anxiety of her situation was relieved only by Paul's own inner strength and the kindnesses of pyschiatric ward nurses who assured her that they knew she was not insane.[45]

By November 9, Wilson's office had received enough complaints regarding the state of affairs to warrant his ordering an immediate investigation. The President appointed W. Gwynn Gardiner, a physician, to investigate and report back to him. Gardiner's report was a whitewash. Whether Dr. Gardiner accepted the statements of prison officials at face value without further investigation, or consciously chose to misrepresent conditions, is difficult to determine. What is clear is the extent to which the report did misrepresent what was happening at Occoquan and at the District Jail. It contradicted charges of abuse and exonerated completely the actions of the prison authorities. The report dismissed forced feeding as "an everyday occurrence . . . to feed patients in this way." The physician charged with carrying out the forced feedings further claimed that the prisoners "took the tube through which the food was to be administered and swallowed it willingly, there being no force or persuasion used . . . and no more than ordinary discomfort."[46] This was at variance with the reports smuggled out of the District Jail by suffragist Rose Winslow.

Yesterday was a bad day for me in feeding. I was vomiting continuously during the process. The tube has developed an irritation somewhere that is painful. . . . Don't let them tell you we take this well. Miss Paul vomits much. I do, too, except when I'm not nervous, as I have been every time against my will. I try to be less feeble-minded. It's the nervous reaction and I can't control it much. . . . We think of the coming feeding all day. It is horrible.[47]

Nevertheless, Wilson accepted Gardiner's report and ordered his secretary, Joseph Tumulty, to send copies of it to persons who expressed concern for the prisoners.[48]

In the meantime, another incident occurred, which became known in suffrage circles as the "Night of Terror." Newly arrested and convicted suffragists had arrived at Occoquan and were in a holding room awaiting further processing. Without warning, Superindendent Whittaker burst into the room, followed by anywhere from fifteen to forty guards. Pandemonium broke out. Whittaker shouted orders to guards to take this prisoner or that prisoner—often identified by name—to the cells. The scene was one of bedlam, intentionally disorienting. Suffragists feared for their lives and the lives of their compatriots. Mary Nolan, a seventy-three-year-old Floridian with a lame leg that she had to take pains to treat gingerly, was literally dragged off between two burly guards, each of whom held an arm, despite her assertions that she would go willingly and despite the pleas of other suffragists to refrain from injuring her leg. Dorothy Day (later of the Catholic Worker's party), had her arm twisted behind her back and was purposefully slammed down twice over the back of an iron bench. Dora Lewis was thrown into a cell with such force that she was knocked unconscious. For several frantic minutes, her companions believed that she was dead. Alice M. Cosu of New Orleans was also thrown forcefully into her cell. She did not fare as well as Dora Lewis. Cosu suffered a heart attack and repeated and persistent requests for medical attention for the obviously stricken woman went unanswered by the authorities throughout the long night. Lucy Burns, who had been arrested once again on November 10, shortly after completing her previous sixty-day sentence, was identified by Whittaker as the ringleader for the group. She was manacled to her cell bars, hands above her head, and remained that way until morning. Later, her clothing was removed and she was left with only a blanket.[49] Eleanor Brannon later testified:

I firmly believe that . . . Whittaker had determined to attack us as part of the government's plan to suppress picketing. . . . It's [the attack] perfectly unexpected ferocity stunned us. . . . Whittaker, in the center of the room, directed the whole attack, inciting the guards to every brutality.[50]

In the face of this persistent abuse and ill-treatment, the Wilson administration began to receive both complaints and inquiries. Responding to one NAWSA letter-writer who enclosed a copy of an article recounting Burns' efforts on behalf of political prisoner status and the treatment being accorded Alice Paul, Wilson replied:

I think our present reply ought to be to the effect that no real harshness of method is being used, these ladies submitting to the artificial feeding without resistance; that conditions. . . . are being investigated for the second or third time . . . but [no abuse] has as yet been disclosed, there being an extraordinary amount of lying about the thing; and that these ladies cannot in any sense be regarded as political prisoners. We have no political prisoners and could not under the law. They offended against an ordinance of the District and are undergoing the punishment appropriate in the circumstances.[51]

Despite these attempts to diffuse the situation, pressure continued to build up and quickly reached unacceptable proportions. The NWP had sent out the "Prison Special," comprised of picket prisoners, to tour the country and advise the public of the conditions in Washington.[52] Traveling in a specially hired train, and dressed in clothing identical to the prison garb they wore at Occoquan, the Prison Special suffragists were effective at getting their story out. Their speeches created havoc among Democrats already fearful of the consequences of adverse publicity on the congressional elections of 1918. "Chances for Democratic success in the Congressional elections are being severely hurt by the unhuman treatment of . . . women in . . . Occoquan," was the assessment of the Democratic State Committee of Illinois chairman, A. P. Blauvelt. "Cannot you use your influence to have these women released and the situation cleared up by passage of the federal amendment?"[53] A speech by Anne Martin in California particularly unnerved Alameda County Democrats, who asked that Wilson "answer by telegram for publication. This speech did much harm."[54] Wilson, it seemed, was being assaulted from all directions on the issue.

By November 20, 1917, Dudley Field Malone had managed to locate Alice Paul in the District Jail, and obtained a writ of *habeas corpus* which allowed him to have her transferred from the psychiatric ward to the regular hospital. Visitors and mail were still restricted, however. Shortly after her transfer to the hospital ward, an unusual visitor was allowed to meet with Paul, as Malone's request and long after the normal visiting hours had ended. The visitor was newspaperman David Lawrence, a close personal friend of Woodrow Wilson. Lawrence insisted to Paul that the visit was entirely his own idea; he denied being a White House emissary. The nature of his visit and the lateness of the hour suggest that Lawrence had indeed been sent by Wilson to talk to the troublesome Paul.[55] On the political prisoner issue, Lawrence told Paul:

The Administration could very easily hire a comfortable house in Washington and detain you all there, but don't you see that your demand to be treated as political prisoners is infinitely more difficult to grant than to give you the federal amendment? If we give you these privileges we shall have to extend them to conscientious objectors and to all prisoners now confined for political opinions. This the Administration cannot do.[56]

It was a remarkable statement. The demand for political prisoner status had, apparently, encouraged the administration to consider the implications of granting political status vs. supporting a federal amendment. According to Lawrence, the federal amendment was the path of least resistance.[57]

Lawrence next asked about the future intentions of the NWP. Would the party agree to abandon picketing if the administration passed the amendment through one house of Congress during the next session, and promised to see that it was passed through the other house within a year? "Nothing short of the passage of the amendment through Congress will end our agitation," Paul reasserted. Lawrence then repeated the scenario he had just gone through and added that, although Wilson did not intend to mention suffrage in his forthcoming Annual Message, he would make his desires known to congressmen before the amendment came up for a vote.[58]

Within days of Lawrence's visit to Alice Paul—on November 27 and 28, 1917—the authorities, without explanation or advance notice, suddenly released all the suffrage prisoners. Between November 1917 and January 1919, picketing was resumed from time to time, but never again with the sustained intensity of that first summer and fall in 1917. And, although more picketers were arrested from time to time, the picketing campaigns were not met with such draconian force as they had been by the authorities in 1917. Even in cases where arrests were made and prison sentences imposed, the sentences were mild in comparison to the six- and seven-month terms experienced previously. The longest term after November 1917 was an eight-day sentence meted out in Boston, Massachusetts, to suffrage protestors who picketed at a rally to celebrate Woodrow Wilson's return from Versailles, France.[59] There were two reasons for this change of tactic from the authorities. First, a series of appeals on behalf of the suffrage prisoners was gradually making its way through the courts' system. The government's position was shaky, at best, and many legal experts expected that the higher courts would condemn the government's actions in denying the suffragists the right to petition under the First Amendment of the Consitution.[60] The ordeal that had begun with the first arrests in June and ended on November 28, 1917, had not been an easy one for the picketers. They had had to endure the wrath of the authorities, abuse from spectators, and condemnation from other women. NAWSA, in particular, had never once protested the loss of civil liberties of the picketers, nor their ill-treatment as prisoners. Indeed, NAWSA often engaged prominently in condemning the activities of the NWP, referring to the pickets as "the enemy with banners," and "those wild women at the gates."[61] Many of the picketers also had to endure the disapproval of family and friends, as well. Elderly Louisine Havemeyer's family flooded her with telegrams after her arrest and accused her of bringing disgrace down upon their heads (one of the few comforting family messages came from her young grandson who desired only to see his "grandmama" again, because, as he noted, she was a "real sport.")[62] Mary Winsor's aunt complained that Mary's ill-considered actions were "reckless" and "harmful" to the family name."[63] Rebecca Reyher later recalled that "While I was on the picket line, among the people who passed me by were many I had gone to high school with, or previous friends and neighbors, and . . . they turned their noses up at me, practically spat at me." One such person was her old friend, Mrs. Walter Lippman, who walked up to Reyher and hissed, "You ought to be ashamed of yourself."[64] Many women, of course, did have the support of their families to some extent, although few were as broadminded as Katherine Houghton Hepburn's husband, Thomas, then a young physician starting out in Hartford, Connecticut. When Hepburn asked him whether he thought her activity might harm his practice, he replied, "Of course it will, but do it anyway. If you don't stand for the things you believe in, life is no good. If I can't succeed anyway, then let's fail."[65] For the thousands of women who picketed, the approximately 500 who were arrested, and the 168 who actually served prison sentences, the picketing was well worth the effort.

The second reason for the change in attitude on the part of the authorities was that the political climate for suffrage had changed markedly. NWP activity accounted for much of the change in attitude. At the same time, NAWSA kept up its courtship of Woodrow Wilson. Beleaguered and pushed on the one hand by the insistent picketing campaign and its attendant publicity, and courted on the other hand by the cooperative NAWSA, Wilson found it both necessary and palatable to begin intervening in a positive fashion to help secure the amendment. With the approach of the New York state referendum in November 1917, Wilson was only too happy to make his prosuffrage views known. Eager to dampen the fires started by the NWP, and for the state to set an example, Wilson conveyed strong endorsements to the people of New York shortly before the election. Lest it appear that he was giving in to the pickets, Wilson cautioned his audiences not to use the pickets as an excuse to reject suffrage and praised the "spirit and capacity and vision of the women of the United States."[66] The amendment passed and in celebration, Wilson arranged a reception at the White House for Catt and Shaw, hosted by his daughter Eleanor Wilson McAdoo.[67] In the months since the picketing had commenced, Wilson had become not only an active suffrage supporter, but a supporter of a federal amendment. In the months to come, he would extend himself time and again, with only moderate backsliding, on behalf of the amendment.

Just as David Lawrence had indicated, Wilson did not discuss suffrage in his Annual Message on December 3, 1917. But less than two weeks later, in mid-December, the House Rules Committee suddenly announced that time could be found on the calendar to bring the amendment to a vote. The announcement took many by surprise because two months earlier, when Representative Pou had announced the formation of a House Committee on Woman Suffrage, he made it clear that consideration for the amendment would have to wait until all current war emergency measures had been dealt with. Under the circumstances, Pou said, the federal suffrage amendment could not possibly be brought to a vote before the Sixty-sixth Congress convened.[68] Now, however, the House was ready to bring the issue to a vote on January 10, 1918.

Two days before the House vote on the amendment, Representative Jouett Shouse (D-Kans.), a member of the Democratic National Committee, fearful that Republicans would seize upon the issue if the vote were defeated, implored Wilson "for the sake of the party" to curb the opposition of recalcitrant southern Democrats who opposed woman suffrage because it would mean enfranchising black women as well as white women.[69] The following day, January 9, Wilson invited Representatives John E. Raker (D-Calif.) and Edward D. Taylor (D-Colo.), along with a committee of ten of their colleagues to the White House. Nine of the congressmen had been present for the previous House vote in January 1915, and six of the nine had voted against the woman suffrage measure.[70] Several of the congressmen had not yet decided how they would vote and they entered the Oval Office looking for some advice and direction from Wilson. In a surprisingly frank move, Wilson publicly acknowledged that he could "frankly and earnestly" advise them to vote for the federal amendment "as an act of right and justice,"[71] Suddenly, the suffrage amendment which only days before had been viewed as having dim prospects for adoption, became a certainty in Washington policital circles. Some observers predicted as high as a fifteen-vote safety margin.[72] When, on January 10, the votes were counted, the amendment had indeed passed, 274 to 136—exactly the two-thirds necessary for success. Significantly, all twelve of the congressmen who had met with Wilson two days earlier voted in favor of passage.[73]

Several publications including the *New York Times* and the *Washington Post* editorialized that success was due to Wilson's last-minute endorsement. The goal of the picketing campaign, indeed of the entire NWP/CU campaign since 1913, had been to convert Wilson to federal suffragism. The process had been a long one and the exact time when Wilson did become a convert to federal suffragism was arguable. For the NWP, however, Wilson's public endorsement of the amendment in January 1918 was crucial. Suffrage had reached a major turning point.[74]

Wilson, like many politicians, had the capacity to transform political necessity into personal advocacy. His wartime speeches indicate a growing awareness of the important role that women played in the war effort. Nevertheless, he viewed issues through the prism of the war and his perception of the political climate was shaped accordingly. Thus he was reluctant to take steps which he believed might upset his political base and possibly do damage to his influence as a wartime leader. For example, while he willingly acceded to NAW-

SA's request to issue a statement urging passage of the New York state referendum on suffrage in 1917, he nevertheless refused to accept the title of honorary president of the Men's League for Women's War Rights, founded in October 1917. "I would not dare to do this," Wilson explained. "If I did, I would be in for it in practically every state in the Union and you know what that might mean by way of weakening the whole of my influence."[75]

Wilson exercised great care in choosing which suffrage requests he would agree to honor. Without exception, the requests he agreed to were from NAWSA, since that was the organization that represented cooperation. But the most forceful steps that he took for instance in publicly supporting the House suffrage vote, were taken because of the pressures exerted by Alice Paul and the NWP. Maintaining that constant pressure on Wilson and the Congress, regardless of how unattractive or unpalatable, provided a sense of urgency, without which the drive for federal suffragism would have been prolonged.

The focus of the pressure campaign shifted in 1918. More emphasis was placed on advertising the fact that only a handful of votes stood in the way of passage of the amendment. Accordingly, Paul organized speaking tours all over the country.[76] Like the anti-Democratic party campaigns, it was not always clear to state workers that the speakers were having the intended effect. "I hope this is my last week here," Alice Henkle wrote back to NWP headquarters. "Kansas City is the limit, but I hope I am bringing something out of the chaos I found here. At least we have a lot of activity and that has stirred up the women to really take an interest."[77]

As a matter of fact, the NWP was pushing exactly the right buttons. "The women of the country are growing more disturbed over the situation. . . . The fact that we are failing to pick up the necessary two votes [in the Senate] . . . is creating the impression that we are not really trying. . . . The so-called Woman's Party is in active propaganda to discredit us," complained Elizabeth Bass, the head of the Democratic National Committee's Women's Division. Bass later complained that because of the criticism coming from the NWP and "all other women over the country," she had to have firt-hand knowledge of what the administration was doing or planned to do to counteract the charges. Still later, Bass reported that even NAWSA, "the

friendly Association," had "gently intimate[d] that if we do not take
the vote soon, the Republicans are going into the congressional campaigns and use the Democrat's delay as an issue."[78] From all quarters,
it seemed, from the NWP, from the DNC's Woman's Bureau, from
the women voters and citizens, and of course from the Republicans,
came the theme that Alice Paul and the NWP had so carefully culti-
vated: "It's all up to Woodrow Wilson now, anyway."[79]

Wilson, the personal advocate, now threw the weight of his office
behind the effort. Following the House vote, the bill went to the Senate where it faced stiffer opposition. In May, the Women's Division
of the Democratic National Committee submitted a list of six Democratic holdouts they believed that Wilson might be able to persuade.
He reported that he had spoken to each of them, to no avail, but that
he would try again.[80] Increasingly, Wilson's appeals tied the fate of
the war—and by implication, the fate of the world—to the suffrage
amendment. Writing to Senator Josiah O. Wolcott (D-Del.), Wilson
stated: "I am writing this letter on my own typewriter (notwithstanding a lame hand). . . . I am deeply anxious—the issues are so tremendous! They are so tremendous as to justify the ardent appeal for your
support."[81] To the unmoving Senator Christie Benet (D-S.C.) he appealed four times in writing and at least once in person.[82] And to Senator John K. Shields (D-Tenn.), Wilson wrote: "Not a little of the faith
which the rest of the world will repose in our sincere adherence to
democratic principles, will depend upon the action which the Senate
takes in this now critically important matter." When the Senator continued to resist, Wilson pursued the matter further, declaring that the
amendment was "an essential psychological element in the conduct of
the war."[83] On June 7, Wilson used the occasion of responding to a
letter from Carrie Chapman Catt to serve notice on the entire Senate.

The full and sincere democratic reconstruction of the world . . . will not have
been completely or adequately attained until women are admitted to the suffrage. The services of women during this supreme crisis of the world's history
have been of the most signal usefulness and distinction. The war could not
have been fought without them, nor its sacrifices endured. It is high time that
some part of our debt of gratitude to them should be acknowledged and paid,
and the only acknowledgement they ask is their admission to the suffrage. Can
we justly refuse it?[84]

When Senator Ollie M. James (D-Ky.) died in office, Wilson asked Kentucky Governor Augustus O. Stanley to appoint a prosuffrage replacement. The governor complied—he appointed himself.[85] Shortly before the scheduled vote, Wilson learned that Senator Robert L. Owen (D-Okla.), was about to leave Washington on an extended trip. He called Owen and persuaded the senator to postpone his departure until after the roll call.[86] In addition to the scores of letters, Wilson continued to schedule personal appointments with various Democratic senators, as well as suffragists, in an effort to coordinate activities as the date of the vote drew near.[87]

Despite the massive effort by Wilson, the vote in the Senate bogged down. Two postponements had already occurred, on May 10 and again on June 27. Alice Paul and members of the NWP, although unofficially *persona non grata* at the White House, continued to pursue their publicity campaign with the public and in the halls of Congress. They also solicited the assistance of influential political figures, some of whom, like Theodore Roosevelt, gave unstinting assistance, and some, like Herbert Hoover and William Howard Taft, who refused point blank.[88] After the second Senate postponement, Paul sent a delegation to call upon Senator Jones, the chairman of the Senate Woman Suffrage Committee. When, they wanted to know, would the Senate reschedule the vote? Jones told them that suffrage would not be placed on the Senate calendar again in the present session. Under the circumstances, Paul and Burns felt their only recourse was a resumption of the picketing campaign.[89]

A meeting was scheduled for Lafayette Park, across the street from the White House. Much to everyone's surprise and chagrin, authorities responded to the meeting by arresting forty-eight suffragists, some released unconditionally and others released on bail and ordered to return to stand trial at some later date when it could be ascertained what they were being charged with. It was a turn of events that left even the most cynical observers nonplussed. What could the administration hope to gain by acquiescing to the arrests after the terrible publicity attendant upon the Occoquan episode of nine months earlier? It was one more in a long line of gross mistakes made either knowingly or unknowingly in an effort to contain the suffrage demonstrations. Several women were sentenced to fifteen days in a facility that, in many ways, was worse than Occoquan because it had been closed down for years and only reopened to accommodate the suffrage prisoners. A hunger strike of five days' duration, amidst many protests from politicians and concerned citizens directed at the White House, resulted in the release of the prisoners.[90]

Finally, however, the administration seemed to find the least offensive way to handle the protests. Alice Paul received a notice from Colonel C. S. Ridley, Wilson's military aide, that the NWP would henceforth be granted permission to hold rallies in Lafayette Park.[91] "We . . . are very glad that our meetings are no longer to be interfered with," Paul responded immediately. "Because of the illness of so many of our members, due to their treatment in prison this last week, and with the necessity of caring for them at headquarters, we are planning to hold our next meeting a little later."[92] The administration had been forced to concede, for neither the first not the last time, under the weight of NWP pressure.

On September 16, Paul added yet a new twist to the NWP campaign. In Lafayette Park, they burned copies of Wilson's "war for democracy" speeches in urns, which they dubbed the "Watchfires of Freedom." The following day, September 17, Senator Jones announced that after careful reconsideration he was rescheduling the suffrage vote for late September. He vowed to keep it before the Senate until it passed.[93]

On Sunday, September 29, two days before the scheduled vote, Wilson's son-in-law, Secretary of the Treasury William Gibbs McAdoo, approached the President with a "desperate" plea. The latest vote tally still indicated a two-vote shortfall for the amendment. McAdoo suggested that Wilson personally address the Senate the next day. When Wilson questioned whether the Senate might resent such a move, McAdoo pointed out that even if he failed to persuade two senators to change their vote in favor of supporting the amendment, public opinion would be so stirred that additional prosuffrage senators would more than likely be elected in November, thus ensuring the amendment's passage by the next Congress.[94] Wilson also had in hand a letter from Carrie Chapman Catt, in which she warned:

If the Amendment fails, it will take the heart out of thousands of women, and it will be no solace to tell them 'it is coming.' It will arouse in them a just suspicion that men and women are not co-workers for world freedom, but that women are regarded as mere servitors, with no interest or rightful voice in the outcome.[95]

Last but not least, the ever-present Woman's Party with their continued demonstrations and speaking tours, added force to McAdoo's suggestion.

The following day, Wilson gave the Senate thirty minutes' notice before proceeding to the Capitol, accompanied by his entire official family save avowed antisuffragist, Secretary of State Robert Lansing. American Presidents rarely invoke their prerogative to address directly a body of Congress on an issue then pending before the Congress. Although his audience knew what Wilson intended to speak on, an air of tension nevertheless filled the august chamber as the President approached the podium. His speech was both eloquent and powerful. He began:

I regard the extension of suffrage to women as vitally essential to the successful prosecution of the great war of humanity in which we are engaged. . . . It is my duty to win the war and to ask you to remove every obstacle that stands in the way of winning it. . . . They [other nations] are looking to the great, powerful, famous democracy of the West to lead them to a new day for which they have long waited; and they think in their logical simplicity that democracy means that women shall play their part in affairs alongside men and upon an equal footing with them. . . . I tell you plainly as the Commander-in-Chief of our armies . . . that this measure is vital to the winning of the war. . . . It is vital to the right solutions which we must settle, and settle immediately. . . . The executive tasks of this war rest upon me. I ask that you lighten them and place in my hands instruments, spiritual instruments, which I do not now possess, which I sorely need and which I have daily to apologize for not being able to employ.[96]

Wilson did insist that "the voices of foolish and intemperate agitators do not reach me at all," lest anyone misinterpret his motives for addressing the Congress.[97] The disclaimer was understandable, but clearly the activities of the NWP had influenced his actions for several months. Even more significantly, in tying the success of the war and the reconstruction to follow to suffrage, Wilson vindicated and validated the war policy adopted by Alice Paul almost two years earlier. Raising the point in February 1917, the NWP had transformed suffrage into an issue of such monumental importance that its passage became imperative in order to maintain public trust in the integrity of the United States both at home and abroad. Nor was the issue of American intentions and integrity a concern only of suffragists. In August 1918, the *New Republic* reported that the American suffrage issue was raising fundamental questions among "English, French, German, and Russian radicals" who wondered if a "nation capable of such flagrant hypocrisy could not be equally capable of arming to safeguard the world for democracy and then using the resulting increase of power . . . for America 'über alles.' "[98] In the eyes of many, woman suffrage had become the measure of America's good intentions and trustworthiness in world affairs. Woodrow Wilson understood this when he agreed to address the Senate.

For all his effort, Wilson was barely out of the Senate chamber when Senator Oscar W. Underwood (D-Ala.) rose to speak against the amendment. The Senate vote, when it was taken the next day, was 62 in favor of the amendment, and 34 against the amendment—two votes shy of the necessary two-thirds majority.[99] Because of the potentially grave consequences that Wilson had enumerated in his speech, it was generally accepted that the two votes would not long stand in the way of success.[100] As McAdoo had predicted, the prosuffrage forces picked up an additional vote in the congressional election. In addition, there were several uncommitted freshmen senators from whom the final vote might be obtained.[101]

With the signing of the Armistice on November 11, 1918, Wilson's time was almost entirely occupied with world politics. Before leaving the country for the Paris Peace Conference, however, at Carrie Chapman Catt's request he did urge Congress to pass the federal suffrage amendment in his Annual Message of December 2, 1918.[102] The new Sixty-sixth Congress would not take up the issue until the following spring.

In the face of almost certain victory, Paul's forces might have wished that their redoubtable leader would use the intervening weeks to recoup their enormously depleted collective energies. Many NWP regulars were exhausted from the months of picketing, touring, speaking, pleading, begging, imprisonment, hunger striking, and forced feedings. But for Paul, the only time to rest would be after the last vote had been counted, the last state ratified, and the federal suffrage amendment added to the list of Constitutional amendments. In the weeks before the final vote, members of the NWP stalked the halls of Congress, ever mindful of weakening support here, a shaky vote there, and doggedly pursuing the uncommitted votes in both Houses. By May, suffrage forces expected the House to repass the amendment by an overwhelming majority. But in the Senate, where the rollcall was scheduled for June 4, every tally indicated they were still one vote short of victory. The key to victory, in Paul's judgment, lay in the hands of three newly elected and as yet uncommitted senators. One of them was William J. Harris (D-Ga.), a personal friend of Wilson's. Late in April, Paul sent her congressional liaison, Maud Younger, to discuss with prosuffrage Democrats—including Joe Tumulty—the possibility of persuading the President to use his influence with Harris, who was then vacationing in Italy.[103] On May 2, Tumulty wired Wilson that the situation was urgent. Wilson thereupon summoned the senator, who arrived in Paris on May 6. After consulting with Wilson, Harris immediately sent word that he would return to the United States at once in order to cast the decisive vote in favor of the amendment. Six days later, with the outcome now seemingly assured, a second uncommitted senator, Henry W. Keyes (R-N.H.), announced that he also would vote for in the affirmative.[104] Finally, on May 20, Wilson cabled yet another message to Congress: "Throughout all the world this long delayed extension of suffrage is looked for. I, for one, covet for our country the distinction of being among the first to act in this great reform."[105] One final senator, Frederick Hale (R-Maine), shifted his vote to the prosuffrage column, and on June 4, with little further debate, the Senate passed the Susan B. Anthony amendment by a vote of 56 to 25. Speaker of the House Frederick H. Gillett (R-Mass.) and Vice-President Thomas R. Marshall signed the joint resolution later that same afternoon.[106]

The ratification process took only fifteen months to accomplish. In part this was because state legislators knew that their constituents favored the measure. The success of the New York state referendum in November 1917 was only the most recent measure of public support. Moreover, the legislators were responding to a climate of opinion that equated equal suffrage with democracy. But rapid ratification succeeded in large measure for two important reasons. First, both the NWP and the NAWSA had excellent state organizations that immediately swung into action when the amendment was passed. Their lobbying techniques, honed to razor-sharpness on the national legislators, were now applied with equal vigor and results to the state legislators. And secondly, ratification was largely unhampered by antisuffrage opposition. All significant opposition melted away with passage of the amendment in Congress for good reason. When the suffrage amendment was reintroduced in Congress for the last time on May 21, 1919, an attempt was made to attach a seven-year ratification rider to the measure. Prosuffrage congressmen, recognizing the proposal for what it was—a last ditch effort by the antis to thwart ratification—roundly booed down the attempt. The leading antisuffragist spokeswoman, Mrs. James Wadsworth of New York, conceded that further opposition would be fruitless.[107]

But ratification was not without its questionable moments. During the fifteen months of work for ratification, Wilson was preoccupied with international treaty negotiations, debates with the Senate Foreign Relations Committee, and a strenuous western states campaign on behalf of the League of Nations—all of which helped to bring about his physical breakdown. On October 2, 1919, Wilson suffered a stroke which left his left side paralyzed. While convalescing, he sent messages to the legislatures of Kentucky, Oklahoma, West Virginia, Louisiana, Delaware, and North Carolina, urging them to ratify the amendment. In addition, he sent messages to the governors of all the southern states.[108]

By the summer of 1920, it seemed that ratification had stalled one state short of the necessary thirty-six required for success. Wilson interceded one last time with the Tennessee legislature. Both the NWP and NAWSA had made repeated appeals for the legislature, which was out of session, to reconvene and vote on the issue. Tennessee, everyone believed, was the state most likely to carry the amendment over the top. Appeals for special sessions went unanswered, however, and anxious suffragists from both factions turned to Wilson once again. "Our only hope lies in Washington," wired a Catt lieutenant in the field. "In Tennessee all swear by Woodrow Wilson. If he will but speak, Tennessee must yield." Wilson telegraphed Governor Albert H. Roberts, imploring him to call a special session of the legislature. His influence prevailed.[109] Tennessee's legislature met and engaged in heated debate for several days. On August 18, by one vote, Tennessee became the thirty-sixth state to ratify the Anthony amendment. On August 26, 1920, Secretary of State Bainbridge Colby signed the proclamation alone in his office, bringing to an end the historic crusade which had begun nearly one hundred years before.[110]

Among the congratulatory messages that Alice Paul and the NWP received after the Senate vote in June 1919, was one from Chief Justice Walter Clark of North Carolina:

Will you permit me to congratulate you upon the great triumph in which you have been so important a factor? There were politicians, and a large degree of public sentiment, which could only be won by the methods you adopted. . . . It is certain that, but for you, success would have been delayed for many years to come.[111]

Three months earlier, Representative Thaddeus H. Caraway (D-Ark.), had told Dora Lewis and Maud Younger that "all this agitation, the lobbying, the persistence never-ceasing, often to us men very irritating like grains of sand in the eyes, has nevertheless hastened your amendment by ten years."[112] Although these and other similar messages were gratifying to Paul and her colleagues in the NWP, she had never doubted the efficacy of their strategy. The NWP had succeeded in its goal of winning over the President's support of federal suffragism, and, as Paul had noted on January 10, 1918: "We knew that it [Wilson's support] and it alone would ensure our success. It means to us only one thing—victory."[113]

CHAPTER 9

From Equal Suffrage to Equal Rights

Winning the suffrage battle brought to a close an important chapter in the women's rights movement. Most women looked to ratification as the end of a long and costly, but ultimately rewarding, campaign. Since the 1890s, when the rationale for suffrage—for most women—shifted from an argument based on justice to one based on expediency, the ballot was seen more and more as a cure-all for society's ills. It was also seen as a cure-all for women's ills within that society. All suffragists were feminists in the broadest sense. But there was a demarcation between the "social feminists" and those who, for want of a better phrase, could be defined as "radical feminists."[1] The dividing line between the two groups tended to coincide with their allegience in the suffrage movement. Most of the older suffragists, although by no means all, were social feminists. Social feminists believed in woman's traditional role in society, that of mother and nurturer. For the social feminists, there existed an immutable difference between women and men that mitigated women's ability to lay claim to equality in the fullest sense of the word. Many social feminists had little desire fundamentally to alter sex roles as society defined them. Where equality could be obtained without endangering woman's place in society, the social feminists pursued it with vigor. For the social feminists, protective legislation for women in industry was a necessary safeguard without which women could not hope to compete in the marketplace. Social feminists thus desired equality insofar as it did not infringe upon their demands for protection for women. For the older suffragists in particular, the Nineteenth Amendment was a culmination of their goals, rather than a beginning. In their view, the Nineteenth Amendment provided the necessary tool with which to insure continuation of traditional roles, provide protection where necessary, and at the same time enable women to exert their "better" natures for the good of society.

The radical feminists, on the other hand, while not necessarily consciously seeking a fundamental change in the structure of society, were willing to accept that as part of their quest for equality. For the radicals, the focus of equality was not immediately clear. They took their cue from the original Declaration of Sentiments, which identified the areas in which women were placed at a disadvantage because of the way society was organized. They were concerned not only with women's status in the public sphere, but with their status in the private sphere as well. Many, like Doris Stevens, saw in the relationships between women and men—husbands, fathers, brothers, sons—the basic ingredient for feminist ideology.[2]

Radical feminists sympathized with and indeed championed many of the same causes espoused by the social feminists, but their views regarding equality inevitably placed them on a collision course with the social feminists. Radicals rejected the prevailing belief in woman's inferiority by virtue of her reproductive function and physical attributes. For them, biology was not destiny. Like their mentor, Elizabeth Cady Stanton, they believed that womanhood was the great fact, and wifehood and motherhood its incidents. Crystal Eastman clearly articulated the kind of fundamental change in society that the radicals sought. The problem of women's freedom, wrote Eastman, is

how to arrange the world so that women can be human beings, with a chance to exercise their infinitely varied gifts in infinitely varied ways, instead of being destined by the accident of their sex to one field of activity—housework and child-raising. And second, if and when they choose housework and child-raising to have that occupation recognized by the world as work, requiring a definite economic reward and not merely entitling the performer to be dependent on some man. . . . I can agree that women will never be great until they achieve a certain emotional freedom, a strong healthy egotism, and some unpersonal source of joy—that in this inner sense we cannot make women free by changing her economic status. What we can do, however, is to create conditions of outward freedom in which a free woman's soul can be born and grow. It is these outward conditions with which an organized feminist movement must concern itself."[3]

But the equality that the radicals sought could not be obtained solely through enactment of the Nineteenth Amendment, although that was a step along the path. What further steps had to be taken to insure eventual equality became the basis for much discussion among the NWP members in the months following ratification.

Even before the amendment was ratified, some women asked, "What next?" And many NWP members, because the party was organized solely to promote a federal equal suffrage amendment, asked, "What—if *anything*—next?" In July 1920, Alva Belmont raised the question at a meeting of the Executive Committee. Belmont suggested that the Executive Committee think about continuing the organization for the purpose of "obtain[ing] for women full equality with men in all phases of life, and mak[ing] them a power in the life of the state."[4] Belmont's proposal seemed simple enough on the surface. In truth, however, the issue was an extremely complex one. For one thing, not all—or even most—of the NWP members wanted immediately to pursue a new program. Most of the members were exhausted by the intensive eight-year-long campaign which they had participated in. These women wanted only to return to a less harried routine and to enjoy the fruits of their struggle to the extent that was possible. Some even felt that they had sacrificed enough for women's rights and were quite ready to turn over the reins to the next generation of women activists.[5] And some, like Lucy Burns, felt exhausted. "I don't want to do anything more," Burns declared. "I think we have done all this for women, and we have sacrificed everything we possessed for them, and now let them . . . fight for it now. I am not going to fight . . . any more."[6]

Whatever course Lucy Burns envisaged her life would take when she first left for Europe to pursue graduate studies more than a decade earlier, the expectation had surely been far different from the reality.

She, with Alice Paul, had coordinated on a day-by-day, hour-by-hour basis, the campaign to win the suffrage. She had organized in the states, helped to coordinate the vast picketing campaign, spent more time in prison than any other American suffragist, endured all the attendant horrors of such confinement, toured the country with the "Prison Special," and in every other way possible helped to secure the end that she and Alice Paul had discussed sitting on the tabletop in the London police station. Now she was exhausted, physically and emotionally. Burns' withdrawal as an activist was prompted not only by fatigue and a desire for a normal life, but by a bitterness as well toward those who had sat out the suffrage movement. She was convinced that single women had borne the cost of suffrage and that married women should now take up the gauntlet.[7] For reasons such as these, many women retired from the NWP or let their memberships lapse after ratification.[8]

While many of the rank-and-file resigned, most of the leaders of the organization did not question the desirability of continuing the party. To them it was self-evident that the NWP must continue to exist, with only its goal and specific program to be determined. At the first postratification meeting of the Executive Committee, this mood was quite evident. Those present at the meeting included Alice Paul, Lucy Burns, Alva Belmont, Doris Stevens, Dora Lewis, Charlotte Perkins Gilman, Crystal Eastman, Florence Kelley, Rheta Childe Dorr, and Harriot Stanton Blatch.

Belmont opened the discussion by reiterating her belief that the NWP ought to be continued as an organization dedicated to abolishing sex discrimination. Blatch, too, saw a "great need of a feminist force in the world," and warned against alliances with other political parties. She felt that the NWP ought to focus on such questions as the endowment of motherhood.[9] Florence Kelley, noting that there was legislation currently before the Congress that ought to receive the support of the NWP, saw a "sublime opportunity to appeal to the conscience of all the women of the world." Kelley argued that the moment ought not to be lost, since there was little guarantee that such favorable circumstances would recur. Gilman, while less enthusiastic about a party structure, did feel keenly that an organization representing "mass power" was desirable.[10]

Crystal Eastman presented the most fully developed set of proposals. Her program was a broad-based one that addressed such issues as occupational and economic independence for women, education, planned parenthood, and the endowment of motherhood. Eastman emphasized the necessity for an organization with an explicitly feminist program. Regardless of which political system women lived with, Eastman pointed out, "the feminist point of view would still have to be projected on society through the efforts of women as a sex." In her view, continuation of the NWP was crucial to the viable presence of a feminist perspective.[11]

Significantly, none of the social feminists at this meeting, like Florence Kelley, expressed any qualms about a possible incompatibility between pursuing complete equality for women and pursuing increased protective legislation for women workers in industry. But whether those present knew it or not, the ideas behind those two goals placed the proponents of each on a collision course that would have resounding effects on the women's movement.

Another question on which there was virtually unanimous agreement was Alice Paul's role in the future of the organization. Indeed, most of those present expressed their belief that any attempt to carry on as an organization would depend largely on Paul's willingness to continue the work.[12] Nor were the members of the Executive Committee the only ones who believed that Paul was necessary for the future of the NWP. "If you don't go on the Woman's Party will not go on, at least not the one we have known and want," wrote one member who expressed the view of many in the organization.[13]

Nevertheless, Paul was not ready to commit herself to another long-term endeavor, whatever it might be. For one thing, the NWP had a debt of $10,000 that had to be cleared off the books.[14] Her first duty, she believed, was to the party's creditors. Consequently, Paul and Maud Younger had agreed to take on the responsibility of raising the required sum to clear the accounts.[15] Then, too, Paul was as exhausted by the previous eight years as anyone else in the organization. She expressed the fear that she simply did not have the physical stamina to continue. During the suffrage years, the stress of running the NWP had resulted in several bouts of illness that required extended rest and/or hospitalization. And, although her health improved markedly in the weeks following ratification, she herself felt such "extreme fatigue" that she thought she could "hardly go any longer."[16]

Paul repeatedly asserted that her resolve to refrain from a new commitment was firm. But it is unlikely that she could ever have disassociated herself permanently from any new endeavor, even without the constant importuning of her followers. As one Washington reporter and friend of Paul observed:

Every other woman in Washington I can imagine without a cause. . . . Even over teacups I think of [Paul] as a political force, a will bound to express itself politically. . . . I remember a long talk we had in 1921 when she was searching her mind for the next plan to advance the freedom of women. She was overwhelmed by the setting up of the League of Nations, which she regarded as a close corporation for deciding the fate of women and of the people. . . . She burned with disgust for the inconsequential part women played in international politics.[17]

The reporter judged, accurately, that Paul was incapable of disentangling herself from the women's rights struggle and predicted that the indomitable Quaker would always be involved in that cause, either on the national or the international level. Paul's hesitancy in immediately taking on new commitments, then, provided her with both the time to renew her physical resources, settle old accounts, and to decide where she personally would be most useful in the women's rights movement.

The standard response, for a while, that Paul gave to those who asked her opinion about where the NWP ought to focus its efforts, was that she was "leaving it up to the women who will have to go on with the work if the organization continues, to decide what they would like to do."[18] She was, however, willing to accept one short-term commitment which, given her aversion to loose ends, allowed her to close the suffrage chapter of the women's movement with the kind of flourish and pageantry that was so satisfying to her. Plans were undertaken to hold a ceremony at the Capitol on February 15, 1921, the anniversary of Susan B. Anthony's birthdate.[19] Years before, a NAWSA committee had commissioned sculptress Adelaide Johnson to make busts of Lucretia Mott, Elizabeth Cady Stanton, and Susan B. Anthony, with the intention of presenting the statues to Congress for permanent placement in the Capitol. In the intervening years the project was placed on a back burner and gradually forgotten. Ida Husted Harper, a member of the original committee, in an effort to revive the project, later discussed the statuary with Carrie Chapman Catt when Catt became president of NAWSA. Catt opposed the idea, because, according to Harper, she believed the statues were too unattractive from an artistic standpoint. Nevertheless, she agreed that Harper should be the one to determine what, if anything, ought to be done. Paul had learned of the statues years before, and in 1920 she discussed the project with Harper. In May 1920, Harper agreed to turn the project over to Paul since no one else expressed any interest at all. The NWP Executive Committee voted to authorize an expenditure of $2,000 to Adelaide Johnson to finish the sculptures.[20] Now, Paul proposed to have the suffrage ceremony revolve around their presentation to Congress. It would be a fitting signature to the suffrage campaign and the idea received unanimous support from members of the Executive Committee.[21]

The Capitol ceremony was more than a celebration just for the NWP. Invitations were sent to every woman's organization in the country which had had anything to do with suffrage, inviting delegates to participate in the event. The ceremony would not only be an opportunity to commemorate their collective victory, but it would demonstrate as well the solidarity of the women's movement.[22]

At the same time, plans were drawn up to hold a national convention of the NWP in Washington after the Capitol ceremony. The convention would decide the future of the NWP. Consequently, discussions within the Executive Committee, expanded to include the National Advisory Committee and the State Chairman's Committee, took on greater urgency. The planners wanted to be able to present a set of recommendations to the convention delegates which they hoped would be acceptable and which would set the organization on its new course. By January 1921, the planners agreed in principle that the primary objective of the NWP would be equality for women. Significantly, they did not define "equality," but rather seemed willing to accept a mutually understood and commonly held—but unarticulated—presumption of what the word meant. The planners were more specific about the immediate focus for achieving their goal, however. The immediate goal would be the "removal of the legal disabilities of women." The organization, the planners determined, would "continue to work for that object until it is accomplished."[23]

Not all the planners were satisfied with this strategy. Some agreed with Edith Houghton Hooker, the Maryland chairwoman, that such a proposal was "too simple, too cold to arouse enthusiasm and obtain support from large numbers of women." It was imperative, Hooker insisted, that any proposal to remove legal disabilities had to be broadly interpreted to cover a variety of concerns including protectionism, birth control, marriage and divorce, child labor, and peace. The great fear, as Hooker perceived it, was that too many women would decide that they could no longer remain in the NWP if the organization chose to define too narrowly what it meant by "legal disabilities."[24]

Hooker's fears were not misplaced. The social feminists in the NWP wanted to use the vote to further very specific interests such as those enumerated by Hooker. The idea of adopting a program, the objective of which was something as vague as undefined "equality," in their view would waste the momentum that had built up and that had made this a propitious time to pursue more concrete objectives. Then, too, even some of the radicals, such as Sara Bard Field, were more eager to pursue different goals because they disagreed that legal inequality was the most important problem immediately confronting women. Field, for example, believed that world peace was the most important issue with which women ought to be concerned.[25] Thus is was clear even before the convention that there was great potential for dissension in the ranks of the party. Unanimity on a specific focus was unlikely at best, and unanimity on principle seemed more and more like wishful thinking on the part of the planners. With these considerations in mind, the planners began to prepare the majority report which would be presented to the delegates at the convention.

The Capitol ceremony took place on the evening of February 15, with representatives of more than 100 women's organizations gathered to observe and to participate. The organizations represented a broad spectrum of interests and included the General Federation of Women's Clubs, the National Business and Professional Women's League, the National Consumer's League, the Women's Christian Temperance Union, the Red Cross Nurses, the Housekeeper's Alliance, the Council of Jewish Women, the Women's Trade Union League, the United Daughters of the Confederacy, the Daughters of the American Revolution, and the Congress of Mothers and Parent-Teachers Association.[26] NAWSA, conspicuously absent, was the only major suffrage organization to refuse to send delegates to the ceremony.[27]

Jane Addams opened the ceremony with a brief welcoming speech that set the tone for the evening. "They [Stanton, Anthony, and Mott] represent not only to their own countrywomen but to women of every globe a new movement destined to become one of the historic movements of all time."[28] To Sara Bard Field fell the task of making the official presentation of the sculptures to Speaker of the House Francis H. Gillette, and of delivering the keynote speech. Her impassioned rhetoric produced an electricity that seemed to infuse the sculpted granite with life.

We commit to your keeping blood-red memories, alive and pulsing—the labor of these women by day and night; the daring attack on entrenched Custom and Superstition and formidable Institution; the defying of even that religious sanction which like a whitened sepulchre had been built about the rotting bones of woman's slavery; the gallant acceptance of the mysterious challenge to live a great life for others at the expense of self rather than a little life for self at the expense of others. . . . Mr. Speaker, I give you—Revolution![29]

It was an inspired speech, but more wish than reality, for Field's revolution would be a long time coming. In large measure, the unanimity demonstrated by the women at the Capitol rang down the curtain on the coalition of interests which had continued so long as women had a common, single, and easily identifiable goal, such as equal suffrage. Thereafter, the diversity of interests led to a fragmentation of the coalition that might have provided the basis for greater gains in the future. Immediately following the impressive ceremony, however, the consequences of the dissolved coalition were not at all apparent to most women, including many NWP delegates who looked forward with optimism to the three-day conference scheduled to convene the following morning.

In a special edition of *The Suffragist*, available to those attending the convention, Paul wrote the lead editorial. She reminded her readers about the Seneca Falls Woman's Bill of Rights of 1848. The Bill of Rights, said Paul, demanded not only the vote for women—that was just one of a number of issues which the women's rights pioneers believed they had to address. Paul pointed out that the Bill of Rights also demanded equality for women with men and the removal of the disabilities which kept women in the position of second-class citizens, both legally and socially. In Paul's view, the vote was important, but it was not sufficient to achieve complete equality between the sexes. The danger, she warned, was that "because of a great victory, women will believe that their whole struggle for independence is ended. They still have far to go." She added, "It is for the woman's Party to decide whether there is any way in which it can serve in the struggle which lies ahead to remove the remaining forms of woman's subordination."[30]

The editorial struck the theme that would be reiterated throughout the convention by the NWP leaders: equality. And Paul, in her opening address on February 16, flung down the challenge to which the 700 delegates and alternates present seemed eager to respond.[31] The NWP must decide, Paul proclaimed, "whether this organization which has battled for eight years for the political freedom of women, shall . . . furl its banner forever, or whether it shall fling it forth on a new battle front."[32] With each reference to equality, the applause and cheers of the audience rolled like waves across the vast convention hall. Clearly, the theme struck a resonant chord in almost all the delegates.

Ample time was provided during the proceedings for minority recommendations and discussions. These included a minority report which proposed that the immediate goal for the NWP ought to be disarmament and peace. After a lengthy discussion, it was voted down. As Elizabeth Rogers later explained, women needed greater power before they could reasonably expect to have an impact on disarmament or war.[33] Crystal Eastman also presented her report recommending a program similar to the one that she had presented to the Executive Committee in September 1920. This proposal, too, was subjected to extensive debate before the delegates voted two-to-one against adoption. The major argument against the Eastman plan was that the specificity of the proposal would limit the scope of the organization.[34]

Representatives of several political parties who had applied for speaking time at the convention appealed to the delegates to work *with* their parties rather than to continue as an independent organization.

"Political campaigns waged upon sex antagonisms is unthinkable," argued Senator Augustus O. Stanley (D-Ky.). "Woman will find her true mission not in the creation of a separate organization but by making both of the old parties better." Simeon Fess, the chairman of the Republican Congressional Committee, declared that "women should counsel, not disturb." Needless to say, Fess, who urged the women to align themselves with the Republican party, did not further his cause with his characterization of the NWP as "disturbers." Similar appeals, although made with considerable more tact, were put forth by Meyer London for the Socialists and J.A.H. Hopkins, speaking for the Progressive alliance, the Committee of Forty-Eight.[35] The delegates were intent on retaining their independence, however, and all such appeals fell on deaf ears.

Delegates also heard from a number of representatives from social service organizations, including Margaret Wilson, Julia Lathrop of the Department of Labor's Children's Bureau, Mary Anderson of the Department of Labor's Woman's Bureau, Florence Kelley of the Consumer's League, Fannie (Mrs. Henry) Garrison Villard of the Woman's Peace Society, and Ethel Smith and Ellis York, both speaking for the Woman's Trade Union League. With the exception of Florence Kelley, no one from an organization representing working women particularly emphasized protective legislation. Kelley, on the other hand, represented the first shot fired in the disagreement over the protective legislation issue that would split the women's movement for more than two decades. Women had to be protected, Kelley asserted, whether they "demanded it for themselves or not."[36] At the time, however, no one recognized the depth of division that would develop over this issue and in any case most delegates were in accord with Mary Winsor, who cautioned: "Don't let's get respectable. The uplift organizations have always been ready to urge us to serve others and subordinate ourselves. I wish to say that before you can serve, you must have power."[37]

The majority resolution was presented to the convention on the final day by the Minnesota state chairwoman, Sarah Colvin. It recommended that the "immediate work of the new organization be the removal of the legal disabilities of women." In a reference to the League of Nations, the resolution also recommended that the NWP work for

equality in that organization as well. Finally, the resolution recommended that the NWP's Executive Committee be allowed the freedom
to pursue whatever program it deemed advisable to implement the spirit
and intent of the convention.[38]

The delegates voted overwhelmingly to accept the majority resolution. Thus, the old NWP, the charter of which specifically limited the
organization to working solely for suffrage, was disbanded. In its place
a new organization, retaining the same name, was immediately organized. The purpose of the new NWP was declared to be equal rights
for women, with the immediate concentration to be the removal of all
legal disabilities. "If," as the *New York Times* observed, "there were
those present who did not believe in the battle cry [of equal rights]
they remained quiet, for they were in the minority."[39]

In a situation reminiscent of the suffrage days, criticism of the NWP
convention of 1921 and disgruntlement over the decisions made by the
delegates began to surface almost immediately. Freda Kirchwey of the
Nation, charged that the leaders of the NWP were racist and out of
touch, and that they did not allow for adequate discussion of the issue.[40] Sarah Colvin, who had presented the majority report, later
claimed, "I have never seen a large crowd so thoroughly deflated as
this one."[41] Emma Wold likened the delegates to being in the "condition of men 'the morning after.' Some of us wish the outcome . . .
had been different."[42] And Florence Kelley criticized the NWP leadership for being totally unconcerned about the problems of working
women.[43] There was a measure of truth in all these criticisms, for they
were all related to a single issue—Alice Paul's desire to bid farewell to
her party in an atmosphere free of dissension and discord. But on the
whole, the records and proceedings of the convention, as well as the
press reports and the response of many more of the delegates who
participated in the convention, contradict the seriousness of the charges
and criticisms. Freda Kirchwey's charge that black women delegates
were refused speaking time was partially true. Black women had repeatedly requested an opportunity to speak to the delegates along with
the other social service organization speakers. But Alice Paul had decided that the black women were "spoilers" and tried to brush them
off. In fact, the black women did get an opportunity to speak during
the convention, although they certainly were not given the coveted spots

accorded to the likes of the Kelleys, Lathrops, and Wilsons. Charges that all minority reports were given short shrift were also partially true and equally distorted. The three-day convention did not allow for open-ended discussion of the various proposals, to be sure, but advocates of minority positions were certainly allowed to voice their opinions.[44] The criticisms, nevertheless, provided graphic evidence that the NWP would have difficulty uniting women for equal rights to the degree that they had been united for suffrage.

The new Executive Committee was chaired by Elsie Hill. Alice Paul, true to her word, elected to "retire" from the NWP. More accurately, Paul took a leave of absence. In the weeks preceding the Capitol ceremony and the NWP convention, Paul had decided that, after the old debts were cleared away, she was going to attend law school. If she was going to pursue the quest for equal rights, Paul reasoned, she had better be well prepared. And, in her view, adequate preparation included a thorough knowledge of precisely what the law was.[45]

Despite the overwhelming vote of support for the equal rights amendment expressed by the convention delegates, it quickly became clear that the NWP was the only organization to advocate such a measure. When the Executive Committee began drawing up a blanket equal rights amendment for the states, as well as a federal equal rights amendment, the extent of the opposition began to surface. The most vociferous opponents focused their opposition on the issue of protective legislation. It was a legitimate issue and the resistance to equal rights on the part of the protective legislationists should not have come as any great surprise. But the bitterness that the protectionists exhibited against the equal rights advocates was surprising. Convinced that equal rights would undo the work of decades in securing protection for women in industry, Florence Kelley, for example, came to perceive her one-time ally Alice Paul as a "fiend" whose only purpose was to hinder the women's movement and undo twenty years of labor legislation.[46] Unfortunately, this characterization which was applied to the NWP as a whole as well as to Paul specifically, fit all too well with the image the NWP had developed among many women during the suffrage campaign. The party had to combat its image as elitist and as an intemperate troublemaker—an image that NAWSA, in large measure, had helped to forge.

From its founding as an organization, the NWP had to contend with constant attacks by NAWSA. Not only did NAWSA disagree with the NWP tactics, but it consistently questioned the motives of the party and its leadership as well. When the NWP picketers were denied their civil liberties during the First World War, NAWSA responded by disassociating itself even further from the militant wing of the woman's movement. NAWSA asserted repeatedly that the NWP did not represent real suffrage feeling and they disavowed any responsibility for the militants. By its silence, NAWSA lent its assent to the treatment accorded the picket prisoners at the hands of the authorities. Both the Wilson administration and the politicians in Congress were quick to point to the circumspect NAWSA as the quintessential example of American womanhood, which, by its work within the system and by its unflagging patriotism during the war, had demonstrated that women deserved equal suffrage. Response to the activities of the NWP was more ambivalent than NAWSA liked to see. In particular, the prison episodes were not appreciated by most Americans, who viewed the actions of the government as heavy-handed at best, and barbaric at worst. Nevertheless, the body of opinion that built up, encouraged by both NAWSA and the political and civil authorities, produced a residual feeling of mistrust towards the NWP in the minds of many Americans, including women. Most women overlooked the crucial role played by Paul's NWP in gaining suffrage. The fact that Paul succeeded in tying the fate of the war and postwar reconstruction to the fate of suffrage so that Wilson had no other choice but strongly to support a federal amendment was, frankly, lost on most Americans. *How* suffrage had been won was less important than the fact that victory had been secured. And, because the mechanics of the suffrage victory were either not understood or ignored, it was all the easier to accept the conventional wisdom that laid all the credit for victory at NAWSA's doorstep. It was an injustice to the women's movement. Women had taken control of their own destinies, had forced the issue, and had won a resounding victory. By downplaying or negating the importance of that element of the suffrage campaign, the probability that women would recognize and use the power they now had, was dramatically decreased. The criticisms of the protective legislationists—the merits of their cause notwithstanding—placed the NWP once again at the center of a conflict which pitted it against virtually every other women's organization. In the circumstances, women tended to accept the pronouncements of the protective legislationists that equal rights would not be beneficial.

Armed with the mandate provided by the convention delegates, the Executive Committee convened a meeting at Seneca Falls, New York, on the seventy-fifth anniversary of the first Seneca Falls Convention. Alice Paul wrote and presented to the convention the new amendment which quickly became known as the Equal Rights Amendment.[47] It was introduced in Congress for the first time in December 1923. The amendment, which instantly became known as the Lucretia Mott amendment, read: "Men and women shall have equal rights throughout the United States and every place subject to its jurisdiction. Congress shall have the power to enforce this article by appropriate legislation."[48] It was a simple and straightforward measure, calculated to avoid entanglements in the myriad issues that equal rights touched upon. Like Crystal Eastman, Alice Paul was well aware that an equal rights amendment, in and of itself, would not automatically insure equality for women. Economics, Paul believed, fundamentally was at the heart of the matter. "The real fight for equality can never be won in legislatures. . . . Women have an economic fight to win. . . . Political forms crystallize long after economic power has established its pattern."[49] Nevertheless, an equal rights amendment would be a major hurdle in achieving equality, as Paul well knew.

The alarm sounded by Florence Kelley during the convention quickly became a call to arms, once the equal rights amendment was introduced in Congress. Lines were firmly drawn, as those who, in early postratification discussions, had believed that the protectionists and the equal righters could accommodate one another, soon realized the degree to which the two positions were at odds. Both sides believed they were right and, indeed, the protectionists had been right in the past and the equal righters would be right in the future. But for the present, each side exhibited a blindness to its moment in history that prevented the gains for women that opportunity had placed in their paths. Compromise would have allowed women to strengthen their ranks and consolidate their new power. In this way, women in the 1920s, in the short run, could have preserved the gains made by them over the past two decades—including their coalition of special interests—that, in the long run, would have provided the foundation to launch an effective equal rights campaign supported by a majority. Since the majority was not ready to embrace such a "radical" idea, they fell in behind the protectionists in support of goals and ideals that seemed both more manageable and more desirable. Neither side considered compromise a really viable solution.

If the NWP had any illusions about the extent to which they were alone on their limb, those illusions were shattered in the course of testimony before a House Judiciary Committee hearing on equal rights in 1925. The NWP was invited to testify, along with representatives from other major women's organizations. In the course of the three-day hearing, it became clear that the NWP was the sole group advocating passage of an equal rights amendment. Congressmen hearing the evidence were persuaded that the amendment would not be as vigorously sought after as the suffrage amendment had been.[50] It also helped to convince Paul that the first task of the NWP would be to secure the support of other women's groups before the party attempted to launch a truly national campaign for equal rights.[51]

Throughout the decade of the 1920s, the NWP worked on two fronts. The organization undertook a massive information-gathering program in the states. In conjunction with their avowed purpose to remove the legal disabilities against women, individual state studies were conducted which ultimately produced a series of reports unique in scope and detail. The studies examined the legal position of women in individual states in areas covering marriage, divorce, custody, work, education, family planning, and career.[52]

The second front, perceived as the more pressing, was to meet the protectionists head-on in an effort to reveal the fundamental inadequacy of discriminatory legislation, regardless of on whose behalf it was passed. It was to that end that Paul—now fully back in the fray—lobbied to get NWP representatives on an investigative panel being formed under the direction of Mary Anderson, the head of the Department of Labor's Women's Bureau. The advisory committee was organized at the request of the Women's Industrial Conference, which met in January 1926.[53] The Conference, mindful of the debate raging between equal righters and protectionists, promoted the Women's

Bureau's "comprehensive investigation of all the special laws regulating the employment of women to determine their effects." The hope was that such an inquiry would answer for once and all the question of whether protective legislation had helped or hindered women workers.[54] (In view of the appointment of three NWP representatives, it is ironic that the Conference program committee refused to allow members of the NWP to speak at the meeting.)[55]

Mary Anderson was hardly an advocate of equal rights, yet in an effort to provide "well rounded advice" on the investigation, she appointed three members of the NWP to the Advisory Committee: Alice Paul, Doris Stevens (now Mrs. Dudley Field Malone), and Maud Younger, whose credentials as a labor leader in California were well regarded. The Advisory Committee was rounded out with Sara Conboy of the American Federation of Labor, Mabel Leslie from the Women's Trade Union League, and Maud Wood Park, the Legislative Counsellor of the National League of Women Voters.[56]

From the start, the Advisory Committee meetings were torn by strife and tension. The three pro-protectionists were convinced that Paul, Stevens, and Younger were concerned with promoting the cause of the NWP and not with conducting a objective inquiry. At issue was the form the investigation would take. The protectionists favored a "technical study by experts and by scientific methods." The NWP sought a series of public hearings.[57] After four stormy meetings dominated by increasingly bitter acrimony, Sara Conboy, Maud Wood Park, and Mabel Leslie resigned in protest, charging that the NWP members had made serious inquiry impossible. According to the Women's Bureau press releases, however, the NWP had agreed to an investigation conducted by a team of technical experts, which included Mary Van Kleeck, Director of the Department of Industrial Studies of the Russell Sage Foundation, Mrs. Frank P. Gilbreth, an industrial engineer (who later wrote the immensely popular *Cheaper By The Dozen*), and Dr. Charles P. Neill, a former Commissioner of Labor of the United States.[58] By this time, the antagonisms had become intensely personal between members of the Advisory Committee, however, rendering continued meetings useless. Sara Conboy's parting shot at Alice Paul and the other NWP committee members was to note that "my experience with the National Woman's Party has shown me that it is composed mostly of women who never knew what it meant to work a day in their lives."[59]

Such criticisms, ill-informed as they were, only served to widen the gap between the NWP and the rest of the women in the country. Alice Paul attempted a show of bravado in the face of the deteriorating situation when she claimed that the resignation of the prolabor people left her "delighted." She went on to assert:

[The] Women's Bureau will now undoubtedly serve a more useful purpose from the point of view of working women than ever before. The attitude of the American Federation of Labor towards women in industry is well known. . . . The National Woman's Party is the one group in this country which stands for giving working women the same chance in industry as the working men and for basing labor legislation upon the job, and not upon the sex of the worker."[60]

With the Advisory Committee a shambles, Mary Anderson announced that future meetings would undoubtedly be fruitless, and therefore all scheduled meetings were indefinitely postponed. At the same time, Anderson noted that the Investigative Committee would proceed with its inquiry "according to the usual methods of the Department and its findings will be available for use by all those, of whatever opinion, who are desirous of securing the facts on this subject."[61]

The makeup of the investigating committee predetermined that the questions asked would elicit responses which would promote the value of protective legislation. When, in November 1928, the findings were released to the public, the report stated unequivocally that protectionism had indeed proved beneficial to women workers. It was not a case of the data being falsified in order to fit a popularly held set of values, but simply that the investigation was carried out along fairly narrow lines of inquiry that eliminated a wider range of responses. The investigators were acting in good faith in conducting an objective inquiry as they perceived it.

The report, entitled "Effects of Special Legislation on Women's Work," noted that there were 8.5 million women employed in American industry, but that only one-third were covered by special labor laws. "In general," the report stated, "the regulatory hour laws as applied to women engaged in the manufacturing processes of industry do not handicap the women, but serve to regulate employment, and to establish the accepted standards of modern, efficient, industrial management." The report also noted that "when applied to specific occupations . . . the regulatory legislation in a few instances has been a handicap to women." Such instances were relatively minor, however, and the conclusion was that legislation helped not only women workers, but that it "raise[d] the standards of working conditions of their male fellow employees."[62]

The report, expected although it was, took what little wind that remained out of the sails of the NWP's equal rights campaign. The organization continued to work on under Paul's direction, but the protective legislationists had clearly won the argument for the time being. And, with the onset of national and then world depression the following year, there was little that Paul could do except hold the ground already won. Even that, in the dark days of the depression, proved too difficult a task at times.[63]

Epilogue

For the remainder of her life, Alice Paul was a prime mover in the equal rights movement. But increasingly, her single-minded strategy in pursuing equal rights alienated colleagues within her own party as well as those outside. Doris Stevens Malone and Sara Bard Field, for example, over time developed strong and outspoken disdain for the tenacity which they had heretofore seen as a positive characteristic in the suffrage days. Paul's tactics fueled a growing discontent, with now younger NWP members asserting that the veteran leader had grown power-hungry, unreasonable, and reactionary. The discontent finally erupted into an open schism in 1947 when Anna Kelton Wiley challenged Paul's hand-picked successor, Anita Pollitzer, for leadership of the party. For several months, both the Wiley and the Pollitzer factions claimed legitimate leadership of the NWP. Even charges of misuse of party funds by Paul were bandied about, forcing the once revered leader to deny the accusations. The split eventually healed and the two groups once again were able to work together, but Paul's influence in the party was greatly diminished.

Nevertheless, she continued to devote her full energies to equal rights. Thanks to her, by the end of the 1940s, most major women's organizations had been converted to the need for a federal equal rights amendment. Then, too, major public figures like Eleanor Roosevelt, long a staunch protective legislation advocate, became converts to equal rights for women. Roosevelt was responsible for incorporating this sentiment into the United Nations Human Rights Charter after World War II, thus helping to persuade many of the Women's Bureau holdouts of the amendment's desirability. The last major holdout, the League of Women Voters, came around in 1959.

With the resurgence of the women's movement at about the same time, equal rights became a rallying cry in much the say way that equal suffrage had fifty years earlier. Paul lived to see the United States Congress pass an ERA amendment, and the nonagenarian jumped right into the campaign for ratification. She died in 1978, convinced that the remaining three states necessary for ratification would be won over and that equal rights would become a reality. Although Alice Paul's ambition has yet to be realized, she did, by dint of her unrelenting efforts, make equal rights a paramount political, social, and economic issue within her party and across her country.

The National Woman's Party remained, for many years, the lone organization with the vision to recognize the importance to women of a federal equal rights amendment. Paul and the NWP were not always on target in their timing, although they were more often right than wrong. By entering the equal suffrage campaign when she did, Paul helped to win the suffrage after a battle that had been waged for seventy years. Since hers was the only organization in the 1920s to perceive of equal rights as the unifying issue around which women could build a new and more powerful coalition, the struggle for equal rights was destined to last at least as long.

Appendix I

Text of the Nineteenth Amendment (Susan B. Anthony Amendment)
August 26, 1920

Article—Section 1. The right of citizens of the United States to vote shall not be denied or abridged by the United States or by any State on account of sex.

Section 2. Congress shall have power, by appropriate legislation, to enforce the provisions of this article.

Text of the Shafroth Amendment (Introduced March 2, 1914)

Section 1. Whenever any number of legal voters of any State to a number exceeding eight per cent of the number of legal voters voting at the last preceeding General Election held in such State shall petition for the submission to the legal voters of said State of the question whether women shall have equal rights with men in respect to voting at all elections to be held in such State, such question shall be so submitted; and, if upon such submission, a majority of the legal voters of the State voting on the question shall vote in favor of granting to women such equal rights, the same shall thereupon be deemed established, anything in the constitution or laws of such State to the contrary notwithstanding.

Text of the Equal Rights Amendment

Version 1 (Written and submitted for approval by Alice Paul at the Seneca Falls meeting, 1923): Men and women shall have equal rights throughout the United States and every place subject to its jurisdiction.

Version 2 (Written and submitted for approval by Alice Paul to members of the Senate Judiciary Committee, 1943):

Equality of rights under the law shall not be denied or abridged by the United States or by any State on account of sex.

Appendix II

Legislative History of the Nineteenth Amendment

| 1875 | Drafted by Susan B. Anthony |
| January 10, 1878 | Introduced by Senator A.A. Sargent |

Reported From Committee

Senate		House	
1878	Adverse majority		
1879	Favorable majority		
1882	Favorable majority, adverse minority		
		1883	Favorable majority
1884	Favorable majority, adverse minority	1884	Adverse majority, favorable minority
1886	Favorable majority	1886	Favorable minority
1890	Favorable majority	1890	Favorable majority
1892	Favorable majority, adverse minority	1894	Adverse majority
		1914	No recommendation
1896	Adverse majority	1916	No recommendation
1913	Favorable majority		

1914   Favorable majority

1917   Favorable majority

1919   Unanimously
         favorable

1917   No recommendation
1918   Favorable majority
1919   Favorable majority

Brought to Vote

January 25, 1887:(Senate):	Yeas: 16 Nays: 34 Absent: 25
March 19, 1914 (Senate):	Yeas: 35 Nays: 34
January 12, 1915 (House):	Yeas: 174 Nays: 204
January 10, 1918 (House):	Yeas: 274 Nays: 136
October 1, 1918 (Senate):	Yeas: 54 Nays: 30
February 10, 1919 (Senate):	Yeas: 55 Nays: 29
May 21, 1919 (House):	Yeas: 304 Nays: 89
June 4, 1919 (Senate):	Yeas: 56 Nays: 25

Notes

INTRODUCTION

1. Conversations With Alice Paul: Woman Suffrage and the Equal Rights Amendment. Interview by Amelia Frye, 1972–73, Suffragists Oral History Project, Bancroft Library, University of California at Berkeley (1976), p. 327 (hereafter: Paul Interview).

2. Ray Stannard Baker and William S. Dodd, eds., *The Public Papers of Woodrow Wilson* (1925–1927), V, pp. 264–267.

3. Max Weber, *The Sociology of Religion*, London: Methuen (1965), pp. 45–59.

4. Inez Haynes Irwin, *Up Hill With Banners Flying*, Penobscot, Maine: Traversity Press (1964), p. 26.

5. See, for example, newspaper coverage in the *New York Times*, March 4, 5, 6, 1913.

6. *New York Times*, June 23 and July 7 and 8, 1917; see also, *Washington Post*, June 23 and 24, and July 7, 1917.

7. See, for example. Aileen Kraditor, *Ideas of the Woman Suffrage Movement, 1890–1920*, New York: Anchor Books (1971); Eleanor Flexner, *Century of Struggle: The Woman's Right Movement in the United States*, rev. ed., Cambridge: Belknap Press of Harvard University Press (1975); and Anne Firor Scott and Andrew Scott, eds., *One Half the People: The Fight for Woman Suffrage*, Philadelphia: Lippincott (1975).

8. Foremost among historians who apply this interpretation to Paul is William O'Neill, *Everyone Was Brave, The Rise and Fall of Feminism in America*, Chicago: Quadrangle Books (1969); and *The Woman Movement: Feminism in the United States and England*, Chicago: Quadrangle 1969; and Robert Riegel, *American Feminists*, Lawrence, Kans.: University of Kansas Press (1963).

9. S. N. Eisenstadt, ed., *Max Weber On Charisma and Institution Building*, Chicago: University of Chicago Press (1968).

10. Robert Wiebe, *The Search for Order 1877–1920*, New York: Hill and Wang (1967).

11. In her interview with Amelia Frye, Paul, on several occasions, expressed wonderment over this fact. She claimed not to understand, for example, the reason why the Pankhursts singled her out of the hundreds of WSPU (Women's Social and Political

Union) members and invested in her a degree of responsibility. She was inclined to attribute it more to the fact that she was an American and therefore more noticeable, than to the fact that her talents were such that she drew people to her almost effortlessly.

12. *Biographical Cyclopedia of American Women*, vol. 1 (New York: The Halvord Publishing Co., 1924–1928), p. 123.

13. Rebecca Hourwich Reyher to Amelia Fye, Rebecca Hourwich Reyher: Search and Struggle for Equality and Independence, Suffragists Oral History Project, Bancroft Library, University of California (1977), pp. 49–50 (hereafter: Reyher Interview).

14. Paul Interview, p. 189.

15. Ibid., pp. 183–189.

16. Ibid., p. 11.

17. Mabel Vernon, "Speaker for Suffrage and Petitioner for Peace," Interview conducted by Amelia R. Frye (1972–1973), Suffragists Oral History Project, University of California at Berkeley (1976), pp. 157–158 (hereafter: Vernon Interview); see also, Freda Kirchwey, "Alice Paul Pulls the Strings," *The Nation*, CXII (March 1921), p. 332.

18. Phyllis Chesler, *Women and Madness*, Garden City, N.Y.: Doubleday (1972), pp. 299–300.

19. Inez Haynes Irwin, *The Story of the Woman's Party*, New York: Harcourt, Brace (1921), pp. 14–15.

20. Paul Interview, p. 110.

21. Ibid., pp. 267–272.

22. Ibid., p. 250.

23. Carroll Smith-Rosenberg, "The Female World of Love and Ritual: The Relations Between Women in Nineteenth-Century America," in Nancy Cott and Elizabeth Pleck, eds., *A Heritage of Her Own*, New York: Simon & Schuster (1979), pp. 311–342; see also, Blanche Weisen Cook, "Female Support Networks and Political Activism: Lillian Wald, Crystal Eastman, and Emma Goldman," *Ibid.*, pp. 412–444.

24. Reyher Interview, pp. 65–66.

25. Dora Lewis to Alice Paul, July 14, 1916; Paul to Lewis, July 25, 1916, Papers of the National Woman's Party, Library of Congress, Washington, D.C. (hereafter cited as NWP Papers).

26. Paul Interview, pp. 195–196.

27. Ibid., p. 198.

28. Ellen DuBois, *Feminism and Suffrage: The Emergence of an Independent Women's Movement in America, 1848–1869*, Ithaca: Cornell University Press (1978), pp. 15–20.

29. Susan B. Anthony, quoted in Doris Stevens, *Jailed for Freedom*, New York: Boni & Liveright (1920), p. xiii.

CHAPTER 1

1. The term "New Suffragists" has little to do with age, although it is true that the National Woman's Party leadership was generally younger than that of NAWSA. It is, rather, a way of distinguishing between that generation of suffragists who adhered to the state-by-state method of campaigning, and those who supported federal suffragism and were willing to employ militant tactics to achieve that end.

2. Thomas Woody, *A History of Women's Education in the United States*, 2 vols., New

York: Science Press (1929); Mary Caroline Crawford, *The College Girl of America and the Institutions Which Make Her What She Is*, Boston: L. C. Page (1905); Lynn Gordon, "Women with Missions: Female Education in the Progressive Era," Ph.D. Dissertation, unpublished, University of Chicago (1980); Sheila Rothman, *Woman's Proper Place: A History of Changing Ideas and Practices, 1870 to the Present*, New York: Basic Books (1978).

3. Rothman, *Woman's Proper Place*; Barbara Kuhn Campbell, *The "Liberated" Woman of 1914, Prominent Women in the Progressive Era*, UMI Research Press (1979); Joseph A. Hill, *Women in Gainful Occupations 1870–1920*, Census Monographs, IX, New York and London, Johnson Reprints (1972); Jennie Croly, *The History of the Woman's Club Movement in America*, New York: Henry G. Allen (1898).

4. Elizabeth Cady Stanton, et al., eds., *The History of Woman Suffrage*, New York: Foster and Wells, 1881–1922, I, p. 70.

5. Kraditor, *Ideas of the Woman Suffrage Movement*, pp. 43–45.

6. National American Woman Suffrage Association, *Victory! How Women Won It*, A Centennial Symposium 1840–1940, New York: H. W. Wilson (1940), pp. 73–74.

7. *History of Woman Suffrage*, I, pp. 310–311.

8. Maud Wood Park, *Front Door Lobby*, Boston: Beacon Press (1960), pp. 1–8.

9. Harriot Stanton Blatch and Alma Lutz, *Challenging Years: The Memoirs of Harriot Stanton Blatch*, New York: G. P. Putnam (1940), pp. 91–128.

10. Caroline Katzenstein, *Lifting the Curtain, The State and National Woman Suffrage Campaigns in Pennsylvania as I Saw Them*, Philadelphia: Dorrance (1955), pp. 168–180.

11. Lydia Kingsmill Commander to Alice Park Lock, June 2, 1908, Alice Park Lock Correspondence, Susan B. Anthony Memorial Collection, Huntington Library.

12. Several full-length studies focus on NAWSA as the preeminent suffrage organization of the time, and discuss in detail the methods it employed. See, for example, Eleanor Flexner, *Century of Struggle: The Women's Right Movement in the United States*, revised ed., Cambridge: Belknap Press of Harvard University Press (1975); Kraditor, *Ideas of the Woman Suffrage Movement*; NAWSA, *Victory! How Women Won It*; Mary Gray Peck, *Carrie Chapman Catt, A Biography*, New York: Octagon Books (1975); Carrie Chapman Catt and Nettie Rogers Shuler, *Woman Suffrage and Politics, The Inner Story of the Suffrage Movement*, New York: Charles Scribner's (1926); Park, *Front Door Lobby*; O'Neill, *Everyone Was Brave*.

13. Stanton, et al., eds., *History of Woman Suffrage*, V, p. 61.

14. Alva Belmont to Mrs. William M. Irvine, Treasurer, New York State Woman Suffrage Association, February 18, 1910; and Harriot May Mills et al., to Alva Belmont, August 10, 1911, NWP Papers.

15. Stanton, et al., eds., *History of Woman Suffrage*, V, Appendix to Chapter X, "Statement by Mrs. Carrie Chapman Catt at Senate Hearings in 1910," pp. 745–746.

16. Irwin, *Story of the Woman's Party*, p. 19; see also, Katzenstein, *Lifting the Curtain*, p. 174.

17. Irwin, *The Story of the Woman's Party*, p. 19; Katzenstein, *Lifting the Curtain*, p. 176.

18. Full suffrage states as of November 1912 were: Wyoming (1890; territory 1869); Colorado (1893), Utah and Idaho (1896), Washington (1910), California (1911), and Oregon, Arizona, and Kansas (1912).

19. Both Susan B. Anthony and Elizabeth Cady Stanton were, of course, much more radical than their successors in NAWSA. In the years after they retired from the scene, NAWSA adopted a more conservative, less political attitude, in an effort to win over

male support. For most of the younger women, the conservatives provided the only visible role models. Critiquing the conservatism of the NAWSA leadership is not intended to be a disparagement of those women who dedicated so much time and effort to the movement. To advocate woman suffrage under any circumstances required a good deal of personal courage, particularly in the days before suffrage became a respectable cause. Nevertheless, a critique of conservatism is necessary in order to understand fully the dimensions of the woman's movement during this critical period.

20. In England, women's rights activists were referred to as "suffragettes," whereas American women were called "suffragists." In all cases throughout the book, an effort was made to subscribe to contemporary usage.

21. On the Pankhursts and the WSPU, see David Mitchell, *The Fighting Pankhursts, A Study in Tenacity*, New York: Macmillan (1967); Mary Phillips, *The Militant Suffrage Campaign in Perspective*, Pamphlet, London (1967), Sophia Smith Collection, Smith College; and Emmeline Pethick-Lawrence, *My Part in a Changing World*, London: Gollancz (1938).

22. Emmeline Pankhurst, Emmeline Pethick-Lawrence and F. W. Pethick-Lawrence, *Suffrage Speeches From the Dock: Conspiracy Trial, Old Bailey, May 15–22, 1912*, (n.d.), Pamphlet, Sophia Smith Collection, Smith College, p. 94.

23. Pethick-Lawrence, *My Part in a Changing World*, p. 299.

24. The following abridged version of the WSPU constitution demonstrates clearly the origins of American militant tactics: "Object: To secure for women the Parliamentary vote as it is or may be granted to men; to use the power thus obtained to establish equality of rights and opportunities between the sexes; and to promote the social and industrial well-being of the community. Methods: 1) Action entirely independent of political parties. 2) Opposition to whatever Government is in power until such time as the franchise is granted. 3) Vigorous agitation upon lines justified by the position of outlawry to which women are presently condemned." Emmeline Pethick-Lawrence, *The Meaning of the Woman's Movement*, Pamphlet, (n.d.), Sophia Smith Collection, Smith College.

25. Inez Haynes Irwin, "The Adventures of Feminism," p. 456, Inez Haynes Irwin Papers, Schlesinger Library, Radcliffe College.

26. Statement of Katharine Houghton Hepburn, n.d., Florence Ledyard Cross Kitchelt Papers, Schlesinger Library, Radcliffe College.

27. On Harriot Stanton Blatch, see, Blatch and Lutz, *The Challenging Years;* and "Harriot Stanton Blatch," in Edward L. James, et al., eds., *Notable American Women, A Biographical Dictionary*, 4 vols., Cambridge and London: Belknap Press of Harvard University Press (1971–1980), I, pp. 172–174; on Nora Blatch, see "Nora Stanton Blatch Barney," *Notable American Women*, IV, pp. 53–55.

28. "Mary Ritter Beard," *Notable American Women*, IV, pp. 71–73.

29. "Letter Written by Mrs. Belmont to a Friend," c. December 1918, NWP Papers; see also, "Alva Erskine Smith Vanderbilt Belmont," *Notable American Women*, I, pp. 126–128.

30. Jane Marcus, "The Divine Rage to be Didactic," foreword to *The Convert*, by Elizabeth Robins, reprint, London: The Women's Press (1980), pp. v–xv.

31. Sara Bard Field to Amelia Fry, Sara Bard Field, Poet and Suffragist, Suffragists Oral History Project, Bancroft Library, University of California at Berkeley (1979), pp. 216–217 and 227–228 (hereinafter cited as Field Interview).

32. "Lucy Burns," *Notable American Women*, IV, pp. 124–125.

33. Anne Herendeen, "What the Hometown Thinks of Alice Paul," *Everybody's*, XLI (Oct., 1919), p. 45.

34. Ernestine Evans, "Women in the Washington Scene," *Century Magazine*, CVL (September 1923), p. 515.

35. Irwin, *The Story of the Woman's Party*, pp. 14–16.

36. Mrs. Medill McCormick to Harriet Vittam, July 31, 1914, Papers of the National American Woman Suffrage Association, Library of Congress (hereafter, NAWSA Papers). The emphasis in the quotation is McCormick's.

37. Stevens, *Jailed for Freedom*, p. 17.

38. Maud Younger, quoted in Irwin, *Up Hill with Banners Flying*, pp. 15–16.

39. Lucy Burns, quoted in ibid., p. 16.

40. Paul Interview, pp. 1–5 and 279–284.

41. Ibid., p. 6.

42. Robert Gallagher, "I Was Arrested, Of Course . . . ," *American Heritage*, XXV (February 1974), pp. 17–18.

43. Paul Interview, p. 31.

44. Paul Interview, pp. 7–8.

45. Herendeen, "What the Hometown Thinks of Alice Paul," p. 45.

46. Paul Interview, pp. 7–8.

47. "LMWW" to Alice Paul, October 26, 1914, NWP Papers. The letter cited, from a friend of Paul's who knew the family quite well, reported on a running argument between Donald Paul and a Paul cousin who supported Alice's activities. There was little doubt that Donald Paul disapproved of his niece's actions.

48. Paul Interview, pp. 68–70.

49. According to Amelia Fry, who conducted the interviews for the Suffragists Oral History Project, the younger children were exposed to music and dance, and their mother even bought a piano. Alice's recollections of her childhood were as stated above, however, and the dance lessons and the arrival of the piano probably occurred after William Paul's death, when Alice had already left home for college.

50. Ibid., p. 16.

51. Vernon Interview, pp. 33–34.

52. Paul Interview, p. 16.

53. Irwin, *Up Hill with Banners Flying*, p. 24.

54. Paul Interview, p. 17.

55. Ibid., pp. 17–18.

56. Ibid., p. 20.

57. Ibid., pp. 31A, 34.

58. Suffrage Scrapbooks I, pp. 80, 95, Sophia Smith Collections, Smith College.

59. Paul Interview, p. 48.

60. Irwin, *The Story of the Woman's Party*, p. 16.

61. Vernon Interview, pp. 35–36.

62. Paul Interview, p. 47.

63. Irwin, *The Story of the Woman's Party*, p. 16.

64. Paul Interview, pp. 225–227; Irwin, *Up Hill With Banners Flying*, p. 18.

65. Ibid., p. 18.

66. Paul Interview, pp. 24, 31A, 34.

67. These women are representative of those who were active in organizing both the Congressional Union and the National Woman's Party. Undoubtedly, there were many

others who were influenced in more or less direct ways by the British suffragette movement, and it is likely that more Anglo-American connections will be uncovered as more and more correspondence and personal paper collections are examined.

68. On Lavinia Dock, see "Lavinia Lloyd Dock," *Notable American Women*, IV, pp. 195–198; on Josephine Casey, see Biographical Data File, NWP Papers; on Anne H. Martin, see "Anne Henrietta Martin," *Notable American Woman*, IV, pp. 459–461, and the Anne Martin Papers, Bancroft Library, University of California at Berkeley (hereafter: Martin Papers); on Elizabeth Brannon, see Paul Interview, pp. 222, 237–238; on Eleanor Doddridge Brannon, see Biographical Data File, NWP Papers; and on Louisine Havemeyer, see Louisine Waldron Havemeyer, "The Suffrage Torch: Memories of a Militant," *Scribner's Magazine*, LXXI (May 1922), pp. 528–539, and Havemeyer, "The Prison Special: Memories of a Militant," *Scribner's Magazine*, LXXI (June 1922), pp. 661–676.

CHAPTER 2

1. *History of Woman Suffrage*, V, pp. 280–281.
2. Ibid., V, pp. 276–280.
3. Frances Squire Potter to William Howard Taft, April 15, 1910; Taft to Potter, April 16, 1910, Papers of William Howard Taft, the Library of Congress, Manuscript Division, Washington, D.C.
4. Statement of Katharine Houghton Hepburn, n.d., Florence Ledyard Cross Kitchelt Papers, Schlesinger Library, Radcliffe College, Cambridge, Mass.
5. Frederick Sullens to Lily Wilkinson Thompson, April 8, 1913, Lily Wilkinson Thompson Papers, Mississippi State Archives, Jackson, Miss.
6. Irwin, *Up Hill with Banners Flying*, pp. 12–13; Paul Interview, pp. 122–131.
7. Paul Interview, pp. 63–64; *History of Woman Suffrage*, V, pp. 380–381.
8. *History of Woman Suffrage*, V, pp. 377–381; Paul Interview, pp. 64–65; Irwin, *Up Hill with Banners Flying*, pp. 12–13.
9. Paul Interview, p. 64.
10. To date there is no full-length biography of Crystal Eastman. However, several biographical sketches do exist, the best of which are, Blanche Weisen Cook, ed., *Crystal Eastman on Women and Revolution*, New York: Oxford University Press (1978), pp. 1–38; June Sochen, *Movers and Shakers, American Women Thinkers and Activists 1900–1970*, New York: Quadrangle Books (1973), passim; and *The New Woman, Feminism in Greenwich Village 1910–1920*, New York: Quadrangle Books (1972), passim; "Crystal Eastman," *Notable American Women*, I, pp. 543–544; and Elaine Showalter, ed., *These Modern Women: Autobiographical Essays from the Twenties*, Old Westbury, N.Y.: The Feminist Press (1978), pp. 86–87.
11. Showalter, *These Modern Women*, pp. 87–92.
12. Quoted in Showalter, *These Modern Women*, p. 5.
13. Cook, *Crystal Eastman on Women and Revolution*, pp. 10–18; Paul Interview, pp. 63–64.
14. Mary Ritter Beard, like Crystal Eastman, has not yet been the subject of a biography, primarily because she destroyed all of her personal papers shortly before her death. The best secondary sources available on Beard are, Anne J. Lane, ed., *Mary Ritter Beard, A Sourcebook*, New York: Schocken Books (1978); and, *Notable American Women*, IV, pp. 71–73.

15. Most of the information available on Dora Kelley Lewis is courtesy of an unidentified granddaughter, who wrote a three-page sketch of Lewis, and a great-granddaughter and namesake, Dora Lewis, of Tivoli, New York. Unaccountably, Dora Kelley Lewis is not included in the 1914–1915 *Woman's Who's Who of America*, although she certainly was a prominent woman both socially and politically at that time.

16. Dora Lewis' work in the Philadelphia Equal Franchise Society is discussed in Katzenstein, *Lifting the Curtain*. Alice Paul also speaks frequently and with admiration of Lewis in the Paul Interview. Lewis also served as chairman of the finance committee of the NWP in 1918, and as treasurer the following year. See also, Stevens, *Jailed For Freedom*, p. 364.

17. Paul Interview, p. 66.

18. Morton Tenzer, "Interview With Elsie Hill," July 30–August 7, 1968, Oral History Project, University of Connecticut at Storrs, Part II, pp. 8–10; Paul Interview, pp. 70–71; "Belva Lockwood," *Notable American Women*, II, pp. 413–416.

19. Christine A. Lunardini and Thomas J. Knock, "Woodrow Wilson and Woman Suffrage: A New Look," *Political Science Quarterly*, XCV (Winter 1980/81), pp. 655–671.

20. National Woman's Party Treasurer's Report, Dec. 7, 1913–Oct. 1, 1920, NWP Papers.

21. See, for example, Avery Collier to Lily Wilkinson Thompson, March 13, 1913, Lily Wilkinson Thompson Papers; and Paul Interview, pp. 70–76.

22. Arthur S. Link, "Theodore Roosevelt and the South in 1912," *North Carolina Historical Review*, XXIII (July 1946), pp. 313–324; and, "Correspondence Relating to the Progressive Party's 'Lily White' Policy in 1912," *Journal of Southern History*, X (November 1944), pp. 480–490; Nancy J. Weiss, "The Negro and the New Freedom: Fighting Wilsonian Segregation;," *Political Science Quarterly*, LXXXIV (March 1969), pp. 61–79; Christine A. Lunardini, "Standing Firm: William Monroe Trotter's Meetings with Woodrow Wilson, 1913–1914," *Journal of Negro History*, LXVI (Summer 1979, pp. 244–264.

23. Reyher Interview, pp. 61–62.

24. Vernon Interview, pp. 157–158; Freda Kirchwey, "Alice Paul Pulls the Strings," *The Nation*, CXII (March 1921), p. 332.

25. Paul Interview, p. 11.

26. Paul Interview, pp. 132–133.

27. *Report of the Committee on the District of Columbia, United States Senate, Pursuant to Senate Resolution 499 of March 4, 1913, Directing Said Committee to Investigate the Conduct of the District Police and the Police Department of the District of Columbia in Connection With the Woman Suffrage Parade on March 3, 1913*, 63rd Congress, 1st Sess., Senate Report No. 53 (May 29, 1913), pp. 10–65 (hereafter: *Senate Suffrage Parade Report*); *Washington Post*, March 9, 1913; Paul Interview, pp. 73–76.

28. Estimates of the number of marchers vary according to the source being used, but the figure of 8,000, although it is lower than the 10,000 marchers claimed by the Congressional Committee, seems to be the figure most often quoted. See, *The Suffragist*, I (December 13, 1913), p. 38; and the *New York Times*, March 3, 1913.

29. On this point, it is instructive that the major United States suffrage organizations and their leaders were actively and continuously involved in the international women's movement, regularly attending international conferences, and serving on international committees with regularity. See, for example, Irwin, *The Story of the Woman's Party;*

Stevens, *Jailed for Freedom;* Peck, *Carrie Chapman Catt;* Blatch and Lutz, *Challenging Years;* Flexner, *Century of Struggle;* Kraditor, *Ideas of the Woman Suffrage Movement;* and O'Neill, *Everyone Was Brave,* all of which contain discussions of American internationalists.

30. *New York Evening Post,* March 4, 1913.

31. Avery Collier to Lily Wilkinson Thompson, March 13, 1913, Lily Wilkinson Thompson Papers; *New York Times,* March 3, 1913.

32. Joint Resolution of the Senate (S.J. Res. 164) and House of Representatives (H.J. Res. 406), *Congressional Record,* 63rd Congress, 3rd Sess., March 1, 1913.

33. *Washington Post,* March 9, 1913; Paul Interview, pp. 74–76.

34. Irwin, *Up Hill with Banners Flying,* p. 31; *New York Times,* March 4, 1913.

35. Ibid., March 4, 1913.

36. Ibid., March 4, 1913.

37. *Senate Suffrage Parade Report,* pp. 77–85.

38. *New York Times,* March 4–5, 1913; *Washington Post,* March 5, 1913.

39. Ibid., March 4–10, 1913; *Washington Post,* March 3–9, 1913; *Senate Suffrage Parade Report,* passim; Stevens, *Jailed for Freedom,* pp. 21–22.

40. *Washington Post,* March 5, 1913.

41. See, for example, the testimony of Major Richard Sylvester, *Senate Suffrage Parade Report,* pp. 136–220, in which considerable time was spent by Sylvester in answering the questions of Senate committee members who wished to determine the extent to which public officials turned a blind eye to a situation they knew to be dangerously unstable.

42. Paul Interview, p. 79.

43. Emma Gillette to Anna Howard Shaw, Joint Inaugural Procession Committee, Finance Statement, April 16, 1913, NWP Papers.

44. Alva Belmont, President, Political Equality Associates, to Alice Paul, April 17, 1913, NWP Papers.

45. Ada Ralls to Alice Paul, April 4, 1913, NWP Papers.

46. Sullens to Lily Wilkinson Thompson, April 8, 1913, Lily Wilkinson Thompson Papers.

47. William A. Clark to Alva Belmont, April 7, 1913, NWP Papers.

CHAPTER 3

1. White House Executive Appointment Diary, 1913, March 17, 1913, Woodrow Wilson Papers, Library of Congress, Washington, D.C. (hereafter: Wilson Papers).

2. Stevens, *Jailed for Freedom,* pp. 22–23; Paul Interview, pp. 89–90.

3. Irwin, *Up Hill with Banners Flying,* pp. 34–35; and Stevens, *Jailed for Freedom,* pp. 22–23.

4. *The Suffragist,* I (November 15, 1913), p. 2.

5. Paul Interview, pp. 95–96; Irwin, *Up Hill with Banners Flying,* pp. 38–39; Alice Paul to Mary A. Burnham, June 12, 1914, cited in Katzenstein, *Lifting the Curtain,* pp. 136–138.

6. *The Suffragist,* I (November 15, 1913), p. 4.

7. Irwin, *The Story of the Woman's Party,* p. 201; *The Suffragist,* I (November 15, 1913), p. 2.

8. Ibid., p. 4.

9. Paul Interview, p. 327.

10. Stevens, *Jailed for Freedom,* p. 13.

11. *The Suffragist*, I (November 15, 1913), p. 2.

12. Mary Ware Dennett to NAWSA Membership Committee, July 2, 1912; Alice Paul to Mary Ware Dennett, June 26, 1913; Laura Clay to Mary Ware Dennett, July 9, 1913; Alice Paul to Laura Clay, July 19, 1913; Laura Clay to NAWSA Membership Committee, October 8, 1913; Mary Ware Dennett to Laura Clay, September 5, 1913, all reproduced in Katzenstein, *Lifting the Curtain*, pp. 61–67.

13. Alice Paul to Mary A. Burnham, June 12, 1914, cited in Katzenstein, *Lifting the Curtain*, p. 138.

14. Senate and House Proceedings, *Congressional Record*, 63rd Congress, 1st Sess., April 7, 1913.

15. Senate Proceedings, *Congressional Record*, 63rd Congress, 1st Sess., July 31, 1913.

16. Senate Proceedings, *Congressional Record*, 63rd Congress, 1st Sess., September 18, 1913.

17. *New York Times*, April 8, 1913; *Washington Post*, April 8, 1913. The lobbying techniques employed by federal suffragists proved to be an effective way of keeping precise tabulations on which senators and representatives favored suffrage, which opposed it, and which were likely candidates for conversion to the amendment. As the technique was refined, it allowed the federal suffragists to make optimum use of their relatively small numbers. Extensive files were kept on each member of Congress. Suffrage organizers just returning to Washington from the states, or individuals who were merely visiting Washington, were provided with information from the files and sent to the Capitol Building. There, they buttonholed the members of Congress from the state they had just come from, impressing upon the congressmen that there was great support for a federal amendment among their home constituents. The suffragists would then report the results of the interview and record the new data on the central card file. In this way, there was always an up-to-date tally of supporters and opponents. See, for example, Report of Mary Ely to Alice Paul on the Congressional Delegation, December 10, 1913, NWP Papers.

18. Senate Proceedings, *Congressional Record*, 63rd Congress, 1st Sess., July 31, 1913; *New York Times*, August 1, 1913; *Washington Post*, August 1, 1913.

19. White House Executive Appointment Diary, 1913; and Head Usher's Diary, White House Diary, March 4, 1913 to March 4, 1921, Wilson Papers; *The Suffragist*, I (November 22, 1913), p. 13.

20. *History of Woman Suffrage*, V, p. 376.

21. "Rheta Childe Dorr," *Notable American Women*, I, pp. 503–505; *A Woman of Fifty*, New York: Funk & Wagnall's (1924), is Dorr's autobiography and provides both an account of the author's life as well as insightful observations about other women activists.

22. *The Suffragist*, I (December 13, 1913), p. 39. While revenues for the first issues did cover costs, which were less than $1,000, in the long run *The Suffragist* had to be subsidized from general revenues of the Congressional Union and later the Woman's Party. Between 1913 and October 1, 1920, revenues from advertising and subscriptions totalled $33,995.23, while costs for that period, including salaries, ran to $89,920.68, leaving a deficit of $55,925.45. National Woman's Party Treasurer's Report, December 7, 1912–October 1st, 1920, NWP Papers.

23. *The Suffragist*, I (December 13, 1913), pp. 38–39. At this time, Congressional Union members paid a joining fee of twenty-five cents, a once-only charge. There were no annual dues.

24. Reyher Interview, p. 84.

25. Ibid., p. 86; Paul Interview, pp. 320–321, 347–348, 560–568; *Notable American Women*, I, pp. 126–128.

26. "Louisine Waldron Elder Havemeyer," *Notable American Women*, II, pp. 156–157.

27. Louisine W. Havemeyer, "The Suffrage Torch: Memories of a Militant," *Scribner's Magazine*, LXXI (May 1922), pp. 528–539; and 'Louisine Waldron Elder Havemeyer," *Notable American Women*, II, pp. 156–157.

28. Paul Interview, pp. 308–312; National Woman's Party Treasurer's Report, December 7, 1912–October 1, 1920, NWP Papers.

29. Reyher Interview, pp. 84–85.

30. Report on Congressional Work, January 1–December 1, 1913; *The Suffragist*, I (December 13, 1913) pp. 38–39.

31. *History of Woman Suffrage*, V, p. 380.

32. Alice Paul to Mary Ritter Beard, October 30, 1913; Mary Ritter Beard to Alice Paul, November 20, 1913, NWP Papers.

33. Katzenstein; *Lifting the Curtain*; p. 107.

34. Catt and Schuler, *Woman Suffrage and Politics*, p. 244.

35. Paul Interview, p. 98.

36. *History of Woman Suffrage*, V, pp. 380–381; Paul Interview, p. 98.

37. Paul Interview, p. 98.

38. *History of Woman Suffrage*, V, pp. 380–381; Paul Interview, pp. 98–99.

39. Alice Paul to Rose Waks, October 8, 1918; also see, "Monthly Treasurer's Statements," 1913–1920; "Annual Reports of the Treasurer's," 1913–1920; and "National Woman's Party Treasurer's Report, December 7, 1913–October 1st, 1920," NWP Papers. The Congressional Union and the National Woman's Party raised nearly $750,000 between 1913 and 1920. The striking thing about the monthly, yearly, and cumulative eight-year reports, is the meticulousness of the records. Pennies are accounted for, and nowhere in the hundreds of pages of financial records is there to be found a category of expenses defined as "miscellaneous" or "petty cash," or anything equally vague. In the cumulative report, for example, one finds itemized expenditures of $1.90 to cover a deputation to the Rules Committee on July 31, 1913, $6.33 for a deputation of Rhode Island women to Congress in 1915, and a $12.00 court fee in 1919.

40. Peck, *Carrie Chapman Catt*, pp. 239–240.

41. Catt's efforts to centralize authority within the suffrage movement at the convention of 1913, are discussed in Flexner, *Century of Struggle*, pp. 281–303.

42. Paul Interview, p. 115.

43. Minutes of the NAWSA 1913 Convention, NAWSA Papers.

44. Ibid.

45. *The Suffragist*, I (December 6, 1913), p. 31.

46. Minutes of the NAWSA 1913 Convention, NAWSA Papers.

47. See, for example, Charles Neu, "Olympia Brown and the Woman Suffrage Movement,." *Wisconsin Magazine of History*, XLIII (1959/60), pp. 277–287.

48. Minutes of the NAWSA 1913 Convention, NAWSA Papers; see also, *History of Woman Suffrage*, V, p. 381.

49. *History of Woman Suffrage*, V, p. 381; "Synopsis of Correspondence and Conferences Regarding the Separation of the Congressional Union and the National American Woman Suffrage Association, 1913–1914," NAWSA Papers.

50. "Synopsis of Correspondence and Conferences Regarding the Separation of the Congressional Union and the National American Woman Suffrage Association, 1913–

1914," NAWSA Papers; see also "Alternative Plans for Congressional Work Presented by Vote of the Board to Miss Burns by Miss Ruutz-Ries on December 11, 1913, Together with Comments by Miss Burns," Ibid.

51. "Alternative Plans for Congressional Work Presented by the Vote of the Board to Miss Burns by Miss Ruutz-Ries on December 11, 1913, Together with Comments by Miss Burns," NAWSA Papers.

52. *New York Times*, January 5, 1914.

53. "Random Notes Taken at the Discussion Between the National American Women Suffrage Association and the Congressional Union, February 12, 1914," NAWSA Papers; William Leavitt Stoddard to NAWSA, December 29, 1913, NAWSA Papers; Lucy Burns to Anna Howard Shaw, December 23, 1913, NAWSA Papers; Wilmer Atkinson to Mrs. Medill McCormick, n.d., NAWSA Papers.

54. Carrie Chapman Catt to Emma Gillette, August 9, 1916, NAWSA Papers; "Random Notes Taken at the Discussion Between the National American Woman Suffrage Association and the Congressional Union, February 12, 1914," NAWSA Papers.

55. Alice Paul to Dora Lewis, January 5, 1914, NWP Papers.

56. *New York Times*, January 12, 1914.

57. Minutes of the 1913 NAWSA Papers; Alice Paul to Anne E. Draper, February 10, 1914, NWP Papers.

58. Anne Howard Shaw to Mrs. Medill McCormick, February 5, 1914, NAWSA Papers.

59. "Synopsis of Correspondence and Conferences Regarding the Separation of the Congressional Union and the National American Woman Suffrage Association, 1913–1914," NAWSA Papers.

60. Ibid.

61. "Random Notes Taken at the Discussion Between the National American Woman Suffrage Association and the Congressional Union, February 12, 1914," NAWSA Papers.

62. Ibid.; also "Synopsis of Correspondence and Conferences Regarding the Separation of the Congressional Union and the National American Woman Suffrage Association, 1913–1914," NAWSA Papers.

63. *New Republic*, I (November 7, 1914), p. 5.

CHAPTER 4

1. Mary Ritter Beard to Alice Paul, August 15, 1914, NWP Papers.

2. Alice Paul to Mary Ritter Beard, August 18, 1914, NWP Papers.

3. Mary Ritter Beard to Alice Paul, August 21, 1914, NWP Papers.

4. Miss MacLemmon to Alice Paul, January 24, 1914; Virginia Hitchcock to Alice Paul, February 5, 1914; Eunice R. Oberly to Alice Paul, February 13, 1914; Lucy Burns to Alice Paul, January 23, 1914; Lucy Burns to Alice Paul, n.d., 1914; Alice Paul to Virginia Hitchcock, February 5, 1914; Alice Paul to Eunice R. Oberly, March 6, 1914, all in NWP Papers.

5. Alice Paul to Eunice R. Oberly, March 6, 1914, NWP Papers.

6. Alice Paul to Virginia Hitchcock, February 5, 1914, NWP Papers.

7. Katherine Houghton Hepburn and Edith Houghton Hooker were the mother and aunt respectively of actress Katherine Hepburn.

8. Lucy Burns to Alice Paul, January 23, 1914, NWP Papers.

9. Constitution of the Congressional Union for Woman Suffrage, 1914, Articles VI–X, NWP Papers. The structure of the National Woman's Party followed closely that of the Congressional Union.

10. Report of the Congressional Union for Woman Suffrage for the Year 1914, with Outline of Congressional Activity during the Preceding Year, January 1915, NWP Papers (hereafter: Report of the Congressional Union 1914).

11. See, for example, Charlotte Whitney to Mrs. William Kent, September 26, 1915, NWP Papers.

12. Alice Paul to Eunice R. Oberly, February 19, 1914, NWP Papers.

13. Anna Howard Shaw to Antoinette Funk, March 20, 1914, NAWSA Papers.

14. Abby Scott Baker, Marie Forest, and Elizabeth Loud to Anna Howard Shaw, April 7, 1914, copy in NWP Papers.

15. Ibid.

16. Mary Beard to Lucy Burns, January 18, 1914, NWP Papers. Beard was quoting Paul.

17. Paul Interview, pp. 103–106. See Appendix for text of Shafroth amendment.

18. Flexner, *Century of Struggle*, pp. 276–277; Kraditor, *Ideas of the Woman Suffrage Movement*, pp. 163–164.

19. Paul Interview, pp. 104–107 and 312–314.

20. *The Suffragist*, II (March 21, 1914), p. 4.

21. Alice Paul to Mary R. DeVou, April 4, 1914, NWP Papers.

22. Alice Paul to Mary Ritter Beard, April 4, 1914, NWP Papers.

23. Anne Howard Shaw to "Dear Friends," April 17, 1914, copy in NWP Papers.

24. Wilson Appointment Books, February 2, 1914, Wilson Papers.

25. Quoted in Report of the Congressional Union 1914, p. 19, NWP Papers.

26. Ibid., p. 19; see also Alice Paul to Harriet Taylor Upton, June 17, 1914, NWP Papers; and the *New York Times*, February 4, 1914.

27. *Congressional Record*, 63rd Congress, 1st Sess., February 4, 1914.

28. Mistake of Calling a Democratic Caucus of the House to Consider the Appointment of a Woman Suffrage Committee, n.d., NAWSA Papers; Antoinette Funk to Anna Howard Shaw, January 21, 1914, NAWSA Papers.

29. Alice Paul to Harriet Taylor Upton, June 17, 1914, NWP Papers; Report of the Congressional Union 1914, pp. 18–19; NWP Papers; Alice Paul, quoted in Stevens, *Jailed for Freedom*, p. 15.

30. *The Suffragist*, II (March 21, 1914), p. 2.

31. Ibid., pp. 2, 5.

32. Report of the Congressional Union 1914, p. 21, NWP Papers; *Congressional Record*, 63rd Congress, 1st Sess., March 19, 1914.

33. Ibid., p. 22.

34. Report of the Congressional Union 1914, p. 24, NWP Papers.

35. *The Suffragist*, III (July 1914); *New York Times*, July 1, 1914; Report of the Congressional Union 1914, pp. 26–27, NWP Papers.

36. Report of the Congressional Union 1914, p. 27, NWP Papers.

37. *The Suffragist*, III (September 1914); Report of the Congressional Union 1914, pp. 27–28, NWP Papers.

38. Irwin, *Up Hill with Banners Flying*, p. 75.

39. Report of the Congressional Union 1914, p. 24, NWP Papers.

40. Ibid., p. 36.

41. Ibid., pp. 36–37.

42. Katherine Houghton Hepburn, quoted in Paul Interview, p. 123.

43. Florence Kelley, quoted in Report of the Congressional Union 1914, p. 37, NWP Papers.

44. Ibid., p. 37.

45. Organizers' Reports, 1914 Campaign of the Congressional Union, NWP Papers; see also Report of the Treasurer, 1914 Campaign of the Congressional Union, NWP Papers.

46. See, for example, Rebecca Reyher's account of the selection process, in chapter II.

47. Sara Bard Field to Anne Martin, September 15, 1916, Martin Papers.

48. The best accounts of the organizers' experiences during the 1914 campaign, in addition to their own letters, are found in the weekly published reports to *The Suffragist*, II (September 19–November 5, 1914); see also Irwin, *Up Hill with Banners Flying*, pp. 76–94; and Stevens, *Jailed for Freedom, passim.*

49. Report of the Congressional Union 1914, p. 38, NWP Papers; see also Biographical Data on Members of the National Woman's Party, NWP Papers.

50. Report of the Treasurer, 1914 Campaign, NWP Papers.

51. Helena Hill Weed to Alice Paul, October 30, 1914, NWP Papers.

52. Jane Pincus to Alice Paul, October 18, 1914, NWP Papers.

53. Lucy Burns to Alice Paul, October 2, 1914, NWP Papers.

54. Quoted in Irwin, *Up Hill with Banners Flying*, pp. 83–85.

55. It must be pointed out that it is difficult to tell how well or badly the organizers were received in the suffrage states with any great accuracy. As one might expect, those who agreed with the methods and goals of the Congressional Union, and from whom letters can be found, praised the efforts of the organizers, while their opponents—notably NAWSA members—were negative in their assessments of the campaign. Similarly, the responses of the press and politicians followed party lines. Still, the evidence available in manuscript collections and in the NWP Papers demonstrates that the public supported the Congressional Union's right to campaign, whether or not they agreed with the Union. Available letters from local citizens seem to be equally divided between supporters and opponents of Union tactics. One thing that can be said is that the Congressional Union organizers rarely lacked for an audience.

56. *Republican Herald*, October 15, 1914, quoted in Irwin, *Up Hill with Banners Flying*, p. 91.

57. *Seattle Sunday Times*, n.d., quoted in Irwin, *Up Hill with Banners Flying*, p. 90.

58. *The Suffragist*, II (November 5, 1914).

59. *Congressional Record*, Vol. 51, Part 17, pp. 1228–1229; see also Irwin, *Up Hill with Banners Flying*, pp. 85–86.

60. *Congressional Record*, October 1914.

61. *Wyoming Leader*, October 6, 1914, quoted in Report of the Congressional Union 1914, pp. 38–39, NWP Papers.

62. *Fountain Herald*, September 25, 1914, clipping in NWP Papers.

63. *Cheyenne Tribune*, October 12, 15, and 16, 1914, clippings in NWP Papers.

64. *Jewel City Republican*, October 16, 1914, clipping in NWP Papers.

65. *Congressional Quarterly's Guide to U.S. Elections* (1971); Report of the Congressional Union 1914, NWP Papers.

66. *Congressional Quarterly's Guide to U.S. Elections* (1971).

67. Harry H. Seldomridge to Mrs. Medill McCormick, June 8, 1915, NAWSA Papers.
68. Helena Hill Weed to Alice Paul, October 30, 1914, NWP Papers.
69. Report of the Congressional Union 1914, pp. 49–50, NWP Papers; Helena Hill Weed to Alice Paul, October 30, 1914, NWP Papers.
70. Report of the Congressional Union 1914, pp. 49–50, NWP Papers.
71. Report of the Congressional Union 1914, p. 50, NWP Papers.
72. Quoted in Report of the Congressional Union 1914, pp. 51–52, NWP Papers.
73. *"The Remonstrance Against Women Suffrage,"* January 1915, p. 2, NAWSA Papers.
74. Alice Paul to Mary Beard, November 9, 1914, NWP Papers.
75. Alice Paul to Mary Beard, November 4, 1914, NWP Papers.
76. *The Suffragist,* II (December 12, 1914), p. 3.

CHAPTER 5

1. Minutes of the National Advisory Committee Meeting, March 31, 1915, NWP Papers.
2. Alice Paul, quoted in the Minutes of the National Advisory Committee Meeting, March 31, 1915, NWP Papers.
3. Mary Beard to Alice Paul, June 24, 1914; Alice Paul to Mary Beard, October 19, 1914; Alice Paul to Mrs. Lawrence Lewis, October 29, 1914, NWP Papers.
4. National American Convention of 1914, *History of Woman Suffrage,* V, pp. 424–425.
5. Ibid., p. 425.
6. Anna Howard Shaw to Anne H. Martin, June 26, 1914, Martin Papers.
7. Anna Howard Shaw to Anne H. Martin, July 16, 1914, Martin Papers.
8. Anna Howard Shaw to Anne H. Martin, September 18, 1914, Martin Papers.
9. See, for example, Alice Paul to Harriot Stanton Blatch, January 21, 1915; Carrie Chapman Catt to Alice Paul, April 12, 1915; and Alice Paul to Carrie Chapman Catt, April 15, 1915, NWP Papers.
10. Harriot Stanton Blatch to Alice Paul, January 21, 1915, NWP Papers.
11. Ibid.
12. Harriot Stanton Blatch to Elsie Hill, January 18, 1915; and Harriot Stanton Blatch to Mrs. Gilson Gardner, January 18, 1915, NWP Papers.
13. Carrie Chapman Catt to Alice Paul, April 12, 1915, NWP Papers.
14. Alice Paul to Carrie Chapman Catt, April 15, 1915, NWP Papers.
15. Carrie Chapman Catt to Harriet Taylor Upton, April 19, 1915, copy in NWP Papers.
16. Carrie Chapman Catt to Alice Paul and Members of the Board of the Congressional Union, May 26, 1915, NWP Papers.
17. Alice Paul to Carrie Chapman Catt, June 24, 1915, NWP Papers.
18. Caroline Katzenstein to Alice Paul, November 7, 1914, NWP Papers.
19. Alice Paul to Carrie Chapman Catt, June 24, 1915, NWP Papers.
20. Caroline Katzenstein to Alice Paul, November 15, 1915, NWP Papers.
21. Clara Ueland to Mrs. Orten H. Clark, August 8, 1915, NWP Papers.
22. Ibid.
23. Anna Howard Shaw to Anne H. Martin, May 11, 1915, Martin Papers.

24. Eunice Dana Brannan and Elizabeth Seldin Rogers to Members of the Executive Committee and Advisory Council of the Congressional Union, June 16, 1915, NWP Papers.

25. Anna Howard Shaw to Anne H. Martin, July 26, 1915, Martin Papers.

26. Ella Rush Murray to Alice Paul, April 9, 1915; Resolution of the Woman's Political Union of Connecticut and Application for Acceptance as an Affiliate of the Congressional Union for Woman Suffrage, April 9, 1915, NWP Papers.

27. Flexner, *Century of Struggle*, pp. 304–318; Kraditor, *Ideas of the Woman Suffrage Movement*, pp. 138–185; and Morgan, *Suffragists and Democrats*, passim.

28. Margaret Kessler to Mrs. William Kent, March 12, 1915, NWP Papers; see also, James P. Louis, "Sue Shelton White and the Woman Suffrage Movement in Tennessee, 1913–1920," *Tennessee Historical Quarterly*, XXII (June 1963), pp. 170–190.

29. Minutes of the First Annual Congressional Union Convention 1915, December 1915, NWP Papers.

30. Ibid.

31. Suzanne Hilton, *Here Today and Gone Tomorrow: The Story of the World's Fairs and Expositions* Philadelphia: The Westminster Press (1978), p. 95.

32. Vernon Interview, p. 144.

33. Irwin, *Up Hill with Banners Flying*, p. 108.

34. Transcripts of Speeches Delivered at the Women Voters' Convention, September 4–6, 1915, NWP Papers; Irwin, *Up Hill with Banners Flying*, pp. 103–110.

35. Minutes of the First Annual Congressional Union Convention for Woman Suffrage 1915, December 1915, NWP Papers.

36. Field Interview.

37. *The Suffragist*, III (October 1915), p. 4; Field Interview, pp. 195–196.

38. Quoted in Irwin, *Up Hill with Banners Flying*, p. 114.

39. Minutes of the First Annual Congressional Union Convention for Woman Suffrage 1915, December 1915, NWP Papers.

40. Irwin, *Up Hill with Banners Flying*, pp. 117–118.

41. *New York Times*, October 7, 1915.

42. *New York Times*, October 20, November 22, and December 8, 1915; The Diary of Edward M. House, December 15, 1915, House Papers, Yale University Library; and Paul Interview, pp. 91–92.

43. *New York Times*, October 6, 1915.

44. Quoted in Arthur S. Link, *Wilson: Confusions and Crises*, Princeton: Princeton University Press (1965), p. 13; *New York Times*, October 12, 1915.

45. Christine A. Lunardini and Thomas J. Knock, "Woodrow Wilson and Woman Suffrage: A New Look," *Political Science Quarterly*, xcv (Winter, 1980–81), pp. 656–662.

46. Ibid., p. 446.

47. Ibid, pp. 445–446 and 455–456.

48. Minutes of the National American Woman Suffrage Association Convention of 1915, *History of Woman Suffrage*, V, p. 452.

49. Ibid., pp. 445–456.

50. "Zona Gale," *Notable American Women*, IV, pp. 7–9.

51. Quoted in *History of Woman Suffrage*, V, p. 469.

52. Hearings of the House Judiciary Committee on the Question of Woman Suffrage, December 16, 1915, copy of transcript in NWP Papers.

53. *History of Woman Suffrage*, V, pp. 453–454; Paul Interview, pp. 202–203.

54. Paul Interview, p. 326.

55. Minutes of the First Annual Congressional Union Convention for Woman Suffrage 1915, December 1915; and, Statement of Receipts and Expenditures of the Congressional Union for Woman Suffrage from January 1, 1915 to January 1, 1916, NWP Papers.

CHAPTER 6

1. In 1912, Democrat Key Pittman won the Nevada race with 7,942 votes (39.8 percent), over Republican candidate W.A. Massey, with 7,853 votes (39.3 percent); a switch of 45 votes would have produced a different winner, *Congressional Quarterly's Guide to U.S. Elections*, p. 493.

2. Alice Paul, quoted in Irwin, *Up Hill with Banners Flying*, pp. 152–154.

3. The card index is contained in the NWP Papers; on Maud Younger, see "Maud Younger," *Notable American Women*, III, pp. 699–700; Maud Younger, "The Diary of an Amateur Waitress: An Industrial Problem from the Worker's Point of View," *McClure's Magazine*, XXVII (March 1907), pp. 543–552, and XXVIII (April 1907), pp. 665–677; "Taking Orders: A Day as a Waitress in a San Francisco Restaurant," *Sunset Magazine* XXI (October 1908), pp. 518–522; and "Revelations of a Woman Lobbyist," *McCall's*, XLX (September, October, and November 1919), passim.

4. Irwin, *Up Hill with Banners Flying*, pp. 134–144.

5. Report of the National Advisory Council, December 1916, NWP Papers; see also, Alice Paul to Mrs. Lucius Cuthbert, April 14, 1916, NWP Papers.

6. Lucy Burns to Alice Park Locke, March 25, 1916, Alice Park Locke Papers, Hunington Library.

7. Margery Ross to Joy Webster, April 8, 1916, NWP Papers; see also, Harriot Stanton Blatch to W. H. Gates, February 25, 1916; Alice Paul to Harriot Stanton Blatch, March 1916; Harriot Stanton Blatch to Alice Paul, March 7, March 15, and March 17, 1916, all in NWP Papers.

8. Ella Reigel to Joy Webster, April 26, 1916, NWP Papers.

9. Ella Reigel to Joy Webster, April 29, 1916, NWP PApers.

10. Olive H. Hasbrook to Joy Webster, April 28, 1916; Margery Ross to Joy Webster, June 1916; Ella Reigel to Joy Webster, April 13 and 29, 1916; Harriot Stanton Blatch, Speech to Audience in Salem, Oregon, May 10, 1916; Annette McCrea to Alden Thomas, May 15, 1916; and Ella Reigel to Joy Webster, May 3, 1916, all in NWP PApers.

11. Report of the Proceedings of the National Woman's Party Convention, June 5–7, 1916, NWP Papers.

12. Constitution of the National Woman's Party, NWP Papers.

13. Report of the Proceedings of the National Woman's Party Convention, June 5–7, 1916, NWP Papers. Paul remained chairwoman of the Congressional Union as well.

14. *New York World*, June 7 and 8, 1916.

15. Report of the Proceedings of the National Woman's Party Convention, June 5–7, 1916, NWP Papers; *New York World*, June 8, 1916; Irwin, *Up Hill with Banners Flying*, p. 161.

16. Charles A. Beard, "Third Party Functions," *The Suffragists*, IV (November 25, 1916), p. 6.

17. *Campaign Text-Book 1916*, NWP Papers.

18. Arthur S. Link and William M. Leary, Jr., "The Election of 1916," in Arthur

Schlesinger, et al., eds., *The History of American Presidential Elections 1789–1968*, III (1917), pp. 2245–2270.

19. *New York Times*, June 17, 1916; see also, *History of Woman Suffrage*, V, pp. 712–715.

20. *New York Times*, June 17, 1916.

21. For a discussion of the various party planks, from the perspective of the NWP, see *The Suffragist*, V: June 17, 1916 (Republican platform); July 1, 1916 (Democratic platform); July 8, 1916 (Progressive platform); July 22, 1916 (Socialist platform); and July 29, 1916 (Prohibitionist platform).

22. Alice Paul to Mabel Vernon, April 20, 1916, Mabel Vernon Papers, Bancroft Library, University of California at Berkeley.

23. Alice Paul to Mabel Vernon, April 20, 1916, Mabel Vernon Papers.

24. *New Republic*, VI (November 21, 1914), p. 4.

25. Ibid., IX (November 18, 1916), p. 59.

26. Charles A. Beard to Carrie Chapman Catt, August 5, 1916, NWP Papers.

27. Speech delivered at Salem, Oregon by Mrs. Harriot Stanton Blatch, May 10, 1916, NWP Papers; Paul Interview, pp. 154–155; Vernon Interview., pp. 191–192.

28. Paul Interview, pp. 155–156.

29. Alice Paul to Harriot Stanton Blatch, July 7, 1917, NWP Papers; Anne Martin to Abby Scott Baker, August 10, 1916, Martin Papers; Paul Interview, pp. 155–156; Ella Reigel to Joy Webster, June 29, 1916, and Anne Martin to Margaret Whittemore, July 22, 1916, both in NWP Papers.

30. Vernon Interview, pp. 191–192.

31. *New York Times*, August 1, 1916.

32. Alice Paul to Mrs. Lucius Cuthbert, August 23, 1916, NWP Papers.

33. Woodrow Wilson to Mrs. E.P. Davis, August 5, 1916, Wilson Papers.

34. Anne Martin to Natalie Gray, July 7, 1916, NWP Papers.

35. Alice Paul to Mrs. Robert Morton, July 5, 1916, NWP Papers.

36. Resolutions Adopted by the National Woman's Party, August 11, 1916; *Campaign Text-Book 1916*, both in NWP Papers; see also Alice Paul to Mrs. Lucius Cuthbert, August 23, 1916, NWP Papers.

37. *Campaign Text-Book 1916*. NWP Papers. Mabel Vernon was Alice Paul's first paid organizer. Vernon had graduated Swarthmore a year ahead of Paul, but the two did not really know each other until the suffrage period. Paul had been apprised of Vernon's varied talents by a mutual friend shortly after the Congressional Union was organized. She invited Vernon to Washington and asked the Baltimore native how much she would need to live on; Vernon, then a schoolteacher, estimated she could get along on $70 a month, Paul guaranteed that amount and the bargain was struck. Neither was ever sorry. A month before the Colorado Springs meeting, during Fourth of July ceremonies in Washington, Vernon achieved national notoriety as the woman who had to be forceably removed from Woodrow Wilson's reviewing stand when she proceeded to heckle the President for his refusal to take up the suffrage issue. The idea was Paul's, but the adventuresome Vernon readily agreed to it. Paul managed to secure platform tickets for Wilson's speech. At appropriate moments during the speech, Vernon called out loudly and clearly, "Mr. President, what will you do for suffrage?" Wilson ignored the question, but after several similar interruptions, Secret Service Agents escorted Vernon off the stage, asking as they went out, "What makes you act that way?" Paul remained on stage, impassively observing the scene. Later, recalling the Secret Service agents'

question to friends, one of them asked Vernon, "Why didn't you say, '*She* does!' ", referring to Paul. See, for example, the *Washington Post* and the *New York Times*, July 5, 1916. Vernon Interview, pp. 61–62, 141–142; and, "Mabel Vernon," *Notable American Women*, IV, pp. 711–712.

38. "Inez Milholland Boissevain," *Notable American Women*, I, pp. 188–190; Paul Interview, pp. 170–173, 339–340, 496; Vernon Interview, pp. 19–21, 64–65; Irwin, *Up Hill with Banners Flying*, pp. 98, 160, 177; Stevens, *Jailed for Freedom*, pp. 48–60.

39. The term "second generation" was Mabel Vernon's description of the new NWP organizers. Vernon referred to those women who were with the Congressional Union from the very beginning as the first generation. Those who came into the organization after 1914 were the second generation, and a third generation, according to Vernon, came in after 1916. Vernon Interview, pp. 141–158.

40. Stevens, *Jailed for Freedom*, Appendix D, pp. 354–371; Vernon Interview, pp. 141–158; Reyher Interview, pp. 33–45.

41. The membership of the Congressional Union and National Woman's Party probably never constituted more than five per cent of the nation's suffragists. At the numerical height of its success, the NWP enrolled fewer than 50,000 members, whereas NAWSA's membership numbered in the hundreds of thousands. The difference was that the NWP members were almost always active and a significant number sacrificed jobs and personal lives to work full-time for the cause. Thus, their relatively small numbers were extremely significant in terms of productivity and influence. Paul Interview, pp. 327–329; Vernon Interview, pp. 190–191.

42. Irwin, *Up Hill with Banners Flying*, pp. 178–179; *New York Times*, October 23, 1916.

43. Iris Calderhead to Anne Martin, October 25, 1916, Martin Papers.

44. Alice Paul to Mrs. Lucius Cuthbert, August 23, 1916, NWP Papers; Alice Paul to Organizers, September 20, 1916, and Alice Paul to Mrs. Stevenson, September 20, 1916, both in Martin Papers; *The Suffragist*, IV (August 19, 1916), p. 6.

45. W. Y. Morgan to John S. Simmons, September 27, 1916, Martin Papers.

46. Abby Scott Baker to Anne Martin, September 21, 1916, Martin Papers; see also, Helen Bonnifield to Mabel Vernon, November 12, 1916, Vernon Papers.

47. Philip S. Triplett to Mabel Vernon, September 30, 1916, NWP Papers.

48. Doris Stevens to Alice Paul, September 20, 1916, NWP Papers. Stevens analysis proved to be accurate, as both the events of the time and later historical analysis demonstrated. See Link and Leary, "The Election of 1916," p. 2257.

49. Alice Paul to Doris Stevens, September 25, 1916, NWP Papers.

50. Anne Martin to Alice Paul, October 3, 1916, Martin Papers.

51. Anne Martin to Alice Paul, September 30, 1916, Martin Papers.

52. Abby Scott Baker to Anne Martin, September 29, 1916, Martin Papers.

53. *Campaign Text-Book 1916*, NWP Papers.

54. Cook, *Crystal Eastman On Women and Revolution*, pp. 15–20, 241–247.

55. Edith Barringer to Anne Martin, September 23, 1916, Martin Papers.

56. Mrs. J. E. Drennan to Alva Belmont, September 27, 1916; Nannie T. Daniels to Alva Belmont, September 28, 1916; Emma Haley Flanagan to Alva Belmont, September 30, 1916, and, Jessie Earnshaw to Alva Belmont, October 1, 1916, all in NWP Papers.

57. Helen Heffernon to Mabel Vernon, October 20, 1916, Vernon Papers.

58. Abby Scott Baker to Mabel Vernon, September 26, 1916, Vernon Papers; see

also, H. V. Castle to Mabel Vernon, October 28, 1916, and Mabel Davis to Mabel Vernon, October 17, 1916, all in Vernon Papers.

59. Margaret Fay Whittemore to Mabel Vernon, September 28, 1916, Vernon Papers.

60. Clara Louise Rowe to Joy Webster, May 21, 1916, NWP Papers.

61. Irwin, *Up Hill with Banners Flying*, p. 183.

62. Report of the Treasury Department of the 1916 Campaign, NWP Papers.

63. Alice Paul to Alice Henkle, September 3, 1916, NWP PApers; Vivian Pierce to Joy Webster, September 21, and September 24, 1916; and Elsie Hill to Joy Webster, September 27, 1916, NWP Papers.

64. Paul Interview, pp. 104, 108–109; Vernon Interview, pp. 37–38.

65. Mabel Vernon to Doris Stevens, October 14, 1916, Vernon Papers.

66. C. F. Clark to Mabel Vernon, September 30, 1916 and October 8, 1916; and, Mabel Vernon to Maud Younger, October 6, 1916, all in Vernon Papers; Gertrude Crocker to Lucy Burns, October 18, 1916, Martin Papers.

67. Alice Park Locke to Anne Martin, November 17, 1916, Martin Papers. A glance at Inez Milholland's itinerary reveals that her speaking schedule was as exhausting as that of any of the candidates and, in retrospect, much too demanding given her physical impairment. After leaving New York on October 4, Milholland was scheduled to speak in forty-three different cities in Wyoming, Idaho, Montana, Oregon, Washington, Utah, Nevada, Arizona, California, Kansas, and Illinois, all in less than one month. Revised Itinerary of Inez Milholland, n.d. (1916), NWP Papers.

68. Baker and Dodd, eds., *The Public Papers of Woodrow Wilson*, IV, pp. 297–300.

69. Bull Moose Progressives were members of the Republican Party who refused to support William Howard Taft in the election of 1912. Bull Moose Progressives, instead, cast their lot with Theodore Roosevelt. This split in the Republican Party is generally credited with throwing the election to Woodrow Wilson.

70. Lunardini and Knock, "Woodrow Wilson and Woman Suffrage: A New Look," *Political Science Quarterly* XCV (Winter 1980/81), pp. 670–671; see also, Arthur S. Link, *Wilson: Campaigns for Progressivism and Peace 1916–1917*, Princeton: Princeton University Press (1965), passim; and Link, *Woodrow Wilson and the Progressive Era 1910–1917*, New York: Harper Torchbooks (1963), passim.

71. Diary entry, June 19, 1876, *The Papers of Woodrow Wilson*, 36 vols., Arthur S. Link et al., eds., III, p. 143.

72. Catt and Shuler, *Woman Suffrage and Politics*, p. 260.

73. Abby Scott Baker to Anne Martin, September 29, 1916, Martin Papers.

74. Beulah Amidon to Anne Martin, November 1, 1916, Martin Papers.

75. *New York Times*, November 10 and 12, 1916; *Literary Digest*, November 18, 1916, pp. 1312–1316; *New Republic*, November 25, 1916, pp. 86–87; see also, Link, *Wilson, Campaigns For Progressivism and Peace*, p. 161 fn.; and, Catt and Shuler, *Woman Suffrage and Politics*, pp. 264–265.

76. See, for example, Alice Paul to Organizers, September 20, 1916; Alice Paul to Mrs. Stevenson, September 20, 1916; and Alice Paul to Organizers, n.d. (ca. October 1916), all in Martin Papers.

77. See, for example, Elizabeth Bass, Chairwoman of the Democratic National Committee's Woman's Bureau, to "Dear Madam," September 18, 1916, NWP Papers; and Harriet E. Vittum, Director of Woman's Work, Republican National Committee, to Anne Martin, September 22, 1916, Martin Papers.

78. *Congressional Quarterly's Guide to U.S. Elections*, Election of 1916: Presidential Results by State; see also Gilson Gardner, "The Work of the Woman's Party," *The Suffragist*, IV (November 25, 1916), p. 4.

79. Quoted in *The Suffragist*, IV (November 25, 1916), p. 8.

80. Ibid.

81. *New Republic*, IX (November 25, 1916), pp. 85–86; see also similar excerpts from the *San Francisco Examiner*, *Wichita Eagle*, *Utica* [New York] *Dispatch*, *Flagstaff* [Arizona] *Sun*, and the *Oroville* [California] *Mercury*, all quoted in *The Suffragist*, IV (November 25, 1916), pp. 4–8.

82. Vance C. McCormick, quoted in Irwin, *Up Hill with Banners Flying*, p. 183.

83. Quoted in *The Suffragist*, IV (November 25, 1916), p. 8.

CHAPTER 7

1. *The Suffragist*, V (January 17, 1917), p. 7.

2. Harriot Stanton Blatch to Woodrow Wilson, quoted in Blatch and Lutz, *Challenging Years*, p. 268.

3. Minutes of the National Executive Committee Meeting, January 5, 1917, NWP Papers; see also, Blatch and Lutz, *Challenging Years*, pp. 275–276.

4. Minutes of the National Executive Committee Meeting, January 5, 1917, NWP Papers.

5. Woodrow Wilson, quoted in Irwin, *Up Hill with Banners Flying*, p. 194.

6. Blatch and Lutz, *Challenging Years*, pp. 276–277; see also Katzenstein, *Lifting the Curtain*, pp. 204–205.

7. Paul Interview, p. 174.

8. Minutes of the National Executive Committee Meeting, January 15, 1917, NWP Papers; Harriot Stanton Blatch to Anne Martin, January 14, 1917, Martin Papers; Blatch and Lutz, *Challenging Years*, p. 277; Paul Interview, p. 179.

9. Alice Paul to Ellen BV. Crump, June 14, 1917, NWP Papers. The exact number of women who picketed can only be guessed at, since even *The Suffragist* could not keep up with a published list of names of every picket volunteer, although it did publish hundreds of names. *The Suffragist*, 1917–1918, passim.

10. Harriet B. Livermore to Alice Paul, June 24, 1917, NWP Papers.

11. Mary E. McCumber to Alice Paul, June 25, 1917, NWP Papers.

12. Edna Buckinan Kearns to Alice Paul, August 1917, NWP Papers (emphasis in original document). See also, for example, Anna M. Kendall to Evelyn Wainwright, January 25, 1921; Agnes Chase to Alice Paul, June 21, 1917; Mabel Haynes to Alice Paul, June 22, 1917; Sophie W. Sage to Lucy Burns, September 5,. 1917; Mabel L. Sippy to Abby Scott Baker, May 2, 1917; and Joseph W. Justice to Alice Paul, May 30, 1917, all in NWP Papers.

13. Mrs. Victor DuPont to Alice Paul, February 27, 1917, NWP Papers.

14. Mrs. Avery Ferry Coonley to Alice Paul, January 31, 1917, NWP Papers.

15. Alice Paul to Mrs. Carle Sprague, June 19, 1917, NWP Papers. An informal survey of NWP correspondence related to the picketing issue revealed that the mail ran three-to-one in support of Alice Paul.

16. *New York Times*, January 11, 1917.

17. See, for example, the *New Republic*, XIII (December 8, 1917), p. 135, and *The Nation*, CV (September 6, 1917), p. 237.

18. *New York Times*, January 17, 1917.

19. Virginia Bratfisch, *The Non-Violent Militant, Alice Paul*, Santa Monica: Women's Heritage Series (1971), p. 7.

20. Edith Bolling Wilson, *My Memoir*, Indianapolis: Bobbs-Merrill (1939), p. 128.

21. Helen Woodrow Bones to Jessie Woodrow Wilson Sayre, January 16, 1917, Wilson Collection, Princeton University.

22. Wilson, *My Memoir*, pp. 122, 128, and 138.

23. Irwin, *Up Hill with Banners Flying*, pp. 204–205.

24. Stevens, *Jailed for Freedom*, pp. 67–68; Irwin, *Up Hill with Banners Flying*, pp. 203–204.

25. Stevens, *Jailed for Freedom*, p. 71.

26. Link, *Wilson, Campaigns for Progressivism and Peace*, pp. 220–339.

27. Alice Paul to State Chairmen, February 8, 1917, NWP Papers.

28. Mary Ingham to Alice Paul, May 15, 1917, NWP Papers.

29. Pauline Clarke to Alice Parke Lock, February 28, 1917, Alice Parke Lock Papers, Huntingdon Library.

30. Florence Bayard Hilles, quoted in Irwin, *Up Hill with Banners Flying*, p. 278.

31. Resolution Passed by the Convention of the NWP and CU, March 1917, NWP Papers.

32. Minutes of the National Convention of the National Woman's Party and the Congressional Union, March 1917, NWP Papers; Blatch and Lutz, *Challenging Years*, pp. 277–278.

33. Minutes of the National Convention of the National Woman's Party and the Congressional Union, March 1917, NWP Papers.

34. Gilson Gardner, quoted in Blatch and Lutz, *Challenging Years*, p. 279. Even the generally unsympathetic *New York Times* commented on the "extraordinary police arrangements" imposed by the administration. *New York Times*, March 15, 1917.

35. Webb, Chairman of the House Rules Committee, to National Woman's Party, reprinted in Stevens, *Jailed for Freedom*, pp. 118–119.

36. Peck, *Carrie Chapman Catt*, pp. 265–271; Stevens, *Jailed for Freedom*, pp. 81–82; William O'Neill, *The Woman Movement*, p. 80; J.A.H. Hopkins to Woodrow Wilson, May 29, 1917, Wilson Papers; *History of Woman Suffrage*, V, pp. 517–518.

37. Lillian Holt to Alice Parke Lock, February 26, 1917, Alice Parke Lock Papers.

38. Edna B. Kearns to Alice Paul, August 1918, NWP Papers.

39. Josephine P. Justice to Alice Paul, May 30, 1917, NWP Papers.

40. Jeannette Rankin was one of fifty dissenting voices voting against United States entry into the war. She served only two terms in the Congress and, by sheer coincidence, in each term she was asked to vote on a declaration of war. The second time, after the attack on Pearl Harbor in 1941, Rankin again voted against entry into war, but on that occasion she was the sole negative voice. Hannah Josephson, *Jeannette Rankin, First Lady in Congress*, Indianapolis: Bobbs-Merrill (1974), pp. 70–76.

41. Paul Interview, pp. 174–177; Josephson, *Jeannete Rankin, First Lady in Congress*, pp. 70–76; United States Congress, *Women in the Congress*, Washington (1976), p. 67.

42. *New York Times*, May to June 1917; Mabel Haynes to Alice Paul, June 22, 1917, NWP Papers; *The Suffragist*, V (May–June 1917), passim; and Irwin, *Up Hill with Banners Flying*, pp. 214–215.

43. Elihu Root, quoted in Stevens, *Jailed for Freedom*, p. 91.

44. *The Suffragist*, V (June 25, 1917), p. 3; *New York Times*, June 21, 1917.

45. *The Suffragist*, V (June 25, 1917), p. 3.

46. *New York Times*, June 21, 1917.

47. Ibid.

48. N.A. Nessaragof to Alice Paul, June 21, 1917, copy in Wilson Papers.

49. Press Release, June 20, 1917, NWP Papers.

50. Stevens, *Jailed for Freedom*, pp. 93–94; Paul Interview, pp. 213–216; *The Suffragist*, V (July 21, 1917), p. 3; Irwin, *Up Hill with Banners Flying*, pp. 214–215; Mabel Vernon to Alice Paul, June 22, 1917, NWP Papers.

51. Paul Interview, p. 264; *The Suffragist*, V (July 21, 1917), p. 3.

52. Paul Interview, p. 216.

53. Arrested on July 4, 1917 were: Francis Green from New York City; Gladys Greiner, a social worker from Baltimore; Dora Lewis of Philadelphia; Vida Milholland, the sister of Inez Milholland Boissevain, from New York City; Lucile Shields of Amarillo, Texas; Elizabeth Stuyvesant, a dancer from New York City; Helena Hill Weed, a geologist from Norwalk, Conn.; Margaret Fay Whittemore from Detroit, Mich.; and Joy Young of New York City. *The Suffragist*, V (July 21, 1917); *New York Times* July 5–6, 1917.

54. *The Suffragist*, V (July 21, 1917), p. 4; *New York Times*, June 28, 1917; Irwin, *Up Hill with Banners Flying*, pp. 227–230.

55. *The Suffragist*, V (June 21 and June 28, 1917), passim; *New York Times*, June 28, July 15, 17, and 18, 1917.

56. *The Suffragist*, V (July 21 and 28, 1917), passim; *New York Times*, July 15, 17, and 18,1917. The sixteen women sent to Occoquan were: Minnie D. Abbott, Atlantic City, N.J.; Anne Martin, history professor from Reno, Nevada; Doris Stevens, journalist and social worker, New York City; Eleanor Brannon, socialite from New York City; Eleanor Calnan, a Congressional district chairwoman of the NWP from Methuen, Mass.; Janet Fotheringham, a teacher from Buffalo, N.Y.; Matilda Hall Gardner, a journalist from Washington, D.C.; Florence Bayard Hilles of Baltimore; Allison Turnbull Hopkins from New Jersey; Julia Hurlburt from Morristown, N.J.; Mary Ingham, a businesswoman from Philadelphia; Beatrice Kinkead from Montclair, N.J.; Louise Parker Mayo, a teacher from Framingham, Mass.; Elizabeth Rogers, a member of New York society; Iris Calderhead, the daughter of a Kansas congressman; and Mrs. Robert Walker, an NWP Maryland state officer from Baltimore.

57. Florence Bayard Hilles, quoted in Stevens, *Jailed for Freedom*, p. 100.

58. *New York Times*, June 28, 1917; Stevens, *Jailed for Freedom*, p. 105.

59. Ibid., pp. 103–104.

60. *The Suffragist*, V (July 21 and 28, 1917), passim; *New York Times*, July 15, 17, and 18, 1917.

61. Press Release, Committee of Public Information, July 3, 1917, reprinted in *The Woman Citizen*, I, no. 16 (Sept. 1917).

62. Dudley Field Malone to Woodrow Wilson, September 7, 1917, Wilson Papers.

63. *New York Times*, July 19, 1917; *The Suffragist*, V (July 28 and August 4, 1917), passim; Stevens, *Jailed for Freedom*, pp. 158–165. (Dudley Field Malone gives a first-person account of his meeting with Woodrow Wilson regarding the suffragists in Stevens' book. Quotes attributed to Wilson and Malone are Malone's recollections of what transpired at that meeting.)

64. Stevens, *Jailed for Freedom*, pp. 161–162.

65. Ibid., p. 162.

66. Ibid., p. 110.

67. *New York Times*, July 19, 1917.

68. Ibid., July 19, 1917. The suffrage story on this day rivaled war news for front page space in the *New York Times*. See also, J.A.H. Hopkins, "An Open Letter to Chairman Webb," *The Suffragist*, V (August 18, 1917), p. 4.

69. Dudley Field Malone, in Stevens, *Jailed for Freedom*, pp. 162–163.

70. Allison Turnbull Hopkins to Woodrow Wilson, July 1917, reprinted in *The Suffragist* V (July 28, 1917), p. 4.

71. Alice Paul, quoted in *Baltimore Sun*, July 20, 1917.

CHAPTER 8

1. Helen Hunt Gardener to Woodrow Wilson, May 10, 1917; Woodrow Wilson to Helen Hunt Gardener, May 14, 1917; and, Woodrow Wilson to Edward W. Pou, May 14, 1917, all in Wilson Papers.

2. Woodrow Wilson to J. Thomas Heflin, June 13, 1917; and J. Thomas Heflin to Woodrow Wilson, June 30, 1917, both in Wilson Papers.

3. Helen Hamilton Gardener to Woodrow Wilson, July 19, 1917, Wilson Papers.

4. Louis Brownlow, *A Passion For Anonymity, The Autobiography of Louis Brownlow*, II (Chicago: University of Chicago Press, 1958), p. 76; see also, for example, *New York Times*, June 21 and 22, 1917.

5. See, for example, David Kennedy's discussion of domestic wartime fervor which led to such extreme reactions, in *Over Here, The First World War and American Society* (New York: Oxford University Press, 1980), passim.

6. An examination of the *New York Times* in June and July, 1917, for example, features articles on IWW unionists, Emma Goldman, antiwar sentiment, draft resisters, and the activities of the suffragists. The articles are often given equal coverage, and sometimes juxtaposed in such a way that readers could not escape the conclusion that all dissent was uniformly harmful. The editors of the *New York Times* made little effort to conceal their own negative bias regarding such dissent.

7. *New York Times*, July 18, 1917.

8. *Canton* (New York) *Advertiser*, June 29, 1917.

9. *Miami Daily Metropolis*, June 30, 1917.

10. Edward Rumley, editor, *New York Evening Mail*, to *The Suffragist*, V (July 28, 1917), p. 9.

11. Richard Bennett to Newton D. Baker, September 22, 1917, reprinted in Irwin, *Up Hill with Banners Flying*, p. 151.

12. *The Suffragist*, V (July 28, 1917), p. 9. For similar response, see also: *New York Call*, June 12, 1917; *Richmond Evening News*, June 22, 1917; *Philadelphia Evening Ledger*, June 24, 1917; *Boston Journal*, June 25, 1917; *Detroit Times*, June 25, 1917; *Topeka* (Kansas) *Capitol*, July 2, 1917; *Boston Evening Record*, July 7, 1917; *Chicago Tribune*, July 2, 1917; *Boston Journal*, July 16, 1917; *New York Evening Mail*, July 18, 1917; *Holyoke Daily News*, July 28, 1917; *Washington Eagle*, July 28, 1917; *Olean* (New York) *Herald*, July 28, 1917; *The New Republic*, July 28, 1917; *Washington Times*, July 29, 1917; *Denver Rocky Mountain News*, August 4, 1917; *Mineapolis Daily News*, August 4, 1917; *Wilmington* (Delaware) *Star*, August 5, 1917; *Colorado Springs Gazette*, August 5, 1917; *New York World*, August 7, 1917; *Richmond Evening Journal*, August 7 and 22, 1917; *Washington Post*, August 8, 1917; *Pueblo* (Colorado) *Chieftain*, August 9, 1917; *Utica* (New York) *Herald Dis-*

patch, August 11, 1917; *New York Tribune*, August 11, 1917; *Washington Herald*, August 16, 19, 21, and 25, 1917; *Boston Journal*, August 16 and 18, 1917; *Raleigh* (North Carolina) *Times*, August 16, 1917; *Fargo* (North Dakota) *Courier News*, August 23, 1917; *Colorado Springs Evening Telegraph*, August 26, 1917; *Los Angeles Times*, August 26, 1917; *San Francisco Examiner*, August 26, 1917; *The Masses*, August 1917; *Buffalo* (New York) *Express*, September 7, 1917; *San Diego Union*, September 12, 1917; *Stamford* (Connecticut) *Advocate*, September 13, 1917; *Philadelphia Press*, September 14, 1917; *Washington Post*, September 25 and 26, 1917. This by no means exhausts the press coverage critical of the official response to the picketing campaign. It is a measure of the concern raised over the issue.

13. Mrs. Ellis Meredith to Joseph P. Tumulty, June 28, 1917, Wilson Papers.

14. Arthur Brisbane to Joseph P. Tumulty, July 20, 1917, Wilson Papers.

15. Memo from Woodrow Wilson to Joseph P. Tumulty, n.d. (ca. July 20, 1917), Wilson Papers.

16. Minutes of the Executive Committee Meeting, August 10, 1917, NWP Papers.

17. See, for example, *The Suffragist*, V (July–November 1917), passim; *Washington Post*, July–November 1917, passim; and the *New York Times*, July–November 1917, passim. One notable exception occurred during the arrests of June 20, when police were hard pressed to protect suffragists from a particularly unruly mob. (*New York Times*, June 21, 22, 1917).

18. House Resolution 171, by Representative Jeannette Rankin, October 5, 1917, reprinted in Stevens, *Jailed for Freedom*, pp. 352–353.

19. Wilson Appointment Books, July 19 and August 8 and 20, 1917, Wilson Papers.

20. The warning, issued in August 1917, apparently was not sufficiently stern enough to prevent servicemen from continued participation in the mob violence.

21. Congressman Charles A. Lindbergh to Woodrow Wilson, August 27, 1917, Wilson Papers; see also, *New York Times*, August 29, 1917.

22. Dudley Field Malone to Woodrow Wilson, September 7, 1917, Wilson Papers; see also *New York Times*, September 8, 1917.

23. Paul Interview, pp. 363–366.

24. *New York Times*, September 16, 1917; Stevens, *Jailed for Freedom*, pp. 171–172.

25. Proceedings of the House, *Congressional Record*, 65th Congress, September 25, 1917; *New York Times*, September 25, 1917. The May 14 letter was the one in which Wilson advised Pou that he, Wilson, approved the establishment of the House Committee on Woman Suffrage.

26. *New York Times*, June 28, 1917.

27. Mary Winsor, "My Prisons," Mary E. Winsor Papers, Schlesinger Library, Radcliffe College; Hallinan Interview, pp. 4–6; Appendix. Vernon Interview. *The Suffragist*, V (August–November 1917), passim; Irwin, *Up Hill with Banners Flying*, p. 271.

28. Mary Winsor, "My Prisons," Winsor Papers.

29. Susan H. Gray to Natalie Gray, September 2, 1917, NWP Papers; see also, Beulah Amidon to Picket Prisoners, August 23, 1917, ibid.

30. Mrs. Walter Adams to Editor, *Survey Magazine*, Calif. October 1917, NWP Papers.

31. Katherine Ralston Fisher, "From the Log of a Suffrage Prisoner," *The Suffragist* (October 13, 1917).

32. Irwin, *Up Hill with Banners Flying*, pp. 269–299. It should be noted that there were no incidents involving black male prisoners and the suffragists.

33. Interview with Hazel Hunkins Hallinan, Appendix I, Vernon Interview, pp. 5–6 (hereafter, Hallinan Interview).

34. Stevens, *Jailed for Freedom*, pp. 215–220.

35. *The Suffragist*, V (November 1917), pp. 3–4.

36. Lucy Burns to Members of the National Woman's Party, November 9, 1917, NWP Papers.

37. Mary E. Winsor, "My Prisons," Winsor Papers; Stevens, *Jailed for Freedom*, pp. 175–183.

38. *The Suffragist*, V (November 1917), passim.; Stevens, *Jailed for Freedom*, pp. 176–177.

39. Petition to the Commissioners of the District of Columbia, n.d. (ca. September 1917), NWP Papers.

40. Stevens, *Jailed for Freedom*, pp. 176–177.

41. Alice Paul to Doris Stevens, quoted in Stevens, *Jailed for Freedom*, p. 220.

42. Ibid., p. 224.

43. Ibid., pp. 221–222.

44. Ibid., p. 225.

45. Paul Interview, pp. 225–226, 230–234, and 397; *The Suffragist*, V (November–December 1917), passim; Stevens, *Jailed for Freedom*, pp. 224–225; Irwin, *Up Hill with Banners Flying*, pp. 294–295; Mary Winsor, "My Prisons," Winsor Papers.

46. W. Gwynn Gardiner to Woodrow Wilson, November 9, 1917, Wilson Papers.

47. Letter from Rose Winslow, n.d. (ca. November 1917), smuggled out of District Jail, NWP Papers; see also Stevens, *Jailed for Freedom*, pp. 190–191, 223–228; Affidavit of Rose Winslow, reprinted in Irwin, *Up Hill with Banners Flying*, pp. 269–299.

48. Woodrow Wilson to Joseph P. Tumulty, Memo, November 10, 1917, Wilson Papers.

49. Statement by Mrs. John Winters Brannon, n.d. (ca. November 1917), NWP Papers; *The Suffragist*, V (November–December 1917), passim; Irwin, *Up Hill with Banners Flying*, pp. 280–286; Stevens, *Jailed for Freedom*, pp. 192–210.

50. Statement of Mrs. John Winters Brannon, n.d., (ca. November 1917), NWP Papers.

51. Woodrow Wilson to Joseph P. Tumulty, Memo, November 21, 1917, Wilson Papers.

52. *The Suffragist*, V (November 1917–November 1918), passim; Louisine Havemeyer, "Prison Special," *Scribner's Magazine*, pp. 640–673.

53. A. P. Blauvelt, Democratic State Committee of Illinois, to Joseph P. Tumulty, November 17, 1917, Wilson Papers.

54. Mrs. S. G. Harrison, Democratic Club of Alameda, to Woodrow Wilson, November 18, 1917, Wilson Papers.

55. Wilson biographer Arthur S. Link, in an interview with the author at Princeton University in 1981, concurred in the probability of Wilson's having sent Lawrence to talk with Paul. Link says that Wilson had, from time to time, used Lawrence as an unofficial emissary in situations where it was not advantageous to use normal channels of commuication. Professor Arthur S. Link to Christine Lunardini, Interview, June 1981, Princeton University.

56. This passage is Alice Paul's recollection of what transpired at the meeting between her and David Lawrence. The quotes attributed to Lawrence were reconstructed by Paul to the best of her recollection. *Milwaukee Leader*, December 18, 1917; Stevens,

Jailed for Freedom, pp. 226–227; Irwin, *Up Hill with Banners Flying,* pp. 261–263; Minnie Bronson to Alice Paul, January 25, 1918, NWP Papers.

57. Doris Stevens reached the same conclusion in her memoir, *Jailed for Freedom,* pp. 226–227.

58. Ibid., p. 227; *Milwaukee Leader,* December 18, 1917.

59. *The Suffragist,* VI (January–February 1919), passim.

60. The predictions for exoneration by the higher courts were correct. Suffrage convictions were overturned, with the courts declaring that the suffragists had been denied their constitutional rights. See, for example, Stevens, *Jailed for Freedom,* pp. 229–240, for a detailed account of the legal battles on behalf of the suffragists.

61. Helen H. Gardener to Joseph P. Tumulty, June 10, 1917; Helen Hunt Gardener to T. W. Brahany, July 1917, both in Wilson Papers.

62. Louisine Havemeyer, "Prison Special," *Scribner's Magazine,* pp. 672–673.

63. Mary Winsor to Mary Howard, July 13, 1950, Winsor Papers.

64. Reyher Interview, p. 49; see also Field Interview, p. 240.

65. Memoir by Katharine Houghton Hepburn, n.d., Florence Ledyard Cross Kitchelt Papers, Schlesinger Library, Radcliffe College.

66. Woodrow Wilson to Carrie Chapman Catt, October 13, 1917, Wilson Papers; NAWSA Press Release, copy in Ray Stannard Baker Papers, Library of Congress; Baker and Dodd, *Public Papers,* 5:109.

67. *History of Woman Suffrage,* V, p. 515.68. *New York Times,* September 25, 1917.

68. *New York Times,* September 25, 1917.

69. Leading southern Democrat John Sharp Williams of Mississippi, made many attempts to divorce black women from voting rights. He suggested, for example, that the amendment read: "The right of white citizens of the United States to vote shall not be denied or abridged by the United States or any state on account of sex." (*Congressional Record,* 63rd Congress, 2nd Sess., March 19, 1914, p. 5104); Jouett Shouse to Woodrow Wilson, January 8, 1918, Wilson Papers.

70. *Congressional Record,* 63rd Congress, 3rd Sess., January 7–23, 1915, pp. 1483–1485; Wilson Appointment Books, January 9, 1918, Wilson Papers; *Washington Post,* January 10, 1918.

71. Press Release, January 9, 1918, Wilson Papers; and Woodrow Wilson to Ray Stannard Baker, January 9, 1918, Wilson Papers.

72. See, for example, the *New York Times,* January 10, 1918; the New York *World,* January 10, 1918; and the *Washington Post,* January 10, 1918.

73. *Congressional Record,* 65th Congress, 3rd. Sess., December 3, 1917 to January 19, 1918, p. 810.

74. *New York Times,* January 10 and 11, 1918; New York *World,* January 10 and 11, 1918; *Washington Post,* January 10 and 11, 1918; Proceedings of the House, *Congressional Record,* 65th Congress, 3rd Sess., December 3, 1917 to January 10, 1918; *The Independent,* February 2, 1918; "Woman Suffrage Crosses Its Jordan," *Literary Digest*(January 19, 1918), p. 15.

75. George Creel to Woodrow Wilson, October 4, 1917; Woodrow Wilson to George Creel, October 5, 1917, Wilson Papers.

76. Minutes of the Executive Committee Meeting, January 11, February 15, March 8, April 2, and April 12, 1918, NWP Papers; Katherine Fischer to Mabel Vernon, August 14, 1918, Vernon Papers; Alice Paul to Anna K. Stimson, July 16, 1918; Alice Paul to Mrs. Lucius Cuthbert, September 21, 1918; Mary Gertrude Fendall to Eliza-

beth Hooker, October 8, 1918; Betty Gram to Mary Gertrude Fendall, October 20, 1918; Julia emory to Joy Webster, October 25, 1918; Caroline Spencer to Natalie Gray, October 31, 1918, all in NWP Papers.

77. Alice Henkle to Mary Gertrude Fendall, June 23, 1918, NWP Papers; see also, Lucy Branham to Mary Gertrude Fendall, April 19 and 28, 1918, NWP Papers.

78. Elizabeth Bass to Woodrow Wilson, May 21, June 13, and June 19, 1918, Wilson Papers.

79. Lucy Branham to Mary Gertrude Fendall, September 1, 1918; and Dora Lewis to Mrs. William G. Brown, Jr., January 12, 1919, NWP Papers.

80. Elizabeth Bass to Woodrow Wilson, May 20, 1918; Woodrow Wilson to Elizabeth Bass, May 22, 1918, Wilson Papers.

81. Woodrow Wilson to Josiah O. Wolcott, May 9, 1918, Wilson Collection, Firestone Library Princeton University.

82. Woodrow Wilson to Christie Benet, May 22, 1918, copy in Wilson Collection; September 18, 26, and 27, 1918, Wilson Papers; Wilson Appointment Book, September 23, 1918, Wilson Papers.

83. Woodrow Wilson to John K. Shields, June 20 and 26, 1918, Wilson Papers.

84. Woodrow Wilson to Carrie Chapman Catt, June 1918, Wilson Papers.

85. Woodrow Wilson to Augustus O. Stanley, August 30, 1918, Wilson Papers.

86. Woodrow Wilson to Robert L. Owen, September 19, 1985, Wilson Papers.

87, Wilson met with Senators John F. Shafroth (D-Colo.), Joseph E. Ransdell (D-La.), Joseph T. Robinson (D-Ark.), Henry F. Hollis (D-N.H.), all supporters of the amendment, on June 24, 1918; he met with Carrie Chapman Catt and Elizabeth Bass on June 13 and again on September 16, 1918; with governor Richard I. Manning (D-S.C.) on September 23, 1918; and with Senator Martin (D-Va.) on September 25, 1918, all in Wilson Appointment Books, Wilson Papers. He also wrote again to Senators Shields, Benet, Overman, Martin, and Wolcott on September 27, 1918, Wilson Papers. See also Woodrow Wilson to Leon S. Haas. Louisiana State Senate, June 4, 1918, and Woodrow Wilson to Senator David Baird (D-N.J.), July 31, 1918, Wilson Papers.

88. Stevens, *Jailed for Freedom*, pp. 259–269.

89. *The Suffragist*, VI (August–September 1918), passim.

90. *The Suffragist*, VI (August–September 1918), passim; Stevens, *Jailed for Freedom*, pp. 271–275.

91. Colonel C. S. Ridley to Alice Paul, August 1918, NWP Papers.

92. Alice Paul to Colonel C. S. Ridley, August 1918, copy in Stevens, *Jailed for Freedom*, p. 275.

93. *New York Times*, September 18, 1918; *The Suffragist*, VI (August–September 1918), passim; Irwin, *Up Hill with Banners Flying*, pp. 370–376; Paul Interview, pp. 363–366.

94. William Gibbs McAdoo, *Crowded Years*, pp. 496–498.

95. Carrie Chapman Catt to Woodrow Wilson, September 20, 1918, Wilson Papers.

96. *New York Times*, October 1, 1918; Baker and Dodd, *Public Papers of Woodrow Wilson*, V, pp. 264–267.

97. Ibid.

98. *New Republic*, XVI (August 10, 1918), pp. 33–35.

99. *New York Times*, October 2, 1918.

100. Ibid., October 2, 1918.

101. For an analysis of the 66th Congress, see Flexner, *Century of Struggle*, pp. 319–328.

102. Carrie Chapman Catt to Woodrow Wilson, November 26, 1918; Wilson's Annual Message, December 2, 1918, Wilson Papers.

103. Irwin, *The Story of the Woman's Party*, pp. 415–416.

104. Joseph Tumulty to Woodrow Wilson, May 2, 1919; Cary T. Grayson to Joseph Tumulty, May 5, 1919; Woodrow Wilson to Joseph Tumulty, May 6, 1919, Joseph P. Tumulty Papers, Library of Congress; see also *New York Times*, May 10 and 16, 1919.

105. Baker and Dodd, *Public Papers of Woodrow Wilson*, V, p. 494.

106. *New York Times*, May 23 and June 5, 1919.

107. Paul Interview, pp. 248–249; *Congressional Record*, 66th Congress, 1st Sess., May 21, 1919; Flexner, *Century of Struggle*, pp. 326–327.

108. *New York Times*, February 26, March 3, May 19, and June 3, 24, and 26, 1920.

109. Woodrow Wilson to Albert H. Roberts, June 24 and August 19, 1920; Albert H. Roberts to Woodrow Wilson, June 25 and August 19, 1920, Wilson Papers.

110. *New York Times*, August 19 and 27, 1920.

111. Walter Clark to Alice Paul, telegram, June 4, 1919, NWP Papers.

112. Report of Dora Lewis and Maud Younger on Interviews with Congressmen, March 1, 1919, NWP Papers.

113. *New York Times*, January 10, 1918.

CHAPTER 9

1. The term "social feminist" was coined by William O'Neill, in "Feminism as a Radical Ideology," in Alfred F. Young, ed., *Dissent: Explorations in the History of American Radicalism* (1968).

2. Doris Stevens, Memoir, n.d., Doris Stevens Papers, Schlesinger Library, Radcliffe College.

3. Crystal Eastman, "Now We Can Begin," (December 1920), reprinted in Blanche Cooke, ed., *Crystal Eastman On Women and Revolution*, pp. 53–54.

4. Minutes of the Executive Committee Meeting, July 9, 1920, NWP Papers.

5. See, for example, Agnes Morey to Elsie Hill, February 24, 1921; Grace White to Alice Paul, February 25, 1921; Agnes Leach to Mabel Vernon, March 1, 1921; Dr. Caroline Spencer to Alice Paul, March 4, 1921, all in NWP Papers.

6. After Lucy Burns left the suffrage movement in February 1921, she returned to her family home in Brooklyn. She spent much of the remainder of her life helping to raise her nieces and nephews. Lucy never returned to public participation in the women's movement. Nor did she, apparently, maintain contact with those women with whom she had been so intimately connected throughout the decade. Paul Interview, p. 257; *Notable American Woman*, IV, pp. 124–125.

7. Paul Interview, p. 257.

8. At a congressional hearing in 1925, Mabel Vernon testified that the number of NWP members at that time hovered around 20,000. If that figure is correct, and even that may be somewhat generous, fully two-thirds of the members resigned from the organization after 1920 or never joined the new organization. *Hearings of the House Committee on the Judiciary on the Equal Rights Amendment*, 68th Congress, 2nd Sess. (Washington 1925).

9. The idea was very popular with feminists at the time. By the "endowment of motherhood," the feminists generally meant a government-sponsored program which

would provide mothers with a stipend. In this way, advocates believed, the nation's mothers would receive the recognition that they deserved in view of the importance of the task they were performing for society.

10. Minutes of the Executive Committee Meeting, September 10, 1920, NWP Papers.

11. Ibid.

12. Minutes of the Executive Committee Meeting, October 8, 1920, NWP Papers.

13. Katherine Morey to Alice Paul, January 30, 1921, NWP Papers; see also, Agnes Morey to Mrs. Richard Wainwright, February 21, 1921; Katherine Day to Alice Paul, February 21, 1921; Kathleen Fischer to Mrs. Richard Wainwright, February 3, 1921; Josephine Bennett to Alice Paul, February 23, 1921; Abby Scott Baker to Psyche Webster, January 29, 1921, all in NWP Papers.

14. Although $10,000 was a substantial sum, in view of the overall costs of the NWP's suffrage campaign—$750,000—it was a relatively modest debt, owing largely to the efficiency and good management of Alice Paul and her lieutenants.

15. Paul Interview, p. 256.

16. Ibid., pp. 256, 307; Minutes of the Executive Committee Meeting, July 13, 1917; Virginia Arnold to Mrs. Richard Wainwright, July 23, 1917; Cora Smith King to Alice Paul, January 25, 1921, all in NWP Papers.

17. Ernestine Evans, "Women in the Washington Scene," *Century Magazine*, CVL (September 1923), p. 514.

18. Alice Paul to Helen Hoffman, January 29, 1921, NWP Papers. See also, Minutes of the Executive Committee Meeting, November 13 and December 10, 1920; and Katherine Morey to Alice Paul, January 30, 1921, all in NWP Papers.

19. Minutes of the Executive Committee Meeting, October 8, 1920, NWP Papers.

20. Minutes of the Executive Committee Meeting, May 14, 1920, NWP Papers; Paul Interview, pp. 351–354.

21. Minutes of the Executive Committee Meeting, October 8, 1920, NWP Papers.

22. Paul Interview, pp. 351–354.

23. Minutes of the Executive Committee Meeting, January 22, 1921, NWP Papers; *New York Times*, December 26, 1920 and January 15 and 29, 1921.

24. Ibid.

25. Field Interview, pp. 425–427.

26. Program of the National Convention of the National Woman's Party, February 15–18, 1921, NWP Papers.

27. Paul Interview, pp. 353–354.

28. Jane Addams' Address at the Capitol Ceremony, February 15, 1921, NWP Papers.

29. Speech of Sara Bard Field at the Capitol Ceremony, February 15, 1921, NWP Papers; see also Crystal Eastman, "Alice Paul's Convention," in Cook, ed., *Crystal Eastman on Women and Revolution*, p. 57.

30. *The Suffragist*, X (January–February 1921), p. 339.

31. The figure is derived from: List of Delegates and Alternates at the National Woman's Party Convention, February 15–18, 1921, NWP Papers.

32. Report of the National Convention of the National Woman's Party, February 15–18, 1921, NWP Papers.

33. Report of the National Convention of the National Woman's Party, February 15–18, 1921, NWP Papers; *New York Times*, February 19, 1921.

34. Report of the National Convention of the National Woman's Party, February 15–18, 1921, NWP Papers; Eastman, "Alice Paul's Convention," in Cook, ed., *Crystal Eastman on Women and Revolution*, pp. 57–63.

35. *New York Times*, February 18, 1921; Report of the National Convention of the National Woman's Party, February 15–18, 1921, NWP Papers.

36. Report on the National Convention of the National Woman's Party, February 15–18, 1921, NWP Papers.

37. *New York Times*, February 18, 1921.

38. Report of the National Convention of the National Woman's Party, February 15–18, 1921, NWP Papers.

39. Ibid., *New York Times*, February 17 and 19, 1921.

40. Freda Kirchwey, "Alice Paul Pulls the Strings," *Nation*, CXII (March 2, 1921), pp. 332–333.

41. Sarah T. Colvin, *A Rebel in Thought*, p. 151.

42. Emma Wold to Mabel Curry, February 21, 1921, NWP Papers. See also, Agnes Leach to Elizabeth Rogers, February 25, 1921, and Agnes Leach to Mabel Vernon, March 1, 1921, both in NWP Papers.

43. Florence Kelley, "The New Woman's Party," *Survey*, XLV (March 5, 1921), pp. 827–828.

44. Report of the National Convention of the National Woman's Party, February 15–18, 1921, NWP Papers. This document provides evidence that minority reports were accorded a great deal of consideration as they were presented. On the mood of the convention, see also *New York Times*, February 16–20, 1921; Alice Paul to Mrs. William Spencer Murray, January 24, 1921; Inez Richardson, Secretary of the National Association of Colored Women, to Alice Paul, February 11, 1921, both in NWP Papers; Ella Rush Murray and Sue Shelton White both wrote rebuttals to the Freda Kirchwey article, in the *Nation* CXII (March 23, 1921), pp. 430, 434; Anita Pollitzer to Bertha Fowler, February 21, 1921; Katherine Day to Alice Paul, February 21, 1921; Caroline Spencer to the National Woman's Party, February 23, 1921; Ida Husted Harper to Alice Paul, February 24, 1921; Agnes Morey to Elsie Hill, February 24, 1921; Grace White to Alice Paul, March 4, 1921; Agnes Morey to Alice Paul, March 7, 1921; and Caroline Spencer to Alice Paul, March 7, 1921, all in NWP Papers.

45. Paul Interview, pp. 459–460. As far as Elsie Hill was concerned, she never considered herself anything other than a temporary replacement for Alice Paul while the latter was busy earning her law degree; see Elsie Hill to Florence Bayard Hilles, February 25, 1921, NWP Papers; and, Interview with Elsie Hill, by Morton Tenczar, University of Connecticut at Storrs, 1968 (unpaginated).

46. Evans, "Women in the Washington Scene," *Century*, CVL (September 1923), p. 515.

47. Paul Interview, pp. 265–266.

48. See Paul Interview, pp. 265–266; the wording of the amendment was changed slightly in 1943. The amendment read then, as it did in its latest form: "Equality of rights under the law shall not be denied or abridged by the United States or by any State on account of sex." Paul dubbed the amendment, the "Lucretia Mott" amendment to honor the nineteenth century women's rights activist.

49. Evans, "Women in the Washington Scene," p. 508.

50. *Hearings of the House Committee on the Judiciary on the Equal Rights Amendment*, Sixty-Eighth Congress, 2nd Sess. (Washington 1925).

51. Paul Interview, pp. 267–268.

52. These reports can be found in the Papers of the National Woman's Party.

53. *Survey*, (June 15, 1926), copy in Mary Van Kleeck Papers, Sophia Smith Collection, Smith College Library.

54. Ibid.; *New York Times*, January 20, 1926.

55. *New York Times*, January 20, 1926.

56. Announcement released by the Women's Bureau of the United States Department of Labor, Washington, D.C., April 2, 1926, and Press Release, Women's Bureau, United States Department of Labor, May 11, 1926, both in Van Kleeck Papers.

57. *Survey* (June 15, 1926).

58. Press Release, Women's Bureau of the United States Department of Labor, Washington, D.C., May 11, 1926.

59. *New York Times*, May 10–12, 1926; *The World*, May 11, 1926.

60. Press Release, National Woman's Party, May 11, 1926, NWP Papers.

61. Press Release, Women's Bureau of the United States Department of Labor, Washington, D.C., May 11, 1926.

62. "Effects of Special Legislation on Women's Work," Report of the Investigating Committee of the Women's Bureau of the United States Department of Labor, November 1928, copy in NWP Papers.

63. In 1932, for example, the government decided that two members in the same family could no longer hold government jobs and that one family member would be dismissed. Women invariably were dismissed regardless of their years of service. See Survey of Dismissed Women Government Workers, NWP Papers.

Bibliography

I. MANUSCRIPT COLLECTIONS

Library of Congress, Washington, D.C.

The Papers of the National American Woman Suffrage Association
(NAWSA Papers)
The Papers of the National Woman's Party 1913–1920, The Suffrage
Years (NWP Papers)
The Papers of William Howard Taft
The Papers of Woodrow Wilson

Archives of the National Woman's Party, Washington, D.C.

The Papers of the National Woman's Party 1913–1974 (Microfilm
Edition) (NWP Papers)

Sophia Smith Collection, Smith College Library, Northampton, Mass.:

The Papers of Jane Addams
The Papers of Florence Ellenwood Allen
The Papers of the Ames Family
The Papers of Helen Tufts Bailie
The Papers of Mary Ritter Beard
The Papers of Vera Biggs

The Papers of the Blake Family
The Papers of Madeleine Zabriski Doty
The Papers of Mary Abby van Kleeck
The Papers of Baird Leonard
The Papers of Rhoda Elizabeth McCulloch
The Papers of Margaret Sanger
The Papers of the Margaret Sanger Research Bureau
The Papers of Florence Tuttle
The Papers of Alice Morgan Wright
Suffrage Scrapbooks

The Schlesinger Library, of Radcliffe College, Harvard University

The Dillon Collection of Suffrage Material
The Papers of Fannie Fern Andrews (Phillips)
The Papers of Susan B. Anthony
The Papers of Florence A. Armstrong
The Papers of Caroline Lexow Babcock
The Papers of Mary Ritter Beard
The Papers of the Beecher-Stowe Family
The Papers of the Laura M. Berrien
The Papers of Mary Williams Dewson
The Papers of Charlotte Perkins Gilman
The Papers of Olive M. Hurlburt
The Papers of Inez Haynes Irwin
The Papers of Florence Ledyard Cross Kitchelt
The Papers of Alma Lutz
The Papers of Jane Norman Smith
The Papers of Doris Stevens
The Papers of Helen Hunt West
The Papers of Sue Shelton White
The Papers of Anna Kelton Wiley
The Papers of Mary Winsor

The Bancroft Library, University of California at Berkeley

The Papers of Anne Henrietta Martin
The Papers of Mable Vernon

The Huntington Library, Pasadena, California

The Papers of Ida Husted Harper
The Papers of Sonia (Levien) Hovey
The Papers of Maude (Anthony) Koehler
The Papers of Alice Parke Lock
The Papers of Maria (Seymour) Severance
The Papers of Una (Richardson) Winter
The Papers of Charles Erskine Scott Wood

Firestone Library, Princeton University

The Holden Collection
The Papers of Miriam Holden
The Wilson Collection

Sterling Memorial Library, Yale University

The Papers of Edward M. House

Mississippi Department of Archives and History, Jackson, Miss.

The Papers of Belle Kearney
The Papers of Lily Wilkinson Thompson

II. SUFFRAGE INTERVIEWS

Sara Bard Field, Poet and Suffragist, Interview conducted by Amelia
    R. Frye 1959–1963, Suffragists Oral History Project, University of
    California at Berkeley (1979).
Interview by Morton Tenczar with Elsie Hill, July 30–August 7, 1968,
    Oral History Project, University of Connecticut at Storrs.
Burnita Shelton Matthews, Pathfinder in the Legal Aspects of Women,
    Interview conducted by Amelia Frye, 1973, Suffragists Oral His-
    tory Project, University of California at Berkeley (1975).
Conversations with Alice Paul: Woman Suffrage and the Equal Rights
    Amendment, Interview conducted by Amelia R. Frye 1972–1973,
    Suffragists Oral History Project, University of California at Berke-
    ley (1976).
Jeannette Rankin, Activist for World Peace, Women's Rights, and
    Democratic Government, Interview conducted by Malca Chall and

Hannah Josephson 1972–1973, Suffragists Oral History Project, University of California at Berkeley (1974).

Rebecca Hourwich Reyher: Search and Struggle for Equality and Independence, Interview conducted by Amelia R. Frye and Fern Ingersoll, Suffragists Oral History Project, University of California at Berkeley (1977).

Mabel Vernon, Speaker for Suffrage and Petitioner for Peace, Interview conducted by Amelia R. Frye 1972–1973, Suffragists Oral History Project, University of California at Berkeley (1976).

III. GOVERNMENT PUBLICATIONS

District of Columbia. *Annual Report of the Commissioners of the District of Columbia, Year Ended June 30, 1917*, Vol.I, Miscellaneous Reports. Washington, 1917.

District of Columbia. *Annual Report of the Commissioners of the District of Columbia, Year Ended June 30, 1918*, Vol.I, Miscellaneous Reports. Washington, 1919.

United States Congress. *Congressional Record*, 63rd Congress, 1st Sess. through 68th Congress, 2nd Sess. Washington, 1914–1925.

United States Congress. *Hearings of the House Committee on the Judiciary on the Equal Rights Amendment*, 68th Congress, 2nd Sess. Washington, 1925.

United States Congress. *Hearings of the Senate Committee on Woman Suffrage 1916.* Washington, 1916.

United States Congress. *House Committee Hearings on Federal Woman Suffrage*, January 3–7, 1918. Washington, 1918.

United States Congress. U.S. Senate Report No.35, *Woman Suffrage*, 64th Congress, 1st Sess., January 8, 1916. Washington, 1916.

United States Congress. U.S. Senate Report No.53. *Report of the Committee of the District of Columbia, United States Senate, Pursuant to S.Res. 499 of March 4, 1913, Directing Said Committee to Investigate the Conduct of the District Police and Police Department of the District of Columbia in Connection with the Woman Suffrage Parade on March 3, 1913*, 63rd Congress, 1st Sess., May 29, 1913. Washington, 1913.

United States Congress. *Women in Congress.* Washington, 1976.

IV. MEMOIRS

Addams, Jane. *The Second Twenty Years at Hull-House*, New York: Macmillan, 1930.

Blatch, Harriot Stanton and Alma Lutz. *Challenging Years: The Memoirs of Harriot Stanton Blatch*, New York: G.P. Putnam, 1940.

Brownlow, Louis. *A Passion for Anonymity, The Autobiography of Louis Brownlow*, Chicago: University of Chicago Press, 1958.

Catt, Carrie Chapman and Nettie Rogers Shuler. *Woman Suffrage and Politics. The Inner Story of the Suffrage Movement*, New York: Charles Scribner's, 1926.

Colvin, Sarah T. *A Rebel in Thought*, New York: Island Press, 1944.

Daniels, Josephus. *The Wilson Era, Years of War and After, 1917–1923*, Chapel Hill, N.C.: University of North Carolina Press, 1946.

Dorr, Rheta Childe. *A Woman of Fifty*, New York: Funk and Wagnall's, 1924.

Duniway, Abigail Scott. *History of the Equal Suffrage Movement in Pacific Coast States with Sidelights on Protection*, Portland, Oregon: James, Kearns, and Abbott, 1914.

Gilman, Charlotte Perkins. *The Living of Charlotte Perkins Gilman, An Autobiography*, New York: D. Appleton-Century, 1935.

Irwin, Inez Haynes. *The Story of the Woman's Party*, New York: Harcourt, Brace, 1921.

——. *Up Hill with Banners Flying*, Penobscot, Maine: Traversity Press, 1964.

Katzenstein, Caroline. *Lifting the Curtain: The State and National Woman Suffrage Campaigns in Pennsylvania as I Saw Them*, Philadelphia: Dorrance, 1955.

McAdoo, William Gibbs. *Crowded Years. The Reminiscences of William Gibbs McAdoo*, Boston: Houghton Mifflin, 1931.

Pankhurst, E. Sylvia. *The Suffragettes: The History of the Women's Militant Suffrage Movement 1905–1910*, New York: Sturgist Walton, 1911.

Park, Maud Wood. *Front Door Lobby*, Boston: Beacon Press, 1960.

Pethick-Lawrence, Emmeline. *My Part in a Changing World*, London: Gollancz, 1938.

Stevens, Doris. *Jailed For Freedom*, New York: Boni & Liveright, 1920.

Wilson, Edith Bolling. *My Memoir*, Indianapolis: Bobbs-Merrill, 1939.

V. NEWSPAPERS

Baltimore Sun (1914–1917)

Boston Evening Record (1914–1917)

Boston Journal (1914–1917)

Buffalo (New York) Express (1917)

Canton (New York) Advertiser (1917)
Chicago Tribune (1914–1917)
Cheyenne (Wyoming) Tribune (1914–1917)
Colorado Springs Evening Telegraph (1914–1917)
Colorado Springs Gazette (1914–1916)
Denver Rocky Mountain News (1917)
Detroit Times (1917)
Fargo (North Dakota) Courier News (1917)
Flagstaff (Arizona) Sun (1916)
Fountain (Colorado) Leader (1914–1916)
Fresno (California) Bee (1916–1918)
Holyoke (Massachusetts) Transcript Telegram (1916–1920)
Los Angeles Times (1914–1918)
Miami Daily Metropolis (1916–1920)
Milwaukee Leader (1915–1918)
Minneapolis Daily News (1917)
New York Call (1914–1917)
New York Evening Mail (1917)
New York Evening Post (1916–1917)
New York Times (1912–1925)
New York Tribune (1916–1918)
New York World (1914–1917)
Olean (New York) Herald (1917)
Oroville (California) Mercury (1917)
Peublo (Colorado) Chieftan (1914–1919)
Philadelphia Evening Ledger (1917)
Philadelphia Press (1917)
Raleigh (North Carolina) Times (1917)
Republican Herald (Salt Lake City) (1916)
Richmond (Virginia) Evening News (1917)
Sacramento Bee (1917)
San Diego Union (1917)
San Francisco Examiner (1914–1918)
St. Paul (Minnesota) Daily News (1917)
Stamford (Connecticut) Advocate (1917)
Topeka (Kansas) Capitol (1914–1917)
Utica (New York) Herald Dispatch (1916–1917)
Washington Eagle (1916–1917)
Washington Herald (1917)
Washington Post (1912–1920)

Washington Times (1916–1917)
Wichita (Kansas) Eagle (1917)
Wilmington (Delaware) Star (1917)
Wyoming Leader, Cheyenne (1914–1917)

VI. PERIODICALS

Congressional Digest (1921–1925)
Equal Rights (1923–1925)
The Independent (1914–1918)
Literary Digest (1914–1918)
The Nation (1914–1920)
New Republic (1914–1923)
The Remonstrance Against Woman Suffrage (1913–1918)
Scribner's Magazine (1914–1918)
The Suffragist (1913–1921)
The Survey (1920–1923)
The Woman Citizen (1917–1919)
The Woman's Journal (1911–1915)

VII. CONTEMPORARY ARTICLES

Beard, Charles A. "The Woman's Party," *New Republic*, IX (July 29, 1916): 329–331.
——. "Woman Suffrage and Strategy," *New Republic*, I (Dec. 12, 1914): 22–23.
Beard, Mary Ritter. "The Legislative Influence of Unenfranchised Women," *Annals of the American Academy of Political and Social Science*, LVI (Nov. 1914): 54–61.
Beyer, Clara Mortenson. "Do Women Want Protection? What Is Equality?" *The Nation*, CXVI (Jan. 31, 1923): 116.
Blackwell, Alice Stone. "Woman's 75-Year Fight," *The Nation*, CXVII (July 18, 1923): 53–55.
Blatch, Harriot Stanton. "Do Women Want Protection? Wrapping Women in Cotton Wool," *The Nation*, CXVI (Jan. 31, 1923): 115–116.
Brooks, Elizabeth. "Future Suffrage Policy," *New Republic*, IX (Dec. 9, 1919): 97.
Cooley, Winifred Harper. "The Younger Suffragists," *Harper's Weekly*, LVIII (Sept. 27, 1913): 7–8.

Debs, Eugene. "Susan B. Anthony," *Pearson's Magazine*, XXXVIII (July 1917): 5–7.

Evans, Elizabeth Glendower and Carol A. Rehfisch. "The Woman's Party—Right or Wrong?" *New Republic*, XIII (Sept. 26, 1923): 123–124.

Evans, Ernestine. "Women in the Washington Scene," *Century Magazine*, CVL (Sept. 1923): 507–517.

Gale, Zona. "What Women Won in Wisconsin," *The Nation*, CXV (Aug. 23, 1922): 184–185.

"Gift to the Republicans," *New Republic*, XIII (Jan. 12, 1918): 301.

Hamilton, Alice. "Protection for Women Workers," *The Forum*, LXXII (Aug. 1924): 152–160.

Harriman, Mrs. J. Borden. "Women in Washington," *The Forum*, LXXII (July 1924): 45–50.

Havemeyer, Louisine Waldron. "The Suffrage Touch: Memories of a Militant," *Scribner's Magazine*, LXXI (May 1922): 528–539.

——. "The Prison Special: Memories of a Militant," *Scribner's Magazine*, LXXI (June 1922): 661–676.

Herendeen, Anne. "What the Hometown Thinks of Alice Paul," *Everybody's*, XLI (Oct. 1919): 45.

"How the Women Voted," *World's Work*, XXXIII (Dec. 1916): 118–119.

Kellor, Frances. "Women in British and American Politics," *Current History*, XVII (Feb. 1923): 831–836.

Kenton, Edna. "Four Years of Equal Suffrage," *The Forum*, LXXII (July 1924): 37–44.

Kirchwey, Freda. "Alice Paul Pulls the Strings," *The Nation*, CXII (Mar. 2, 1921): 332–333.

"Labor's Position on Woman Suffrage," *New Republic*, VI (Mar. 11, 1916): 150–152.

Martin, Anne H. "Equality Laws vs. Women in Government," *The Nation*, CXV (Aug. 16, 1922): 165–166.

Pankhurst, Emmeline, Emmeline Pethick-Lawrence and F.W. Pethick-Lawrence. *Suffrage Speeches from the Dock: Conspiracy Trials, Old Bailey, May 15–22, 1912*. Pamphlet, Sophia Smith Collection, Smith College.

Pethick-Lawrence, Emmeline. *The Meaning of the Woman's Movement*. Pamphlet, Sophia Smith Collection, Smith College.

Robinson, Helen Ring. "What About the Woman's Party?" *The Independent* (Sept. 11, 1916): 381–383.

"Special Feature: The Equal Rights Amendment," *The Congressional Digest*, III (Mar. 1924): 192–207.

"The Spokesman for Suffrage in America," *McClure's Magazine*, XXIX (July 1912): 335–337.

Stevens, Doris. "The Blanket Amendment: A Debate," *The Forum*, LXXII (Aug. 1924): 145–152.

"Three Cheers for the Poor," *New Republic*, XIII (Jan. 26, 1918): 364–365.

Wold, Clara. "We Don't Want Nothin' New: A Suffragist's Interview With a Delaware Legislator," *The Independent*, CII (April 17, 1920): 79–80, 115.

"Woman Suffrage and Congress," *The Independent*, LXXXIV (Dec. 27, 1915): 522.

"Woman Suffragists and Party Politics," *New Republic*, IX (Dec. 9, 1916): 138–140.

Younger, Maud. "The Diary of an Amateur Waitress: An Industrial Problem from a Worker's Point of View," *McClure's Magazine*, XXVII (Mar. 1907): 543–552, and XXVIII (April 1907): 665–677.

——. "Revelations of a Woman Lobbyist, *McCall's Magazine*, XLX (Sept./Oct./Nov. 1919): passim.

——. "Taking Orders: A Day as a Waitress in a San Francisco Restaurant," *Sunset Magazine*, XXI (Oct. 1908): 518–522.

VIII. SECONDARY WORKS AND ARTICLES

Andrews, John B. and W.D.P. Bliss, *History of Women in Trade Unions*, Vol. X, *Women and Child Wage-Earners in the United States*. Washington: Government Printing Office, 1911.

Baker, Ray Stannard and William S. Dodd, eds. *The Public Papers of Woodrow Wilson*, 6 vols., New York: Harper & Row, 1925–27.

Beard, Mary Ritter, *Woman as Force in History*. New York: Macmillan, 1946.

Beatty, Bessie, *A Political Primer for the New Voter*. San Francisco: Whitaker & Ray-Wiggin, 1912.

Berkin, Carol E. and Mary Beth Norton. *Women of America: A History*, Boston: Houghton Mifflin, 1979.

Berkin, Carol E. and Clara M. Lovett, eds. *Women, War, and Revolution*, New York: Holmes and Meier, 1980.

Blum, John Morton. *Joe Tumulty and the Wilson Era*, Boston: Houghton Mifflin, 1951.

Bond, Horace Mann. *The Education of the Negro in the American Social Order*, New York: Octagon Books, 1966.

Bratfisch, Virginia. *The Non-Violent Militant, Alice Paul*, Santa Monica: Women's Heritage Series, 1971.

Brownlee, W. Elliot and Mary M. Brownlee. *Women in the American Economy: A Documentary History, 1675–1929*, New Haven: Yale University Press, 1976.

Campbell, Barbara Kuhn. *The "Liberated" Woman of 1914: Prominent Women in the Progressive Era*, Ann Arbor: UMI Research Press, 1979.

Carroll, Berenice A., ed. *Liberating Women's History: Theoretical and Critical Essays*, Urbana: University of Illinois Press, 1976.

Chafe, William E., *The American Woman: Her Changing Social, Economic, and Political Roles 1920–1976*, New York: Oxford University Press, 1972.

——. *Women and Equality: Changing Patterns in American Culture*, New York: Oxford University Press, 1977.

Chesler, Phyllis. *Women and Madness*, Garden City, N.Y.: Doubleday, 1972.

Clinton, Catherine. *The Plantation Mistress, Woman's World in the Old South*, New York: Pantheon Books, 1982.

Congressional Quarterly's Guide to U.S. Elections, Washington: Congressional Quarterly, 1971.

Conway, Jill. "Women Reformers and American Culture," *Journal of Social History*, V (Winter 1971/72): 164–177.

Cook, Blanche Weisen. "Female Support Networks and Political Activism: Lillian Wald, Crystal Eastman, and Emma Goldman," in Nancy Cott and Elizabeth Pleck, eds., *A Heritage of Her Own*, New York: Simon & Schuster, 1979.

——, ed. *Crystal Eastman on Women and Revolution*, New York and London: Oxford University Press, 1978.

Crawford, Mary Caroline. *The College Girl of America and the Institutions Which Make Her What She Is*, Boston: L. C. Page, 1905.

Croly, Jennie. *The History of the Women's Club Movement in America*, New York: Henry G. Allen, 1898.

Davis, Allen F. *Spearheads for Reform: The Social Settlement and the Progressive Movement 1890–1914*, New York: Oxford University Press, 1969.

——. "Welfare, Reform, and World War I," *American Quarterly*, XIX (Fall 1967): 516–533.

Degler, Carl M. "Charlotte Perkins Gilman on the Theory and Practice of Feminism," *American Quarterly*, VII (Spring 1956): 21–39.

Degnan, Mary Louise. *The History of the Women's Peace Party*, Baltimore: Johns Hopkins University Press, 1939.

Dobkin, Marjorie Houspian, ed. *The Making of a Feminist: Early Journals and Letters of M. Carey Thomas*, Ohio: Kent State University Press, 1979.

DuBois, Ellen Carol. *Feminism and Suffrage: The Emergence of and Independent Women's Movement in America, 1848–1869*, Ithaca: Cornell University Press, 1978.

Eagle, Mary Cavanaugh Oldham, ed. *The Congress of Women, World's Columbian Exposition*, 2 vols., Chicago: W. B. Conkey, 1894.

Eisenstadt, S. N., ed. *Max Weber on Charisma and Institution Building*, Chicago: University of Chicago Press, 1968.

Evans, Richard J. *The Feminists: Women's Emancipation Movements in Europe, America, and Australia 1840–1920*, New York: Barnes & Noble, 1977.

Faber, Doris. *Petticoat Politics: How American Women Won the Right to Vote*, New York: Lothrop, Lee, & Shepard, 1967.

Flexner, Eleanor. *Century of Struggle: The Women's Right Movement in the United States*, rev. ed., Cambridge: The Belknap Press of Harvard University Press, 1975.

Gilman, Charlotte Perkins. *Herland, A Lost Feminist Utopian Novel*, New York: Pantheon Books, 1979.

——. *Women & Economics: The Economic Factor Between Men and Women as a Factor in Social Evolution*, New York: Harper Torchbooks, 1966.

Gluck, Sherna, ed. *From Parlor to Prison: Five American Suffragists Talk About Their Lives*, New York: Vintage Books, 1976.

Goldman, Eric. *Rendezvous with Destiny*, New York: Vintage Books, 1955.

Gordon, Lynn. "Women and the Anti-Child Labor Movement in Illinois 1890–1920," in Frank R. Breul and Steven J. Diner, eds., *Compassion and Responsibility: Readings in the History of Social Welfare Policy in the United States*, Chicago: University of Chicago Press, 1980.

——. "Women with Missions: Female Education in the Progressive Era," Ph.D. Dissertation, unpublished, University of Chicago (1980).

Gruberg, Martin. *Women in American Politics: An Assessment and Sourcebook*, Oshkosh, Wis.: Academia Press, 1968.

Hill, Joseph A. *Women in Gainful Occupations 1870–1920*, Census Monographs, IX, New York and London: Johnson Reprints, 1972.

Hilton, Suzanne. *Here Today and Gone Tomorrow: The Story of the World's Fairs and Expositions*, Philadelphia: The Westminster Press, 1978.

James, Edward L., et al., eds. *Notable American Women, A Biographical Dictionary*, 4 vols., Cambridge, Mass. and London: The Belknap Press of Harvard University Press, 1971–1980.

Johnson, Ann. "The National Woman's Party," M.A. Dissertation, University of California at Berkeley, 1972.

Josephson, Hannah. *Jeannette Rankin, First Lady in Congress: A Biography*, Indianapolis: Bobbs-Merrill, 1974.

Kennedy, David M. *Birth Control in America, The Career of Margaret Sanger*, New Haven: Yale University Press, 1970.

Kessler-Harris, Alice. *Women Have Always Worked, An Historical Overview*, Old Westbury, N.Y.: The Feminist Press, 1981.

Kraditor, Aileen. *The Ideas of the Woman Suffrage Movement, 1890–1920*, New York: Anchor Books, 1971.

——. ed. *Up From the Pedestal*, New York: Quadrangle/New York Times Book Co., 1968.

Lagemann, Ellen Condliffe. *A Generation of Women, Education in the Lives of Progressive Reformers*, Cambridge: Harvard University Press, 1979.

Lane, Anne J., ed. *Mary Ritter Beard, A Sourcebook*, New York: Schocken Books, 1978.

Lasch, Christopher. *The New Radicalism in America*, New York: Alfred A. Knopf, 1965.

Lemons, J. Stanley. *The Woman Citizen: Social Feminism in the 1920s*, Urbana, Ill.: University of Illinois Press, 1973.

Leonard, John William, ed. *Women's Who's Who of American 1914–1915*, New York: American Commonwealth Corp., 1914.

Lerner, Gerda. *The Majority Finds Its Past. Placing Women in History*, New York: Oxford University Press, 1979.

——. *The Woman in American History*, Menlo Park, Cal.: Addams-Wesley, 1971.

Link, Arthur S. *Wilson: Campaigns For Progressivism and Peace 1916–1917*, Princeton: Princeton University Press, 1965.

——. *Wilson: Confusions and Crises*, Princeton: Princeton University Press, 1965.

——. *Wilson: The New Freedom*, Princeton: Princeton University Press, 1956.

——. *Wilson: The Road to the White House*, Princeton: Princeton University Press, 1947.

——. *Woodrow Wilson and the Progressive Era 1910–1917*, New York: Harper Torchbooks, 1963.

——. "Correspondence Relating to the Progressive Party's 'Lily White' Policy in 1912," *Journal of Southern History*, X (Nov. 1944): 480–490.

——. "Theodore Roosevelt and the South in 1912," *North Carolina Historical Review*, XXIII (July 1946): 313–324.

—— and William M. Leary, Jr. "The Election of 1916," in Arthur Schlesinger, Jr., et al., eds., *The History of American Presidential Elections 1789–1968*, III, New York: Chelsea House Pubs. in association with McGraw-Hill, 1971.

——, *et al.*, eds. *The Papers of Woodrow Wilson*, 36 vols., Princeton: Princeton University Press, 1966—.

Louis, James P. "Sue Shelton White and the Woman Suffrage Movement in Tennessee, 1913–1920," *Tennessee Historical Quarterly*, XXII (June 1963): 170–190.

Lunardini, Christine A., "Standing Firm: William Monroe Trotter's Meetings With Woodrow Wilson, 1913–1914," *Journal of Negro History*, LXVI (Summer 1979): 244–264.

Lunardini, Christine A. and Thomas J. Knock. "Woodrow Wilson and Woman Suffrage: A New Look," *Political Science Quarterly*, XCV (Winter 1980/81): 655–671.

McGovern, James K. "The American Woman's Pre-World War I Freedom in Manners and Morals," *Journal of American History*, LV (Sept. 1968): 315–333.

Mahoney, Joseph F. "Woman Suffrage and the Urban Masses," *New Jersey History*, LXXXVII (Autumn 1969): 151–172.

Mitchell, David. *The Fighting Pankhursts, A Study in Tenacity*, New York: Macmillan, 1967.

Morgan, David. *Suffragists and Democrats*, East Lansing, Mich.: Michigan State University Press, 1972.

Mowry, George E. *Theodore Roosevelt and the Progressive Movement*, Madison: University of Wisconsin Press, 1946.

National American Woman Suffrage Association. *Victory! How Women Won It. A Centennial Symposium 1840–1940*, New York: H. W. Wilson, 1940.

Neu, Charles, "Olympia Brown and the Woman Suffrage Movement," *Wisconsin Magazine of History*, XLIII (1959/60): 277–287.

O'Neill, William J. *Everyone Was Brave, The Rise and Fall of Feminism in America*, Chicago: Quadrangle Books, 1969.

——. *The Woman Movement: Feminism in the United States and England*, Chicago: Quadrangle Books, 1969.

Oppenheimer, Valerie Kincade. *The Female Labor Force in the United*

States: Democraphic and Economic Factors Governing Its Growth and Changing Composition, Population Monograph Studies No. 5, Berkeley: University of California Press, 1970.

Paul, Alice. "The Legal Position of Women in Pennsylvania," Ph.D. Dissertation, University of Pennsylvania, 1912.

Peck, Mary Grey. *Carrie Chapman Catt, A Biography*, New York: Octagon Books, 1975.

Phillips, Mary. *The Militant Suffrage Campaign in Perspective*, Pamphlet, London, 1967, Sophia Smith Collection, Smith College.

Proceedings of the Women's Rights Conventions Held at Seneca Falls and Rochester, New York, July and August 1848, New York: Robert J. Johnston, 1870.

Randall, Susan Louise. *A Legislative History of the Equal Rights Amendment 1923–1960*, Ann Arbor, Mich.: University Microfilms, 1979.

Riegel, Robert. *American Feminists*, Lawrence, Kans.: University of Kansas Press, 1963.

Robins, Elizabeth. *The Convert*, London: The Woman's Press, 1980.

Rothman, Sheila M. *Woman's Proper Place, A History of Changing Ideas and Practices, 1870 to the Present*, New York: Basic Books, 1978.

Ryan, Mary P. *Womanhood in America: From Colonial Times to the Present*, New York: New Viewpoints, 1975.

Scott, Anne Firor and Andrew Scott, eds. *One Half the People: The Fight for Woman suffrage*, Philadelphia: Lippincott, 1975.

Showalter, Elaine, ed. *These Modern Women: Autobiographical Essays from the Twenties*, Old Westbury, N. Y.: The Feminist Press, 1978.

Silbey, Joel H. and Samuel T. McSeveney, eds. *Voters, Parties, and Elections: Quantitative Essays in the History of American Popular Voting Behavior*, Lexington, Mass.: Xerox College Publishers, 1972.

Smith-Rosenberg, Carroll, "The Female World of Love and Ritual: The Relations Between Women in Nineteenth Century America," in Nancy Cott and Elizabeth Pleck, eds., *A Heritage of Her Own*, New York: Simon & Schuster, 1979.

Smuts, Robert W. *Women and Work in America*, New York: Schocken Books, 1971.

Sochen, June. *Movers and Shakers, American Women Thinkers and Activists 1900–1970*, New York: Quadrangle Books, 1972.

——. *The New Woman, Feminism in Greenwich Village 1910–1970*, New York: Quadrangle Books, 1972.

——. *The New Woman, Feminism in Greenwich Village 1910–1920*, New York: Quadrangle Books, 1972.

——. *The New Woman, Feminism in Greenwich Village 1910–1920*, New York: Quadrangle Books, *1972*.

——, ed. *The New Feminism in Twentieth Century America*, Lexington, Mass.: D. C. Heath, 1971.

Stanton, Elizabeth Cady, *et al.*, eds. *The History of Woman Suffrage*, 6 vols., New York: Foster and Wells, 1881–1922.

Trecker, Janice Law, "The Suffrage Prisoners," *The American Scholar*, XXI (Summer 1972): 409–423.

Weber, Max. *The Sociology of Religion*, London: Methuen, 1965.

Weiss, Nancy J. "The Negro and the New Freedom: Fighting Wilsonian Segregation," *Political Science Quarterly*, LXXXIV (March 1969): 61–79.

Wiebe, Robert H. *The Search For Order 1877–1920*, New York: Hill and Wang, 1967.

Wilner, Ann Ruth. *Charismatic Political Leadership: A Theory*, Princeton: Center for International Studies, Princeton University, 1968.

Wood, Ann Douglass, "The War Within A War: Women Nurses in the Union Army," *Civil War History*, XVIII (Sept. 1972): 197–212.

Woody, Thomas. *A History of Women's Education in the United States*, 2 vols., New York: Science Press, 1929.

Young, Alfred F. ed. *Dissent: Explorations in the History of American Radicalism*, DeKalb, Ill.: Northern Illinois University Press, 1968.

Zimmerman, Loretta Ellen, "Alice Paul and the National Woman's Party 1912–1920," Ph.D. Dissertation, Tulane University, 1964.

Index